The
Sugar Girls

Duncan Barrett & Nuala Calvi

The Sugar Girls

Tales of Hardship, Love and Happiness
in Tate & Lyle's East End

Collins

First published in 2012 by Collins
an imprint of HarperCollins*Publishers*
77–85 Fulham Palace Road
London W6 8JB

www.harpercollins.co.uk

1 3 5 7 9 10 8 6 4 2

While every effort has been made to trace the owners of copyright material
reproduced herein and secure permissions, the publishers would like to
apologise for any omissions and will be pleased to incorporate missing
acknowledgements in any future edition of this book.

A catalogue record for this book is
available from the British Library

ISBN 978-0-00-744847-0

Printed and bound in Great Britain by
Clays Ltd, St Ives plc

MIX
Paper from
responsible sources
FSC
www.fsc.org
FSC™ C007454

FSC™ is a non-profit international organisation established to promote
the responsible management of the world's forests. Products carrying the
FSC label are independently certified to assure consumers that they come
from forests that are managed to meet the social, economic and
ecological needs of present and future generations,
and other controlled sources.

Find out more about HarperCollins and the environment at
www.harpercollins.co.uk/green

For Margaret Denby

Preface

Heading east out of the City of London, just past Poplar and the Isle of Dogs, you'll find the artificial peninsula of Silvertown: a narrow strip of land two and a half miles long, sandwiched between the Royal Docks and the broad sweep of the Thames.

By the mid-twentieth century this area was home to a score of factories, from British Oil & Cake Mills at one end to Henley's Cable Works at the other. The factories were a major employer, both for people living in the rows of slum houses in Silvertown and those in the surrounding areas north of the docks: Canning Town, Custom House and Plaistow. While the thriving docks provided work for the men in the local community, the factories offered employment for women as well.

When working-class girls left school there were a limited number of options available to them: dressmaking, service, clerical work perhaps, and, for the vast majority, a job in a factory. With the near full employment that followed the Second World War, most young people could simply take themselves along to a factory of their choice, ask for work and be hired on the spot. If they found they didn't like it there, they could walk out at lunchtime and be taken on somewhere else before tea.

Among the most sought-after factories to work at were the two operated by Tate & Lyle, the Plaistow Wharf and Thames refineries, at either end of the Sugar Mile (so called because, in addition to the sugar and syrup they produced, Keiller's jam factory was also located there). Tate & Lyle offered the best wages, generous bonuses three times a year, and a social life that was unrivalled in the neighbourhood thanks to the Tate Institute, a subsidised bar and entertainment hall. Unsurprisingly, the company inspired fierce loyalty among its employees – many young men and women working there in the post-war years were the fourth generation of their families to do so.

There were plenty of positions for young 'sugar girls', thanks to the many female-dominated departments: the great sugar-packing operation known as the Hesser Floor, the Blue Room where the sheets of paper were printed for the sugar bags, and the can-making and syrup-filling floors where the tins of Lyle's Golden Syrup were put together and filled. The jobs could be heavy, exhausting and repetitive, but for the women who undertook them the rewards outweighed the hardships. Most stayed until they married or fell pregnant (the rules varied between departments as to when they were forced to leave). Nearly all of them looked back on their time at the factories as a kind of golden era in their lives – of independence, friendship and romance, before the responsibilities of marriage and motherhood took over.

Originally the two refineries had been run by rival companies. Henry Tate, a Liverpool grocer turned sugar magnate, put up his London factory in 1877, when much of Silvertown was still marshland. His great business adversary was Abram Lyle, who built his own sugar and syrup factory a mile upstream four years later. Lyle was a pious Scot whose ruddy cheeks belied his commitment to teetotalism: he once declared he would rather see a son of his carried home dead than drunk.

For many decades the two firms competed in sugar production, but with an important unspoken agreement: the Lyles would not encroach on Tate's trademark cubed sugar, while the Tates would not produce a single drop of the golden syrup the Lyles had invented. But a cold war developed between them, and when the Lyles heard rumours that the Tates were about to launch a syrup onto the market, they hastily knocked together a cube plant in response. Leaking word of its existence was enough to ensure that it never had to be used.

The families were scrupulous in keeping up professional boundaries – although the senior Tates and Lyles took the same train from Fenchurch Street Station every morning, they made sure to sit in separate carriages, and never acknowledged each other.

By the end of the First World War it was clear that the competition was actually hurting both companies, but neither had a clear upper hand: the Lyles had the edge in profitability, but the Tates' output was not to be rivalled. A merger was the obvious way forward. Negotiations began, and for three years Ernest Tate and Charles Lyle tore their hair out in frustration as proposal after proposal was rejected by their respective boards. A deal was finally agreed in 1921.

The new Tate & Lyle company retained both London factories – Tate's Thames Refinery in the heart of Silvertown and Lyle's Plaistow Wharf Refinery a mile upriver. The management of the two factories, however, remained in the hands of the respective families. The original Tate and Lyle, Henry and Abram, were both long dead by now, and had never known the fate of their companies. In fact, they had never even met.

The old rivalry didn't die out completely, though, and from 1937 onwards it was played out in a more friendly fashion, on the company's new shared sports ground. There, the workers from 'Tates-es' and 'Lyles-es' (as the two factories continued to be known by the locals) would compete against each other in football and cricket.

The Second World War brought great changes to both refineries, as their workforces became female-dominated for the first time. As men were called up, the management were forced to blur the strict distinctions between 'men's' and 'women's' jobs, with female workers tackling even the most physically demanding and high-status roles, including that of the panmen who boiled up the sugar liquor. The women were thrilled to see their wages go up when they took on such new jobs, but they were still only paid 75 per cent of what their male counterparts had earned.

After the war the men reclaimed their old roles, but a shift had taken place and the crucial part that the sugar girls played in the company's success could no longer be ignored. In 1948 a mixed-sex canteen was built at the Plaistow Wharf Refinery, and for the first time the women were able to eat alongside their male colleagues.

Today, after the closure of the docks and almost all of the local factories, much of Silvertown has the feeling of a ghost town. It is overshadowed by the planes taking off and landing at City Airport – whose runway cuts between the Royal Albert and

King George V docks – and the looming concrete viaducts of the Docklands Light Railway. Many of the old Victorian terraces have been replaced by blocks of council flats, and the pubs, shops and cafés that once lined the North Woolwich Road opposite the Plaistow Wharf Refinery are all gone. The close-knit neighbourhoods, and the way of life that once thrived there, have vanished and can never be recovered.

Tate & Lyle is unusual in having retained its Silvertown factories, although from the late 1960s much of the Plaistow Wharf Refinery was demolished as its sugar refining activities were wound down. Many loyal workers took redundancy rather than accept a transfer downriver to the Thames Refinery. Even there, the company now employs only a small fraction of its former workforce, and the jobs once done by the sugar girls are all performed by machines.

Tate & Lyle has long since stopped being a family firm, and in 2010 it was bought by an American sugar giant. However, the legacy of its original founders lives on. In 2006 the iconic Lyle's Golden Syrup tins were officially recognised by the *Guinness Book of Records* as the oldest brand in Britain. Meanwhile, the philanthropic work of the Tate family is remembered in the libraries and art galleries that bear its name.

But the contribution of those ordinary young women who played such a central role during Tate & Lyle's East End heyday is not widely recognised, and their lives have not generally been recorded.

This is the story of those women, the teenagers who left school and gave the best years of their lives to Tate & Lyle. This is the story of the sugar girls.

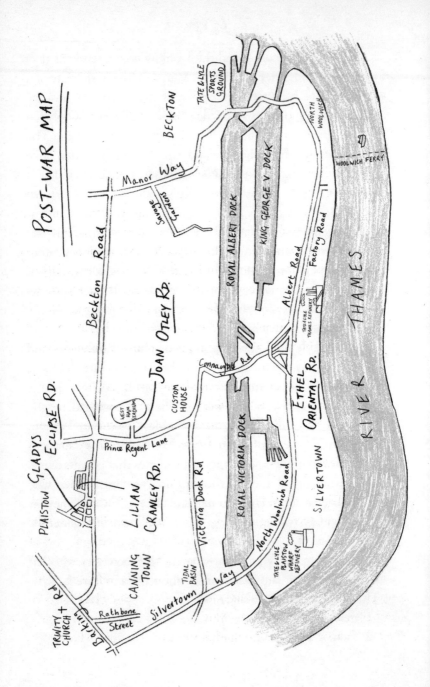

1

Ethel

On a crisp September day in 1944, Ethel Alleyne stood outside Tate & Lyle's Plaistow Wharf refinery, looking up at the giant gate with its elaborate wrought iron and shining white clock.

A wiry, frizzy-haired girl with light-brown skin and keen dark eyes, she was wearing her best dress for the occasion – black with red trimmings. In one hand she clutched her headmaster's testimonial, already proudly committed to memory:

> *Ethel's attendance has been regular and punctual. She is a very willing, cheerful girl, always ready to give her best. Her neatness and tidiness and general attention to detail are very pleasing. I can recommend her to any employer as a conscientious worker.*

At 14, Ethel had never been inside a factory, but she felt as if she'd been preparing for this moment all her life. She had grown up in the heart of Silvertown and was used to living in the shadow of the Sugar Mile – the stretch of colossal factories that ran between Tate & Lyle's sugar and syrup refineries. The factory life was in her blood – her mother's family had lived in the area for generations, working in Keiller's jam and marmalade factory, and her grandfather would tell anyone who would listen that he remembered when Silvertown was little more than a marsh.

From a hut on the left of the entrance emerged a fierce-looking man in the smart, military-style uniform of a commissionaire, his navy-blue tunic buttoned up to the collar and the silver buttons gleaming in the sunlight.

'Yes, darlin'?'

Ethel drew herself up to her full height and did her best to hide her nerves. 'I'm here about a job,' she told him.

'In here.' He gestured for her to follow him into the little hut.

Inside, Ethel stood anxiously while a man in a white boiler-suit glanced over her testimonial and noted down a few details on a form. 'Hesser Floor, I reckon,' he told her briskly, 'but the surgery will need to check you out first. I'll get a girl to take you.'

Before long a smartly dressed young woman who looked to be in her late teens arrived at the door. 'Hesser girl?' she asked Ethel, as they stepped out of the hut.

'Um, I think so,' Ethel replied, 'but I'm not sure what that means.'

'Oh, Hesser of Stuttgart make the sugar-packing machines, but we try to keep that quiet these days! Come on.'

The two girls headed into the refinery.

Ethel was quite unprepared for the sight that met her eyes. She knew that the factory was big, but seeing it up close, from the inside, was another matter. Ahead of her, slightly to the right, the enormous grey-brick hulk of the Hesser building towered over her. At its base a team of boys and burly-looking girls were standing on a raised level open to the yard, loading up great haulage lorries with tonne-weight boards of sugar bags.

To her left, another large building housed the factory's bar and Recreation Room, and in front of her wagon tracks criss-crossed all over the ground, branching off straight ahead towards the syrup shed, where the Lyle's Golden Syrup tins were filled. Underneath it was the Blue Room, where the sugar bags were printed, and beyond was the can-making depart-ment, where girls produced the famous tins. In the distance she could make out the looming white concrete of the pan house, where sugar liquor was boiled into crystals, and next to it an even taller set of chimneys from the boiler house.

Ethel searched in vain for the shining curve of the Thames, where the boats of raw sugar were unloaded. She knew it must be at the far end of the site, but through the jungle of ware-houses in between she couldn't catch a glimpse of the water.

As the two girls hurried across the yard, a musty, malty smell of damp sugar hit them in a cloying wave – shortly followed by another, ranker odour that almost made Ethel retch. She knew what it was, but tried her best not to think about it: the pile of rotting carcasses just the other side of the factory wall, at John Knight's soap works. It was a smell that every Tate & Lyle worker had to learn to ignore.

In the surgery, a young nurse listened to Ethel's heart, took her blood pressure and checked the movement and strength of her limbs. Then she carefully scoured her frizzy hair for nits, before passing her fit for service.

Ethel followed the other girl back towards the dark-grey Hesser building, on the outside of which a black metal staircase zigzagged up all eight floors. 'It's a long way up but you get used to it,' said the girl, as they began to climb the steps.

As they neared the top, Ethel was beginning to lose her breath, so she was relieved to spot a sign that read:

SMALL PACKETS. They went into a cloakroom, where Ethel deposited her coat and bag, and then through a pair of double doors onto the factory floor.

The noise as they stepped through the doors was overwhelming. The large room echoed with the rattle and grind of a dozen machines, huge lumps of iron around which stood teams of young women. Over the top of the noise there was music blaring out, and some of the girls were singing along.

They went up some stairs to an office on a mezzanine level, and as the door clicked shut behind them Ethel was aware of a blissful quiet settling around her. The girl left her in front of an impeccably tidy desk on which stood a little sign: IVY BATCHELOR, FORELADY. Behind the desk sat a tall, upright woman in a long white coat. Her brown hair had evidently been expertly styled, and her nails and make-up were immaculate.

'Take a seat,' she said calmly, gesturing to a chair on the other side of the desk.

Ethel did so, sitting up as straight as she could. She was determined to make a good impression.

The forelady looked at her kindly, reached for a form from a pile on her desk and took down Ethel's name and address. 'Is there any particular reason you want to work at Tate & Lyle?' she asked.

Ethel hesitated. She had dreamed of working at one of the giant sugar factories ever since she was little and her dad had taken her to the Tate Institute, the social club opposite the Thames Refinery. They had gone to see a show laid on for local residents and employees, and Ethel had been transfixed – not merely by the dancers onstage, but by the glamorous young women who thronged the hall watching them. They were the factory's female workforce and her dad had told her they were known as the sugar girls.

She felt self-conscious at the idea of telling that story, though. 'I only live down the road,' she offered instead.

Ivy Batchelor laughed gently. 'Now, I'm afraid we can't offer you a uniform at present, unless you have ration coupons to spare, but we should be able to lend you an apron for the day.' She rummaged around under the desk and came up with a rather worn-looking pinny. 'Your hours are eight to four Monday to Friday and eight to twelve on Saturday. You're allowed half an hour for dinner and two toilet breaks a day. Any questions?'

Ethel shook her head.

'Good. Then Mary will see you to one of the machines.'

As if on cue, a stern-looking woman with dark hair marched through the door of the office and gestured for Ethel to follow her. She was Mary Doherty, one of the department's three supervisors, known as charge-hands.

'This way,' she commanded. Ethel jumped up and followed her onto the floor.

At each machine, paper bags were moving along a conveyor belt and being filled with sugar from a chute overhead. They were then sealed with a spurt of glue and a girl took them off the belt, piling them up ready to be packed. A packer then pulled down a sheet of brown paper and flipped the bags onto it in layers until they had made up a parcel, sealing it like an envelope with a bit of cold water and heaving it onto a board. When a tonne-weight of sugar had been assembled, it was taken away on a trolley down to the lorry bay. In charge of each machine was a driver, who paced around keeping an eye on everything. The girls' various repetitive movements combined to give the impression of an elaborate ballet.

Mary led Ethel across to a machine at the far side of the room, where a woman with giant hands was parcelling up the sugar bags.

'This is Annie Stout,' Mary told Ethel. 'She'll show you how the packing is done.' She strode off across the floor and back up to the office.

Ethel noticed that on the ends of Annie's fat fingers were ten little paper thimbles. 'You'll need some of these,' she told her, 'or your hands'll be bleeding by lunchtime.'

Without once interrupting her flow, Annie instructed Ethel in how to make her own thimbles from some spare scraps of paper. Then she stood back and let her have a go at packing.

At first Ethel found it hard holding several bags at once in her hands, but if she applied enough pressure to the sides, and lifted them in a clear, fluid arc, twisting them rapidly before they had a chance to slip, she found that she could manage it without dropping any.

'That's it,' Annie told her approvingly. After a while, she leaned in close and Ethel thought she was going to offer to take over the job again, but instead she whispered something in her ear.

'Got any sweetie coupons you don't want, darlin'?'

'Any what?' said Ethel, taken aback by the question.

Annie whispered more emphatically: 'Ration coupons.'

'No, sorry,' Ethel replied briskly. She screwed up her face as if focusing intently on her work, and tried to avoid catching Annie's eye.

Before long Ethel's wrists were aching from flipping layer after layer of sugar bags, and she was beginning to wonder whether it was too soon to ask for one of her two toilet breaks.

Just then there was a sudden dimming of the lights, and a voice crackled out from the loudspeakers which were stationed around the room.

'All personnel to shelters, please. All personnel to shelters.'

The driver of Ethel's machine swiftly pulled a lever, and the whole mechanism ground to a halt. Carefully, Ethel laid down the bags in her hands to complete a layer, and then looked up, hoping that Annie would tell her what to do next. But Annie was gone, lost in the stream of bodies filing in an orderly but hurried fashion towards the exit.

Four years after the start of the Blitz, Tate & Lyle had got evacuations down to a fine art, and could gather nearly all 1,500 of their wartime workforce into shelters within the space of four minutes. A command centre under the can-making department received signals from the national telephone exchange, and four spotters permanently stationed on the pan-house roof provided visual confirmation. Those whose jobs meant that they couldn't simply leave their posts – such as the men on the boilers and turbines, which were not easily shut down – were provided with blast-proof shielding to keep them safe, while the rest were immediately ordered to evacuate.

Ethel rushed to join the back of the queue of sugar girls streaming out of the door. It was only now that she heard sirens outside the factory as well.

In front of her was one of the smart girls from the office. 'You're new, aren't you?' she asked.

'Yes, it's my first day,' said Ethel wryly.

'Poor you!' the other girl replied. 'Well, don't worry, the shelter's just downstairs – we can't have them underground because of the river. I'm Joanie, by the way. Joanie Warren.'

Ethel followed Joanie back down the black iron staircase to the second floor of the building. It was the same size as the Hesser room up above, but whatever machinery it had once housed had been removed, and blast walls had been built, dividing it into compartments. The windows were all bricked up, and wooden boards lined the floor for the workers to sit on. Ethel tried hard to suppress the feeling that she was cooped up in a dungeon.

Before long, the room was packed with bodies, mostly women and girls but a fair number of men as well. By now only a third of the refinery's employees were male, and women who had previously been forced to leave when they got married were hurriedly being recalled by an army of door-knockers. Many had taken over jobs formerly held by men – working on the lorry bank under the Hesser Floor, manning the centrifuges and working as fitters in the can-making department. Others had been assigned a variety of unusual new roles: dehydrating vegetables to be sent out in tins to the troops (often with a hopeful note containing the name and address of the girl who had sent them) and even producing aeroplane and gun parts.

A woman pushed a steaming mug of cocoa into Ethel's hand and offered her a Matzo cracker. 'Could be in here a while,' Joanie advised her, 'so you might as well have one.'

Ethel took the Matzo and they sat huddled together, straining their ears for any sound from the skies. Eventually it came: the familiar phut … phut … phut … of a doodlebug passing overhead.

* * *

When the bombs first came to Silvertown four years earlier, Ethel was living in Charles Street, a stone's throw from the

Connaught Bridge which divided the Victoria and Albert docks. The seventh of September 1940 was a balmy summer's day, and the Alleyne family, like the rest of their neighbours in the East End, had no idea what was in store for them.

It was Ethel's 11th birthday, and a special tea of jelly and fruit had been planned. Louise Alleyne was busy bathing her three daughters in the tin bath – first her eldest, Dolly, then Ethel and finally little Winnie. She always took great pride in making sure they were squeaky clean and smartly turned out, with spotless white socks and gleaming ruby-red shoes. Louise had high hopes for her three girls and sometimes even made them walk around the house with books on their heads to improve their posture, just as long as the neighbours weren't looking. A strict mother, she wasn't averse to taking her hand to her daughters if their behaviour fell short of what was expected.

Her husband, a more laid-back character, was tinkling away contentedly on the keys of a battered old upright piano. Jim Alleyne used to say that he must have acquired his musical skill from his father, a black Saint Lucian who had married a white lady and emigrated to England. When Jim was only a few years old his parents had left him and his sister Etty with a lady he knew only as Aunty Lyle, and never returned. Aunty Lyle was white, but had married a Caribbean sailor herself, and had adapted herself to the requirements of a mixed-race household, making the best rice 'n' peas this side of the Atlantic. Jim had become a sailor like his stepfather, but when he had children he packed it in and took a job as a greaser on the Woolwich Ferry.

Jim and his two older girls often played music together, he on the piano, Dolly on guitar and Ethel on an old accordion. He also entertained the locals at the Graving Dock Tavern on the North Woolwich Road, and at the Tate Institute. Louise could never understand how he did it, since she herself was practically tone deaf. But that didn't stop her being an appreciative audience.

As the sirens began to sound, Jim jumped up from his stool. 'Louise!' he called, 'Get those girls dressed. We've got to get into the shelter.'

Louise briskly dried the girls down, and passed around a set of clean clothes from the pile she had stacked neatly by her side. Then she hurried them out into the yard, where their father stood watch by the side of the brick hut that now took up most of their outdoor space.

Louise – ever the house-proud mother – had done her best to add a touch of style to the shelter, with sheets draped down the walls to keep out the damp, a little rug on the floor offering a splash of colour, and even a double bed, which barely fitted between the four cramped walls but at least meant that no one would have to spend the night on the floor.

She and the girls had just clambered onto the squeaky mattress when they heard the faint sound of planes flying overhead, followed by a series of gentle 'crump' sounds in the distance. Hauling the door shut behind him, Jim caught his wife's eye for a moment as the rumbling above them grew louder.

Before long it had turned into a roar, punctuated every few moments by deep, hollow thuds of increasing ferocity. There was a sudden whoosh overhead and Jim flung himself down on top of his wife and children, spreading him arms wide to shield them from the menace above.

The noises grew louder still, and this time the sounds were more distinct: the crumbling of bricks and masonry, the jagged tinkling of shattered glass falling from windows, and, most terrifying of all, the merciless low beat of the detonating explosives, which seemed to pound the shelter walls on all sides.

With one giant blast the brick hut shook, and lifted momentarily from the ground. Then, gradually, the storm overhead began to pass, and the noises receded into the distance.

Ethel clutched her mother and sisters close as Jim sat up on the bed and looked around him. There was a trickle of bright-red blood snaking down his brown forehead. 'Dad,' she shouted, 'they got you!'

Jim put a hand up to feel for the wound, smarting as he tested the cut with his finger. He let out a laugh of relief.

'What is it, Dad?' Ethel asked. 'Are you all right?'

'Don't worry, my darlin',' he replied, wiping his hand on his trousers. 'Just caught myself on the bedhead is all.' He leaned forward so that Ethel could see he was telling the truth. 'I'll be more careful next time.'

Jim hugged his wife and children to him once again, tousling Dolly's blonde locks with one hand and squeezing Ethel close with the other, while Winnie clung on to Louise for dear life. Ethel noticed that her mother had become very quiet.

At six-thirty p.m. the all-clear was sounded and the Alleyne family emerged to see what was left of their home. Half the house had been destroyed altogether, and the half that remained was in a very bad way. Windows had been blasted out of their frames, stray tiles from the roof littered the yard, and the door had been blown off its hinges.

Carefully they picked their way through the ruined building, avoiding the scattered pieces of broken crockery that should have been serving Ethel's birthday tea, and clambering over the remains of Jim's beloved piano, its black and white keys strewn all over the floor.

It was only once they were on the road outside that they realised how lucky they had been. Charles Street was a scene of devastation. There were piles of rubble where some houses had once stood. Others were still standing, but gaping holes revealed the pitiful sight of their inhabitants' ruined possessions.

A grey dust was beginning to settle all around, and Ethel coughed violently as it caught in her lungs.

Jim turned and addressed the family. 'We can't stay here,' he told them. 'We'll head for the rest centre at Woodman Street School, and I'll come back later and pick up some clean clothes.'

Hand in hand, the family set off on the mile-long journey, passing street after street in no better state than their own. Wardens were out with stretcher-bearers, pulling injured people out of the rubble. By the side of the road were blackened bundles, some large and some small. Ethel tried to make out what they were, but her mother pulled her close, and told her not to look.

Along the docks many warehouses were ablaze, and burning butter, sugar, molasses and oils oozed out into the water and the surrounding roads, creating boiling hot puddles, thick smoke and overpowering smells.

By the time the family arrived at the rest centre, Louise Alleyne's head was pounding and she was beginning to feel queasy. 'I've got to lie down,' she told her husband. 'I'm getting one of my migraines.'

Jim walked with her arm in arm until they found a quiet spot where she could have a rest. 'You stay here for a while,' he whispered in her ear.

The main hall of the school was thronging with anxious families, most of whom looked dishevelled and miserable. Jim took one look at the scene and bounded up to the front of the hall, where an old upright piano had been pushed to the side of the stage. 'Excuse me, mate,' he said to a man who was leaning on it. 'Do you mind?'

The man seemed to shake himself out of a stupor. 'Nah, go ahead,' he replied. 'Bleedin' good idea.'

As Jim sat and began tinkling away, a crowd started to gather and a throng of young women descended on the piano. Jim was used to it – his light-brown skin and musical talent had always brought him attention from the local women, and he had learned how to handle it.

'This is my wife's favourite song,' he told them. 'I reckon she thinks it was written for her.' He began singing Maurice Chevalier's 'Louise', and the women soon joined in.

Before long, other members of the crowd were singing along as well.

That night Jim played into the small hours, just happy, like the enthusiastic crowd around him, for the opportunity to clutch at something beautiful amid all the destruction and fear. Outside, the raids had started up again. By the end of the night 250 German bombers had dropped 625 tonnes of high explosive, and more than 400 lives had been lost.

The next morning Jim kept his word, and before the rest of the family had woken up he made the journey back to their bombed-out home. Officially the road had been cordoned off, but he knew that having clean clothes for the kids would mean a lot to Louise.

When Jim arrived at 23 Charles Street and carefully made his way back inside the wrecked building, he realised that his wife was going to be disappointed. What little the bombs had spared had already been looted, and drawer after drawer fell open empty. The family would have to manage with what they had on their backs.

Before long, the Alleynes were relocated to Waunlwyd, a little village near Ebbw Vale in South Wales, where Jim had accepted a job in a munitions factory. It could scarcely have been more different from the bomb-damaged East End, and for the three girls it was an adventure in an utterly unknown world.

As the train pulled into the station Ethel leapt up from her seat. 'Look, Dad,' she cried, barely able to believe her eyes, 'there are sheep and geese and donkeys just walking around in the street!'

The family lived in a little house on a hill, where Louise learned to cook on a fire instead of a stove. Ethel and Dolly went to the local school, while little Winnie stayed at home with their mother.

Dolly took to the rough-and-tumble of rural life more than Ethel, who was forever trying to get the mud off her shoes. Always the more sensible sister, Ethel was frequently mistaken for the eldest by people who met the two of them. While Dolly soon made friends with a group of local Welsh children, Ethel was not admitted into their gang, who considered her too 'miserable and boring'.

Dolly's favourite new pastime was playing kiss-chase with the country boys, and Ethel could never understand how her sister, who was normally such a fast runner, would keep getting caught. Ethel always ran for her life, and no one ever seemed to catch up with her.

The country life proved quite a shock to Ethel, and not just because of the farm animals. One afternoon she was walking some way behind Dolly and the other children on their way to Sunday school, when a man leaped out of the bushes and exposed himself to her. She turned on the spot and ran home at full-pelt, screaming her lungs out all the way back up the hill to the house.

'Dad! Dad!' she exclaimed when her anxious father opened the front door, 'there's a man down there with a broom handle in his trousers!'

Jim Alleyne may have been a laid-back father, but when it came to protecting his girls he was fearsome. He legged it all the way down the hill in hot pursuit of the pervert, but by the time he got there both the man and his broom handle had retreated.

By 1942, although the war raged on in Europe, for Londoners the horrors of the Blitz seemed to be behind them. Like many families, the Alleynes took the decision to return to the East End. They found a house in Oriental Road, not far from Charles Street and still in the heart of Silvertown, and Jim got a job at the Spencer Chapman chemical factory. The girls' old school had been levelled by the Luftwaffe, so they were sent to a makeshift classroom in the local swimming pool, which until recently had served as a morgue.

Ethel was thrilled to be admitted to a gang of local kids: Archie Colquhoun, Gladys Rawlins, Johnny Jay, Alf Gosford and Lenny Bridges. After being teased by Dolly and her friends for being boring, it felt wonderful to have a group of her own to lark about with at last.

Her favourite in the new gang was Archie, a ginger-haired boy a year older than her who lived on her new road, and who was as cheeky and playful as she was serious. As they ran about the streets together, playing gobstones and knock down ginger, Ethel realised that she was smitten.

There was just one unfortunate obstacle to her future happiness: Archie preferred her sister Dolly, whose tumbling blonde curls were a far cry from Ethel's dark, frizzy hair. When he turned up at their door one afternoon asking if 'Blondie' would like to go for a walk, poor Ethel was horrified.

She wasn't one to give up easily, however, and when Archie and Dolly left the house together she followed them in secret, borrowing her grandfather's dog from across the road as an alibi in case her stalking was discovered. She did her best to stay well back, even though she was desperate to know what they were saying to each other, and kept a beady eye out for any hand-holding or kissing.

Ethel made it as far as the Connaught Bridge before her cover was blown. 'Ooh, she's jealous, Archie,' Dolly called out, loudly enough to ensure that her sister could hear her. Ethel was mortified and hurried home, dragging the unfortunate dog behind her.

She decided the best strategy was to bide her time. Dolly had no shortage of male attention and would hopefully tire of Archie's before long. Meanwhile, Ethel made sure to remind him of her presence. At 14, Archie had already left school and was working at the Hollis Bros timber yard. Every day, Ethel was out on the front step when he walked past on his way home for dinner.

Soon enough, Archie's interest in Dolly waned, and one day he asked Ethel if she fancied going to the pictures together at the Imperial cinema in Canning Town. She tried not to jump for joy as she accepted the invitation.

Being alone with Ethel seemed to have a sobering effect on Archie, and around her he kept his cheekiness in check, behaving like the perfect gentleman. That night he didn't dare do more than sneak an arm around her, even in the dark of the picture house.

In fact, after several months of courting, Archie still hadn't plucked up the courage to kiss her. One day they were walking to the park together and chatting, when one of Ethel's friends spotted them from across the road. 'Just do it, Arch!' she shouted. 'Go on!'

Archie froze like a rabbit caught in the headlights, but he knew it was now or never. While Ethel was still chatting away he suddenly turned, grabbed her and planted a great big smacker on her lips.

'Archie!' she chastised him, as soon as their lips unlocked, 'I was in the middle of a sentence!'

But after that she let him kiss her whenever he liked. By the time Ethel joined Tate & Lyle, she and Archie were inseparable.

* * *

Phut … phut … phut …

Ethel and Joanie held their breath, along with the hundred or so other inhabitants of the factory shelter, as they listened to the distinctive splutter of the doodlebug. They willed the noise to continue, knowing that if the engine cut out it meant the warhead was about to fall.

The flying bombs, launched from occupied Europe, had become a regular feature of East End life ever since the D-Day landings the previous summer. But at least the doodlebugs, which flew like regular aircraft, provided enough warning to get civilians into shelters. Far more menacing were the V2 rockets, which travelled so fast – at four times the speed of sound – that the explosion was the first anybody knew of them. The shock wave alone was enough to kill unsuspecting victims far from the point of impact, and in the aftermath of a V2 strike it was not uncommon to see a normal-looking bus full of passengers, apparently sitting patiently in their seats but on closer inspection all quite dead.

At the height of the V2 menace the Royal Docks were sustaining a strike every two or three days, but Tate & Lyle's two factories escaped a single direct hit. Plaistow Wharf had suffered its fair share of battering earlier in the war, with 54 incendiary bombs landing inside the factory, all but one of which were quickly extinguished. There was only one fatality, a Mr Kinnison who ran into an exploding bomb on his way to a shelter. Downriver, the Thames Refinery was also hit many times, but only two minor casualties were reported.

Various rumours had sprung up to explain the firm's apparent lucky streak. At the Thames Refinery, the most popular theory was that their iconic chimney – the tallest in the area – provided such a good landmark for the docks that the Luftwaffe were reluctant to damage it. At Plaistow Wharf, the story went that the mysterious Hesser company had begged Hitler not to damage their precious packing machines.

Fortunately for Ethel, Tate & Lyle's good luck continued to hold out, and the splutter of the doodlebug finally began to recede into the distance. The inhabitants of the shelter were able to relax, and Ethel let out a sigh of relief.

Moments later the all-clear siren began to sound, and the men and women around her were suddenly getting to their feet.

'Back to work then,' Joanie said cheerfully, munching on the last of her cracker and brushing a few stray crumbs from her lap onto the floor. Ethel followed as they made their way back up the black iron stairs.

On the Hesser Floor, Joanie retreated up to the office, while Ethel returned to her machine, determined to perfect her packing technique. But a friendship had already been forged. Before they left work that day, the two young women had arranged to go to the pictures together.

To begin with, the rigours of her new job took their toll on Ethel. At the end of each day her hair was grey with sugar dust and her clothes were stiff with it. Every night her wrists ached painfully from the twisting movement that she had to repeat over and over again packing hundreds of sugar bags. At work, when it got really bad, she would be sent to the factory surgery, where a nurse would rub ointment on her wrists and bandage them up temporarily, before sending her straight back to the Hesser Floor. But as time went on her muscles grew accustomed to the exertions, and she found herself growing stronger and more robust.

While the work of a sugar girl was building up the muscles in Ethel's body, her mind soon got some exercise as well. The packers had to tally up the number of sugar bags that had been packed each day and display the result on a board at the base of each machine. Ethel had always been good at maths in school and had no problem with this, but she noticed that a girl on the next machine was struggling. Before long she was doing the other girl's tally as well as her own.

Her efforts did not go unnoticed up in the office, where the forelady Ivy Batchelor stood gazing out through the glass window over her Hesser girls. Soon she had invited Ethel up to the office to try her out on a new job, calculating the overall tonnage of the entire department. Ethel was delighted, especially since it meant working with Joanie and the other office girls. She hadn't made any friends on the factory floor and spent most lunchtimes eating a sandwich in the cloakroom on her own while the others all went to the canteen.

Louise Alleyne could not have been more proud of her daughter's promotion, especially since Gladys Rawlins, from Ethel's group of friends at home, had now also joined Tate & Lyle and was not progressing beyond sweeping the floor. When Ethel informed her mother of her friend's dead-end job, she responded in no uncertain terms, 'They put you on a broom, you come straight home. No girl of mine's going to sweep floors for the rest of her life.'

The words stuck in Ethel's mind, making her all the more determined to distinguish herself at work and win her mother's approval.

As the war moved into its final months, trips to the factory shelters grew increasingly rare. At eight p.m. on 8 May 1945 the voice of company telephonist Nellie Franks was heard over the loudspeaker system announcing that Victory in Europe had been declared. Production was shutting down immediately, and it was time to down tools and begin the party.

Most of the workers congregated in the Recreation Room, where the celebrations were soon underway, carrying on until well after midnight. Outside the factory gates, the locals had lit a huge bonfire made from railway palings and were dancing around it. Even the refinery director, Oliver Lyle, was spotted enjoying a quick jig with them on his way home.

Few parts of the country had as much reason to celebrate the end of the war as the East End, and the area lived up to its reputation for enjoying a good knees-up. Flags and bunting from the King's coronation nine years earlier were scavenged from old cupboards and strung up all over the houses, effigies of Hitler and his generals hung from the lamp-posts, and more bonfires sprung up in the war-damaged streets, those same East Enders who had fought the blazes caused by the Luftwaffe now raiding telephone kiosks for directories to keep the fires burning. Some enthusiastic souls let off fireworks they had been storing for six years, although the explosions, however beautiful, weren't universally popular among the battle-weary population.

While some grateful Christians hastened to church as soon as they heard the news, the majority of people hit the local pubs, where the sawdust was trampled underfoot more furiously than ever before. The amount of alcohol consumed was prodigious, and before long the drunkenness had spread to every street. Any pianos that had survived the bombing were dragged outside, along with accordions and radiograms, to provide the soundtrack to a party on a scale never seen before, and the locals sang and danced into the early hours of the morning.

Ethel and Archie headed to a pub in North Woolwich. Unfortunately, even on such a joyous occasion, not everyone was intent on celebrating the peace. As they got onto the bus,

Archie accidentally brushed past a drunk man, who took offence and tried to lunge at him.

The man hadn't counted on Archie's lady friend, however. Ethel may have been thin, but she was wiry, and before the man could get to her beloved Archie she had clouted him round the ear.

The nervous 14-year-old who had stood outside the gates of the factory had gone. Ethel was a sugar girl now.

2

Lilian

When Lilian Tull came to Tate & Lyle shortly after the end of the war, she was older than most new arrivals. A lanky, fair-haired woman of 23, she worked in the can-making department, where the Golden Syrup tins were assembled. Lilian had arrived on the job with a heavy heart, and her colleagues noticed a sad, far-away look in her eyes. At break times she could often be seen gazing at a small photograph that she kept in the pocket of her dungarees.

Lilian's job was to check that the bottoms of the syrup tins were properly sealed. She would pick up five at a time using a long fork and then suction test each one on a special disc. The ones that were faulty fell off and were sent for resealing, while the others continued on their way to the syrup-filling department.

The can-making suited Lilian, because the machines were so noisy it was difficult to talk. Many of the girls had developed the ability to lip-read, but even so the forelady, Rosie Hale, kept an eye out for anyone who seemed to be neglecting their machines, patrolling the room on a balcony above the girls and shouting 'No talking! Back to work!' She never had need to scold Lilian, who lacked the high spirits of her chirpy colleagues.

From her earliest years life had been a struggle for Lilian, and she knew the bitter taste of poverty well, having grown up in the dark days of the Great Depression. The Tull family had all slept in a single room on the ground floor of 19 Conway Street, Plaistow. The children shared a bed with their parents, which became increasingly crowded since their mother Edith seemed always to be pregnant or nursing a newborn. Nine babies came along altogether, and were kept quiet with dummies made from rags stuffed with bread and dipped in Tate & Lyle sugar.

The children were clothed in handouts from the church, chopped down to child-size proportions and re-hemmed by their mother. Their father's Sunday suit was a hand-me-down from the Pearces across the road – the only family in the street rich enough to afford a Christmas tree, and therefore considered 'posh'. Whenever he wore the suit, Harry Tull was painfully aware that all the neighbours recognised it from its previous owner.

Harry did shift work at the ICI sodaworks in Silvertown, coming home each night covered in cuts from the sharp pieces of soda he chopped up all day. Lilian's mother Edith would tenderly dress his wounds with strips of cloth covered in Melrose ointment. Keeping a large family on his wages wasn't easy, and life was lived constantly 'on the book', with this week's money going to pay off last week's shopping bill at Weaver's, the shop on the corner. The children were sent down to the greengrocers each weekend to ask for a ha'pence of specks – bad apples – to supplement their diet, and happily gorged on the bits of fruit that were left over once the rotten parts had been cut out.

Despite their poverty, Edith Tull was extremely house-proud. Every morning she could be seen on her hands and knees, scrubbing and whitening the doorstep until it glowed. Next, the shared toilet in the back yard was swilled down with hot water and new squares of newspaper were threaded onto the rusty nail that served as a loo-paper dispenser. Then the coconut matting came up and the place was swept and dusted vigorously until lunchtime. Monday was wash day, when Edith would rub the family's dirty linen on her washboard until her arms were covered in angry red blisters. Friday was the day for baths, with water heated in the copper by burning old shoes and boots if there was no money for fuel.

Before her husband returned from work each evening, Edith got a fresh piece of newspaper for a tablecloth and carefully laid out the mismatched cutlery and crockery she had got from the rag-and-bone man. Harry would come home and nod in approval. A strict, Victorian-style father, he regarded family teatime as sacred, and tapped his children with his knife if they weren't sitting up straight. The children themselves were too scared to speak at the table for fear of their father's disapproval, so mealtimes generally passed in silence. Secretly, they all looked forward to the weeks when he was on the late shift and their more soft-hearted mother allowed them to stay up past their bedtime.

Death seemed to hover over the Tull household. Baby boys Bernard and George came into the world and departed it the same day. When Lilian was six, her grandfather passed away suddenly, and not long afterwards her three-year-old brother Charlie died from unknown causes.

The latest death shook the normally restrained Harry Tull to the core. 'There's a curse on this family,' he cried bitterly.

Harry's greatest shame was that, since there was no money for a private burial, Charlie would have to be laid to rest in a communal grave at West Ham Cemetery, without a headstone. 'No son of mine's going to be buried in an unmarked grave,' he said, storming out to the back yard.

Lilian went to follow him, but Edith put a hand on her shoulder. 'Leave him be, love,' she said. 'Leave him be.'

Several hours later, Harry was still outside. 'What's Daddy doing?' Lilian asked her mother.

'Don't you worry about that,' came the reply.

Finally, Harry came back into the house, a look of silent suffering on his face. In his hand was a wooden cross he had made himself, the words 'RIP CHARLIE' lovingly carved into it.

'It's beautiful, Harry,' Edith said. Lilian saw that her eyes were filling with tears, and felt her own well up, too.

As was the custom, Charlie was laid out in his little coffin in the front room, for family and neighbours to pay their respects. Lilian watched the people come and go, wondering who they all were and why they wanted to stare at her brother.

As night fell the visitors no longer came and Edith told the children it was time for bed. 'What about Charlie?' Lilian asked.

There was nowhere else to put him, so the family bedded down in the same room as the coffin. 'Don't worry, love, he'll be sleeping too,' Lilian's mother reassured her, gently stroking her blonde hair.

Lilian lay awake all night, thinking about her dead brother lying just feet away from her and wondering if he was going to wake up in the morning.

When Charlie was buried the whole family laid flowers on the grave and Harry hammered the little cross into the earth. Out in the open it looked smaller and more delicate than it had in the house, flimsy in comparison with the real headstones elsewhere in the cemetery.

Harry shook his head. 'It ain't right,' he muttered to Edith.

When they got back to Conway Street, Harry sat with his head in his hands for a long time. Then, suddenly, he got up and marched over to the family's rickety old marble-topped washstand – virtually the only piece of furniture in the otherwise barren room – and began dismantling it.

'Harry – what on earth are you doing?' Edith cried, rushing over to him.

'If I can't afford to buy a headstone, then I'll just have to give this to Charlie,' he said, yanking the marble away from the wood.

Edith and the children watched open-mouthed as their father heaved the large slab under his arm and walked out of the door.

That Sunday, the children went with their parents to lay flowers at the cemetery. Lilian looked for the little wooden cross but couldn't find it. 'Where's Charlie's cross gone?' she asked her mother anxiously.

'Charlie doesn't need it any more, sweetheart,' Edith told her. 'Look.'

There in the earth was a marble heart, carved out of the washstand, with the name 'CHARLIE' engraved upon it.

When Lilian was 12 the Tulls were rehoused in a block of flats near West Ham station. The local fruit and veg seller lent them his horse and cart, and Harry and Edith piled into it what few possessions they had, followed by their children. 'I'm not sorry to see the back of that place,' said Edith, as they set off.

The Tulls couldn't believe their luck when they saw their new home. There were three bedrooms, which meant that Harry and Edith could sleep alone for the first time in more than a decade, and the boys and girls now had separate rooms, even if they did still have to share beds. 'Look, Harry!' said Edith in delight. 'There's a bathroom!'

Edith's enthusiasm for vertical living quickly waned, however. Their flat was on the top floor, and with no lifts in the building, climbing the stairs loaded with her shopping from Rathbone Market in Canning Town left her utterly exhausted. She had never been a robust woman, but now she had less energy than ever.

For Lilian, a shy, awkward child, the move to the flats brought her first true friend – a girl by the name of Lily Middleditch. The two soon became thick as thieves.

As the children grew older, Harry consoled himself over the loss of three sons by putting all his hopes into his eldest child, Harry Jnr, who was proving to be something of a brainbox at school. When he passed his exams, his father, glowing with pride, took Harry Jnr to work with him and got him a job in the offices at ICI. He himself might still be chopping soda, but now he went to work with his head held high, knowing his son was working 'upstairs'.

Lilian, meanwhile, was increasingly feeling like the school dunce. She was persistently coming bottom of the class and becoming shyer and shyer as a result. When she left school at 14, she and Lily Middleditch got themselves jobs at the RC Mills bakery in Hermit Road. For Lilian the bakery was a haven, where, unlike at school, she found something she enjoyed and that didn't make her feel stupid. She loved to help the baker make his fairy cakes and breathe in the sweet smells seeping from the ovens as they rose. The fresh ones went to the shop at the front, but the stale ones Lilian collected to sell off at the back door for a penny each to the long queues of hungry people who waited there each day.

Lilian was accident prone, however, and one day she burned her hand badly. 'Someone take that girl to the hospital,' shouted the baker, horrified, and Lily Middleditch quickly ran over, wrapped the wound in a tea towel and led Lilian away. The accident scarred her for life, but she refused to give up her job in the bakery.

Lilian was 16 when war broke out, and when the Blitz began a year later her mother and the younger children were evacuated to Oxfordshire. Since Lilian and Harry Jnr were in work and the family needed the money, they stayed in London with their father. Her brother had tried to volunteer for the Air Force but had failed the medical on account of an irregular heartbeat.

One Saturday, Lilian and Lily Middleditch had planned a trip to Green Street to look around the market. They worked the morning in the bakery as usual, then dusted the flour off their clothes and headed to West Ham station, arm in arm, to get the train.

The girls entered the station, bought their tickets and went up the stairs to the platform. As they waited for the train, they chatted excitedly about what they were going to buy. After a few minutes, they heard the mournful whine of an air-raid siren. 'Oh God,' said Lily Middleditch. 'It had to be on our afternoon off, didn't it?'

'Lily, look,' said Lilian, in a shaky voice, her eyes fixed on the sky over her head. Lily followed her gaze. There in the near distance was a line of tiny black planes, growing closer by the second. Lilian could already hear the distant grind of the engines, pulsing insistently. It was clear there was no time to get to a shelter and the station wasn't underground. She felt a sickening dread wash over her.

People began running along the platform towards the exit. Lily set off, but Lilian was still rooted to the spot, staring at the planes as if mesmerised by them.

Lily ran back and yanked at her arm. 'What are you doing? Come *on*!' she yelled, pulling Lilian behind her.

They made it to the top of the stairs and had just begun to hurry down them when they heard the first bombs drop. People started to panic, missing their footing and stumbling as they ran down the steps. A little girl screamed in her mother's arms. At the bottom a knot of confused people bumped into each other. 'Where do we go? Where do we go?' they asked frantically.

'Get down, everyone,' a man shouted. All around him the crowd obediently dropped to the floor. Lilian and Lily lay as flat as they could, their hands over their heads. No one said a word. They heard another explosion, then another. Lilian was shaking, and Lily reached out and held her hand, squeezing it hard.

Just then there was an almighty blast and a terrible crashing sound. The whole station seemed to shake and a hot wind rushed over Lilian's body, almost blowing her over. It was followed by the sensation of something soft raining down on her head and back. Lilian realised she had been holding her breath and now desperately needed to breathe, but as she gasped she seemed to be drawing not air into her lungs but thick, bitter powder, causing her to splutter and retch.

Beside her she could hear coughing, which soon gave way to screams. There was a horrible crunching sound and she could feel something heavier now dropping onto her back, as if she was being pelted with pebbles.

This is it, she thought, the station's collapsing. I'm going to die.

Lilian tried to tuck her head even closer into her body, protecting her neck from the onslaught as well. She had lost Lily's hand but didn't dare reach out for it again. After a while she couldn't feel the debris hitting her body directly any more, but the mass on top of her grew heavier and heavier. Her mouth was on the arm of her cardigan and she tried to suck air through it to avoid breathing in more dust. Time seemed to stand still, and in her mind Lilian could see her parents' faces, dropping in despair as they were told they had lost another child, while behind them someone cried 'Lilian … Lilian … Lilian.'

Suddenly the faces disappeared and the sound of her name being called rushed to the fore. It wasn't in her head now but above her, and it was accompanied by a raking sound. She felt hands reaching through the debris and encircling her upper body, and she was lifted out of the rubble, dust and stones streaming off her. Lily Middleditch was there, and Lilian realised it was her voice she had heard. She grabbed her friend's hand and they followed the other people, stumbling and gasping, out into the sunlight.

Although she was outside, Lilian found it was still impossible to breathe through her nose because her nostrils were completely blocked with dirt and dust. It was in her ears too, and in her eyes, which were itchy and sore. Her fair hair was coated in grey, and everyone's faces and clothes were grey too, as if the colour had been drained out of them.

She and Lily hugged each other and then without a word began to run down Manor Road back towards her block of flats.

All around lay the wreckage of other buildings destroyed in the raid, and dirty, bloodied people were everywhere, some of them desperately pulling at piles of bricks, others simply standing around in shock. But Lilian didn't have time to think about anyone else. All she wanted to know was whether her brother and father – who would have finished his Saturday shift around the same time as her – were all right.

As they turned the corner, Lilian's heart sank. The block of flats had been hit and her mother's beloved apartment, with its bathroom and separate bedrooms, had been blown to smithereens.

Panic-stricken, she ran towards the remains of the building shouting, 'Dad! Harry!' Her throat was so dry from breathing in the dust that it came out as a rasping noise.

She had lost Lily Middleditch in the chaos but as she scoured the scene her eyes landed on a familiar face – that of their neighbour, Mrs Draycock. Seeing Lilian distressed and dirty she hurried over.

'Lil, don't worry, there was nobody in,' she said. 'You all right?'

'Yes, I'm – all covered in dust,' Lilian blurted out. For the first time, she realised she was shaking.

Mrs Draycock put her arm around her. 'Never mind about that now, love. You come with us – we're going to the country to get away from all of this.'

Lilian could do nothing but nod mutely. She followed Mrs Draycock, her daughter Rosie and son Bobby, and boarded a bus heading out to Essex.

A short time later, they arrived at the village of Dunmow and were assigned a condemned cottage to stay in. Lilian was still covered in dust and had nothing to change into, but the local church was handing out old clothes and she gratefully took a bundle. When she unfolded it later back at the cottage, out fell the most beautiful thing she had ever seen: a man's dressing gown in hand-embroidered satin. She had never owned a dressing gown before.

While Lilian was safe in Dunmow, her father and Harry Jnr had returned to the flats to find them destroyed, and no sign of Lilian anywhere. They went all round the area asking those neighbours and friends who were still left there, but nobody had seen her.

Over the next few days, Harry Tull switched his search for a living, breathing daughter to one for her remains, fearing that the family curse had struck again. He went to the nearest mortuary, where he was told the corpse of a young blonde woman had been brought in and, convinced that it must be Lilian, asked to see it. He watched, trembling, as the body was uncovered – but to his relief it wasn't her.

He went to another mortuary, and then another, always filled with a sickening certainty that this time he would find his daughter. Each time, he would breathe a sigh of relief when he discovered she wasn't there, before the creeping dread set in again and he continued his search.

After a week, Mrs Draycock thought it safe to send her son, Bobby, back to London to let Lilian's family know where she was. He returned the same day with Lilian's father, who clasped his daughter so tightly in his arms that she could hardly breathe.

Then he straightened himself up and assumed his usual, Victorian manner. 'You're going to Oxfordshire to be with your mum from now on,' he said, briskly. 'You'll be safer there.'

Mr Tull was right that his daughters were safe from the bombs in the countryside, but little did he know what other perils lay in wait for them there.

Without their father's strict discipline and sobering presence, the younger Tulls and their mother were having the time of their lives. They were one of two evacuee families put up in the gamekeeper's cottage on the estate of Kirtlington Park, a grand country house a few miles north of Oxford with 50 acres of parks and gardens designed by Capability Brown. An area of the park that was normally a polo ground had been cultivated by the Dig for Victory campaign, while a farm had been turned into an RAF airfield. Hundreds of evacuees and land girls were living in the great house itself.

Coming from the bombed-out East End, Lilian thought her new home was a paradise, and without her father around she felt freer than she had for a long time. One of the first notable effects of this new freedom was the possibility of fraternising with the opposite sex.

At home, Lilian's father had kept a close watch over his daughters, making it nigh on impossible for boys to get anywhere near them. A few months earlier, Lilian and Lily Middleditch had met some boys at Memorial Avenue Park, and as they were walking back towards the flats one of the boys, who had taken a shine to Lilian, flirtatiously pulled the scarf she was wearing off her neck. Up on the top floor, Harry Tull was leaning out of the window, intently watching the proceedings through a sixpenny toy telescope belonging to his youngest son, Leslie. As soon as he saw the scarf slipping from his daughter's neck his head popped back into the house, the telescope dropped to the floor and he rushed as fast as he could down the stairs and out of the flats. He marched up to the group of terrified teenagers, clamped his hand on Lilian's shoulder and commanded: 'Home!'

In Oxfordshire, far away from the long arm of Harry Tull, Lilian and her sister Edie – who was just a year her junior – were brave enough to venture into the village alone in the evenings. There they attended the Kirtlington village hall, which was becoming quite a hub for dances at the time, what with all the land girls looking for some distraction in the countryside. Unfortunately there were never enough men to go around, which left many of the girls standing at the side of the room or resorting to dancing with each other for most of the evening. Lilian didn't mind – her natural shyness meant she was happy just watching the spectacle.

One night, however, as the band was striking up a waltz, she saw a handsome, dark-haired young man walking across the room towards her. Instinctively, Lilian glanced over her shoulder to see who he was looking for, but Edie and all the girls behind her had moved away to get drinks.

'Would you like to dance?' he asked, holding out his hand. Lilian was gobsmacked. He sounded so gentlemanly and grown-up, and must be at least ten years her senior. Why on earth would he want to dance with a lanky teenager like her?

She gave him a shy smile. 'I don't know how to waltz,' she said.

'Never mind, just follow me,' he replied, taking her hand and leading her onto the dance floor.

To begin with, Lilian tried awkwardly to follow his steps, but her limbs were rigid. 'Just relax,' the man whispered gently. Suddenly the two of them seemed to be in perfect unison, and she was twirling across the floor as if she did this every night. Lilian caught sight of Edie at the side of the room, staring at her with a look of surprise and disbelief. She quickly closed her eyes before her sister's expression ruined her composure.

With her eyes closed, Lilian could focus completely on the sensation of being held by another human being. It wasn't one she was used to, and it felt so safe and secure.

Over time, Lilian learned that the handsome stranger's name was Reggie, that he was 27, and that he had been born and brought up in Kirtlington. He worked at the Morris Motor Company factory in Cowley, near Oxford, which to his delight was now producing mine sinkers and Tiger Moths instead of cars.

Suddenly Lilian's life was full of music, dancing and laughter. She and Reggie went dancing in the village hall every Friday and Saturday, and for long country walks together on Sundays. Reggie always escorted her home to the gamekeeper's house on the outskirts of the village, and with no Harry Tull around they smooched on the doorstep for as long as they liked.

'He's such a lovely-looking fella,' swooned Lilian's mother Edith. 'Such nice manners, too.'

'It's not fair,' complained Lilian's sister Edie. 'Why can't I meet someone like Reggie?'

'We'll find you a nice man soon enough, don't you worry, my girl,' said her mother.

Edith's promise was fulfilled sooner than she expected. A few days later, she returned from shopping in the village to see a lorry parked at the side of the road and a young soldier standing next to it.

Wandering over to see if he was all right, she discovered that the young man's vehicle had broken down and he was waiting for assistance, but it was likely to be a while coming. He was shy and sweet-looking, and Edith took to him instantly. 'Come inside for a cuppa, why don't you?' she said, smiling to herself, and he happily followed her into the game-keeper's house.

'Edie,' she called, as she came in, 'there's a young soldier here's broken down and wants a cup of tea.'

Edie came rushing to the door, smiling her most winsome smile, and the man looked at her as if he had just walked through the gates of heaven.

Harry, as he was called, was a farm labourer from Suffolk who was down in Oxfordshire with the Army on manoeuvres, and soon he and Edie were a couple of lovebirds like Lilian and Reggie. Their mother looked on in pleasure at her two daughters and their handsome young men.

'We're Edith and Harry, just like you and Dad!' Edie told her. 'Ain't it perfect?'

'What would Dad do if he could see us now?' Lilian chipped in.

The question hung in the air and she and Edie both shuddered slightly. Then they burst out laughing.

The country idyll ended all too soon for Lilian when she was called up for war work and assigned a job at the Plessey electronics factory in Ilford, which was now producing shell cases and aircraft components. Her Aunty Hilda, her father's sister, had found the family a new house in Cranley Road, Plaistow, and Lilian was to move back in with her father and brother. She was devastated.

'Reggie,' she sobbed, 'promise me you'll write.'

'Course I will,' he said, holding her tight. 'I've got a little something for you for when you're not with me.'

He reached into his pocket and drew out a small photograph. 'I had it taken in Oxford,' he said, proudly.

Lilian clasped it to her breast, grateful to have something of Reggie to take with her.

Back in the East End, the days at Plessey's were long and the work was frequently interrupted by air-raid sirens. Lilian was sad to discover that her friend Lily Middleditch had joined the forces and was no longer around. She lived only for Reggie's letters now, rushing to the door to be the first to get her hands on the post so that her father wouldn't see them, and squirrelling them away until she was safely on the bus out of Plaistow. She would read every letter slowly, making each word last. Every break time the latest missive would come out again and Lilian would reread it, until the creases in the paper had worn thin.

At first, Lilian was sending two letters for every one she received from Reggie. Then it became three, then four. To her desperation his correspondence was petering out. She wrote to him again, begging him to reply, and his letters became more frequent. Lilian's heart soared. But it was short-lived, and soon the letters were thinning out once more.

At work, Lilian found it hard to concentrate and before long her clumsiness got the better of her again. A piece of machinery came down on her finger, leaving a scar.

'What's wrong with you, girl?' asked her forelady.

'I'm sorry,' she cried. 'I just wasn't quick enough.'

To avoid the long evenings at home with her father, and to take her mind off Reggie, Lilian volunteered as an air-raid warden. Every night she donned her blue uniform and set out on the lookout for fires. But no matter how many flames she doused, her love for Reggie burned all the stronger.

When her mother and siblings returned to London, however, she discovered she wasn't the only one with problems stemming from those carefree country days.

Lilian was walking along Cranley Road on her way home from work when she heard the unprecedented sound of shouting coming from her house. Nervously, she pushed open the front door, slipped inside and closed it quickly behind her.

Her father was in a rage the like of which she had never seen before. 'It's a disgrace,' he was shouting, 'a disgrace to the whole family!' Before him stood her mother and, sobbing in her arms, a distraught Edie. As Lilian entered the room, Harry Tull stormed out of it, and Edie collapsed to the floor.

'Edie, what's happened?' asked Lilian, rushing over to her, but Edie was too upset to speak.

'She's pregnant, love,' said her mother, quietly. Lilian looked down at her sister's shaking body. 'I should have done something,' Edith continued, miserably. 'I should have done something.'

'No, Mum,' said Edie, suddenly looking up, her face wet and patchy with redness. 'It's not your fault.' Then she looked at Lilian. 'Oh Lil,' she said, 'what am I going to do?'

'We'll just have to write to Harry and get you two wed,' said her mother, hopefully. 'It'll all work out fine, just you see.'

If Harry had been close at hand, no doubt Edie's father would have marched him to the altar immediately, but he was far away, fighting abroad. The agonising wait for letters to be sent and received ensued, and when the response finally came it was worse than they could have feared. Harry, it turned out, was already married.

The girls' upstanding, Victorian father was facing the unthinkable: an unmarried daughter giving birth to a child under his roof, with no hope of being made an honest woman. The disgrace to the family was beyond measure. How would Harry Tull cope with the shame? Would he disown Edie? His wife knew she had to do something fast.

'I've found out about a lovely little place run by the Salvation Army,' she told Edie a few days later. 'It's in Hackney, up in North London, so no one from round here will know where you are.'

Edie nodded silently. She knew there was no point in protesting. Lilian said goodbye to her sister, and for the next few months Edie disappeared from their lives, seen only by their mother in discreet visits.

In the autumn of that year, Edie returned, looking older and more womanly than Lilian remembered. In her arms was a little baby boy. 'I named him Brian,' she said. 'Brian Tull.'

Her father looked down at the sleepy face of the baby, not so unlike little Charlie who had been lost before the war, and his heart melted.

Before long Harry Tull was out in the yard once again, this time whistling away as he built a cot for Brian out of some scraps of wood. He duly proved himself the most doting grandfather in the East End.

Meanwhile his daughter Edie lived in hope that once her Harry came out of the Army he would return to her and meet the son he had fathered.

By the time Lilian joined Tate & Lyle, soon after the war was over, Reggie's letters to her had stopped completely. Yet something about him, about the way he had made her feel when she danced in his arms, meant she just couldn't let him go, and she felt that she never would.

Lilian kept the little black-and-white photograph he had given her when she left Kirtlington, and when she thought no one was looking she would take it out and look at it longingly. She read his last letter over and over again, trying to decipher the meaning behind the words. Had he met someone else? Had she done something wrong? The questions hanging over the end of their affair tortured her constantly.

Meanwhile her best friend, Lily Middleditch, wrote to say she had met and married a soldier while in the forces and would be moving to his home town of Blackpool. Lilian had never felt more alone.

* * *

At the factory, Lilian found she wasn't the only one whose mind kept drifting back to the events of the war years. In her department, a girl called Winnie Taylor told of her friend Olive, who had been buried in the rubble when the shop she worked in was hit by a doodlebug. She escaped with her life but was deeply traumatised, unable to cope with any sudden noises, and thereafter always had a stammer. Many Tate & Lyle workers found it hard to escape their memories, particularly the scenes of violence and bloodshed they had witnessed. On the Hesser Floor, Anne Purcell couldn't shake the image of a neighbour she had found lying on the ground after a bombing raid, her arteries and veins hanging out of her arm; in the Print Room, Pat Johnston was haunted by the memory of a bus conductress she saw running up her road with one eye blown out. Meanwhile, Pat's teenage cousin was losing his hair from the stress of witnessing a woman's head being blown off by a bomb, seconds after she had pushed him out of harm's way.

In the factory offices, a girl called Barbara Bailey still bore the scars she had suffered when a window had blown in during a bombing raid and filled her face with glass. Her mother had told her to get under the kitchen table, but Barbara was reading a book at the time and had insisted on getting to the end of the page.

The men of the factory had their own traumatic memories to deal with. Some had been interned in Japanese prisoner-of-war camps and now struggled when they saw oriental boats on the Thames – whenever one passed the raw sugar landing, the men there shouted for 'the bastards' to be thrown overboard. Others had been involved in the liberation of Belsen, and told stories of the terrible scenes they had witnessed.

Many refugees had settled in the East End after the war, and among them, at Tate & Lyle, was a Polish man called Bassie. His steel-grey eyes always seemed to be staring at unknown horrors, but nobody dared ask what they were.

One bitterly cold day it was snowing, and Bassie was pulling the handle of a truck carrying bags of sugar on steel pallets. Two younger men were meant to be helping, but were slacking off and complaining about the cold.

'You think this is cold?' Bassie demanded suddenly.

'Yeah, Bassie, it is,' they replied.

'You don't know cold,' he said. 'You don't know hard. I've chopped trees at 50 below zero in Siberia. When the Russians invaded our country they took us away in cattle trucks and gave us rotten fish eggs and old bones to eat. They made us dig holes to live in. If you couldn't do it, kneel down and bang, you're dead.'

The boys were shocked by Bassie's words, but fascinated to hear the normally reticent man speak about his past, and were determined to question him further. They learned that he had come to Britain under an arrangement to take Polish prisoners into the forces.

'Why didn't you go back to Poland after the war?' asked one of the young men, Erik Gregory.

'I can't go home,' Bassie replied. 'There is nothing there.'

'What about your family?' Erik asked him.

Bassie shook his head. 'Auschwitz,' he said quietly. 'Gassed by the Germans. You don't know what hardship is, and I never want you to. But don't you take the piss with me.'

The boys nodded respectfully, and never complained to Bassie about their work again.

3

Gladys

While Lilian Tull's family seemed to live under a curse, Gladys Taylor's had something of a lucky streak. Although their house had received a direct hit on the first night of the Blitz, seven-year-old Gladys, her four brothers, baby sister and parents had survived – emerging blinking from their Anderson shelter just a few feet away, completely unscathed.

They had just been admitted to the local rest centre, in the basement of South Hallsville School in Canning Town, when they were intercepted by Gladys's Aunt Jane. 'Don't even bother staying here, the place is packed to bursting,' she advised them. 'We can hitch a ride to Kent instead, and go hopping till things quieten down.'

Soon the whole family was huddled in the back of a lorry, relieved to be getting out of harm's way. They began to curse their decision, however, when a German fighter plane swooped and began machine-gunning the vehicle as it was going over Shooter's Hill. They passed the rest of the night cowering underneath the lorry, wishing they hadn't listened to Aunt Jane, before finally making it safely to the hop fields in the morning. But little did they know how fortunate they had been.

While the Taylors spent the next two days hop-picking, the 600 people at South Hallsville School continued to wait for the coaches that were due to pick them up and take them to the countryside. Sunday and Monday went by, and still the vehicles hadn't arrived. They were offered no explanations, just endless cups of tea. A rumour went round that the drivers had mixed up Canning Town with Camden Town in North London and gone to the wrong place.

As darkness fell again on Monday night, so too did the bombs. One made a direct hit on the school, demolishing half the building and causing many tons of masonry to collapse onto the people huddled below. Hundreds of terrified men, women and children lost their lives, in one of the worst civilian tragedies of the Second World War.

Five days later, when the Taylors returned to London to pick through the wreckage of their home, neighbours' mouths gaped at the sight of them. Their names had been on the list of those declared dead, and if not for Aunt Jane they too would have ended their days in the wreckage of Hallsville.

Some attributed the Taylors' luck to the fact that Gladys's mother Rose was from a well-known gypsy family, the Barnards. A tiny Romany woman with long, plaited hair rolled into enormous coils on either side of her head, Rose had been expected to marry inside the gypsy community. But after a childhood spent roaming the fields of Kent and Sussex in a caravan, she had been determined to give her own children a more settled existence.

To that end she married a young man from Tidal Basin, near the Royal Victoria Dock, moving into a flat on Crown Street right next door to his parents. The neighbourhood was full of sailors who had married and settled down there – many of them black men who had taken up with local white girls, lending the road the nickname Draughtboard Alley.

Rose may have wanted a settled life, but her new husband Amos, a red-headed and rebellious seaman, had other ideas. Perhaps she should have heeded the warning lying in his parents' garden – Amos's uniform, helmet and gun, which had been hastily buried there when he deserted from the Army and ran off to sea during the First World War.

After fathering three sons with Rose, Amos did a second disappearing act, going AWOL from the family for 18 months without a word. When Rose could bear his silence no longer, she threw off her pinny and marched up to the shipping office, demanding that her husband be traced. The errant father was discovered to be working as a professional footballer in New Zealand, and duly returned with his tail between his legs.

The arrival on the scene of Gladys, with a shock of red hair just like her father's, prompted the final showdown between Rose and Amos, whose seafaring could no longer be tolerated now that there were six mouths to feed. 19 Crown Street trembled to the sounds of the almighty row, which ended in his service book being ripped up and thrown onto the fire. Amos accepted his fate, and a job in the docks – where he would wistfully sing the dirty sea ditties of his youth. But he never quite forgave his daughter for thwarting his ambition.

Fourteen years later, Gladys's own ambition in life was to become a nurse. Playing doctors and nurses had been a favourite game ever since, aged three, she had fallen ill with diphtheria and had her life saved by the staff at Sampson Street fever hospital. She had also been told more than once that, compared to other girls, she was remarkably unsqueamish, a virtue she assumed was much needed in the medical profession. Having been brought up with four brothers, she was a natural tomboy who didn't think twice about picking up spiders or other creepy-crawlies, to the horror of the girls at school – a habit which frequently landed her in the headmaster's office. One day she had pierced her own ears out of curiosity, and she was soon piercing those of the local gypsy boys as well. She was used to the sight of blood, thanks to her dad's hobby of breeding chickens and rabbits to sell at the pub, which he would slaughter and nail upside down in the back yard to drain.

With no qualifications to her name, save for a half-hearted reference from her long-suffering headmaster stating that she was a trustworthy sort, Gladys headed straight to the hospital on Sampson Street as soon as school was out, and collected an application form.

She returned excitedly to Eclipse Road, clutching the papers in her hand.

'What've you got there, love?' her mother asked.

'It's my papers from Sampson Street. I'm going to be a nurse!'

'Oh yeah?' said her father, raising his red eyebrows. 'And do you know what you have to do when you work in a hospital?'

'Well, look after people and all that,' said Gladys.

A mischievous grin spread across Amos's face. 'You have to get old men's willies out and hold them while they wee!'

'I'm not doing that!' shrieked Gladys, who had never seen a grown man's willy in her life.

'Well you're not going to be a nurse then, are you?' said her father, erupting into a loud belly laugh.

Gladys tore up the papers in disgust and threw them onto the fire, watching her own ambitions fly up the chimney. 'What am I going to do then?' she moaned.

Her dad grinned with satisfaction. 'What do you think? Go down Tate & Lyle's like everyone else.'

On Monday morning, Gladys found herself outside the Personnel Office at the Plaistow Wharf Refinery. A shiny new sign on the door read: MISS FLORENCE SMITH, LABOUR MANAGERESS.

Gladys knocked reluctantly and a deep voice issued from the other side of the door. 'Come in.'

Inside the pokey little office, three women were seated behind a single long table. In the centre was Miss Smith, a huge, broad-shouldered boulder of a woman with a stern, matronly look. Her blonde hair was cut in a short, severe crop, and her grey suit and white blouse were buttoned up so tight over her enormous bosom that it was a wonder she could breathe. She was a recent appointment to the top woman's job at the factory, although no one who met her would ever have guessed.

The other two women in the office were both called Betty. To Miss Smith's left was the young Personnel secretary, Betty Harrington, and on her right sat her deputy, Betty Phillips, a thin woman with glasses.

Miss Smith nodded to a chair opposite the three of them. 'Sit down,' she ordered.

Gladys slumped into the seat. Miss Smith took in her boyish frame and messy ginger hair. 'Have you left school yet?' she asked suspiciously.

'Yeah, of course,' Gladys retorted.

'Name? Address?'

'Gladys Taylor, 38 Eclipse Road, Plaistow.'

Miss Smith scribbled on a white form.

'Do you have a letter of recommendation?'

Gladys fished around in her pocket and handed over a crumpled piece of paper. Miss Smith read the headmaster's carefully chosen words.

'Well, that's certainly concise,' she said, handing it back.

What a cow, thought Gladys, stuffing the paper back into her pocket.

'And why did you wish to work at Tate & Lyle in particular?'

'I didn't really,' Gladys said, before she could stop herself. The two Betties shuffled nervously in their seats.

Miss Smith looked up from her form and glared at Gladys. 'I have four rules in this factory,' she said. 'No make-up, no jewellery, no swearing – and no cheek. Is that understood?'

'Yes, Miss,' muttered Gladys, beginning to feel she had walked straight out of one headteacher's office and into another.

'Good. I think we'll start you in the Blue Room and see how you fit in there.' Gladys could have sworn she saw a glint in Miss Smith's eye. 'You'll be on six-to-two one week and two-to-ten the next. Report to the gate at six a.m. sharp tomorrow and ask for Julie McTaggart. She'll be your charge-hand.'

Six a.m.? Gladys was horrified. But before she could protest, Miss Smith had stamped the form and handed it to one of the Betties for filing.

Gladys's first week at Tate & Lyle made her school record look flawless by comparison. On Tuesday morning she was woken by her mother at four-thirty a.m. 'Your shift starts at six – you'd better be quick,' Rose said, shaking the snoring bundle under the sheets.

'Can't,' Gladys protested.

'Well, you'll be on two-to-ten next week – you can sleep then,' said her mother, plonking a bowl of bread and hot milk down next to her.

Gladys dragged herself into a sitting position and slurped her breakfast down. She grabbed the nearest available clothes and put them on, before attempting to pull a comb through her unruly red hair.

'Time to go or you'll miss your bus!' called her mother. Gladys gave up the battle with her hair and ran down the stairs, passing her father as she went. 'Have fun!' he chuckled, and she gave him a scowl.

From Eclipse Road it was only a couple of minutes' dash to the bus stop, where Gladys hopped on the back of a 175 trolleybus along the Beckton Road. At Trinity Church she caught a second bus, the 669 to North Woolwich, which she knew would drop her at the gates of the factory.

The bus travelled down the Barking Road, passing Woolworths, the men's outfitters Granditers and the women's clothes shop Blooms. They went by the corner of Rathbone Street, home to the area's thriving market, where anything and everything could be bought for the right price, from eels still wriggling in their buckets and freshly beheaded chickens to broken biscuits, soaps made from the pressed-together pieces collected from hotel bathrooms, and steaming cups of sarsaparilla.

At the end of the high street, the bus turned left onto Silvertown Way, passing the Liverpool Arms pub and the

Imperial cinema as it began the gentle climb up to the familiar twin protractors of the Silvertown Viaduct, which crossed over the railway lines heading further east. It was here that Winston Churchill had stood during the early days of the Blitz to survey the horrors meted out on the dockside community, and from the same vantage point seven years later Gladys could see the extent of the devastation suffered in her former stomping ground of Tidal Basin. The area had been virtually flattened, and the old Victorian dwellings were now being replaced with the modern flats and houses of the Keir Hardie Estate, the most ambitious building project in West Ham's history.

As the road dropped down towards Silvertown, the great expanse of the Royal Victoria Dock stretched out to her left, where the giant ships unloaded cargo from all over the world. She passed the lock that linked the dock to the Thames, and then suddenly they were in the heart of industrial West Silvertown, with British Oil and Cake Mills, Pinchin Johnson's paint factory and Ohlendorff's fertiliser plant spewing out smoke from their giant chimneys. A swarm of shift workers was descending on the factories lining the river on her right, and on her left was the parade of little shops and cafés that served the local community, as well as the Jubilee pub where many a Tate & Lyle worker celebrated the week's end. Before long she could see the refinery itself, and the bus conductor called out, 'Tate and Lyle, Plaistow Wharf. Disembark here for the knocking shop!'

A peal of gruff laughter went around the bus, which was largely filled with dockers and factory men, among whom Tate & Lyle had something of a reputation for promiscuity.

But one young sugar girl on the bus was not amused. 'Excuse me, mate,' she shouted angrily, 'I work there and I'm not a tart, so I think you ought to shut your mouth!'

There was another roar from the crowd, this time of approval for the plucky teenager. The cowed conductor muttered an apology, before the tough young woman marched off the bus. Gladys followed close behind, a little in awe.

Near the bus stop was a coffee stall and newspaper stand where the workers were picking up their morning's necessities. The crowd thronging towards the gates of Tate & Lyle was particularly heavy, but amid the bustling movement one man stood perfectly still. He was a slim, elegant-looking fellow in a pale mackintosh, with grey hair slicked back across his scalp, and he stood scribbling in a little notebook.

His name was Bob Tyzack and he had never got over being given the sack from Tate & Lyle. He stood outside the factory day in, day out, noting down the lorries coming and going, for reasons known only to himself. This was particularly awkward for his brother Bill, the head commissionaire, who was charged with making sure he never stepped onto the factory grounds. The Tyzacks were a well-known Tate & Lyle family, and their name was soon to become famous across the country when Bill's niece Margaret became a film star.

Gladys headed across the road with the rest of the throng. She looked up at the big white clock above the factory gates, which read two minutes to six: she wasn't late yet.

Suddenly a collective groan went up from the crowd – a train was about to pass along the tracks in front of the gate. They waited impatiently for it to go through. 'That's it, we'll be docked a quarter of an hour's pay now!' grumbled one girl.

Gladys turned to her. 'But the train won't take that long, will it?'

'Don't matter,' said the girl. 'You're even one minute late here, they close the gate and make you lose 15.'

This harsh rule prompted some Tate & Lyle workers to risk their lives by scrambling under the trains as they slowed down, and stories went round the factory of the injuries suffered by those who had miscalculated.

When the gates finally reopened there was a great rush towards a board on the wall, where clocking-in discs were waiting on hooks to be collected and taken to the various departments. Gladys was almost knocked over in the fray, but fought her way to the commissionaire and asked for the Blue Room charge-hand, Julie McTaggart.

Before long, she saw a stern-looking woman with very dark hair marching towards her, hands clasped firmly behind her back.

'Gladys Taylor?'

Gladys nodded.

'You're late.'

Defiance welled up in Gladys's chest. 'It weren't my fault,' she retorted. 'It was the train. Silly place to put it, if you ask me.'

Julie looked at her straight-faced. 'I didn't.'

They headed to the surgery, where a nurse checked Gladys over and passed her fit for work. Then Gladys followed Julie into another building. 'We're in here, underneath the syrup-filling,' Julie said, leading her into a cloakroom and pushing a bundle of clothing into her hands. 'Don't be long.' The door swung closed, leaving Gladys alone in the little room.

She laid out the pile of clothes on a wooden bench: a pair of dark-blue dungarees and a blue-and-white checked blouse – plus a spare set of each. Like going into the bleedin' Army, she thought ruefully.

Gladys changed into her new uniform. The dungarees hung loosely on her boyish frame, the crotch resting somewhere down by her knees and the backside looking like a crumpled sack waiting to be filled with potatoes. The short-sleeved blouse seemed to have been designed with a buxom matron in mind, and one with arms as thick as her legs, not a skinny, flat-chested 14-year-old. What kind of monstrous creatures worked in this Blue Room?

Then Gladys noticed the final addition, which had fallen to the floor by her feet – a piece of checked cloth which was evidently intended for a turban. 'How am I supposed to wear that?' she muttered, scooping it up. She twisted it around her head a few times, shoved the end under the rim, and tried unsuccessfully to poke her red hair beneath the material.

As she left the cloakroom, the dungarees flapping between her legs almost tripped her up. She followed Julie McTaggart into a long, narrow room which was painted blue. 'This is where we print the packets for the sugar,' Julie told her.

Around twenty girls were standing at machines of varying sizes. They were chatting and laughing loudly, singing along to music, or talking to young men who were hauling great reels of paper onto one end of the machines. Behind a glass partition was an office where the forelady Peggy Burrows sat, busy with her paperwork.

As Julie approached, a hush immediately fell and several girls rushed back to their machines from other parts of the room.

Gladys stared at them open-mouthed. Far from the monstrous creatures she had expected, they were all extremely young, slim and glamorous, their dark-blue uniforms neatly tailored to show off their figures and their checked turbans not roughly assembled cowpats like her own, but towering works of art that gave them the stature of models. As they returned her gaze, some of them began to giggle and Gladys's pale skin turned bright red as she remembered the baggy dungarees swinging between her legs.

'Be quiet, the lot of you,' snapped Julie. She turned to Gladys. 'Let's get you to work.'

At each machine, a girl stood watching the progress of the paper, checking for smudging as it turned dark blue and the white letters 'TATE AND LYLE PURE GRANULATED SUGAR, UNTOUCHED BY HAND' emerged. The machine then cut the papers down to the size of sugar bags and spat them out at the other end onto a pallet which, when full, was taken away by one of the boys to the Hesser Floor for filling. Every now and then the girl would pick up one of the stacks of paper, fanning them out and expertly counting them in fives up to 1,000. Everybody, Gladys noticed, had blue ink-stained fingers.

Julie led Gladys over to a machine. 'If your reel starts running out, call one of the boys to replace it immediately, and keep an eye on the ink duct – if it's running low, get an engineer to top it up,' she told her. 'And if you need the loo, put your hand up so someone can take your place. We can't have the machines stopping for anything.'

Gladys nodded.

'Maisie!' Julie shouted across the room. 'Stop flirting with the reel boys and come and show Gladys the ropes.'

Gladys turned to see a young blonde woman saunter across the floor. She was without doubt the prettiest and most glamorous of all the Blue Room girls, and that was no mean feat. Her uniform seemed to be a few centimetres tighter even than everyone else's, and the top few buttons of her blouse were undone. She walked with a distinctive wiggle, which the best-looking boy on the floor was currently doing an impressive job of imitating behind her back. When she heard the other boys begin to whistle at the spectacle, she swung her head round with a swish of her beautiful hair. 'Give it a rest, Alex, you ain't got the hips for it,' she told him.

Julie McTaggart looked at Maisie disapprovingly before marching off, her hands behind her back.

Maisie walked over to Gladys, and leaned in to whisper in her ear. 'She was in the ATS in the war,' she said, nodding to Julie. 'Thinks she still is.'

Gladys giggled. Then, looking up at Maisie, she found herself mesmerised by her eyes. Each one was framed by the thickest, darkest, most luscious curled lashes she had ever seen.

'Like 'em?' Maisie asked, batting them seductively. 'I bought them myself. Now let me introduce you. That's Joycie and Eileen – they're sisters – and Rita their cousin. Over there's Ruthie, Annie, Blanche and Joanie,' she said, pointing to girls who looked no more than 14 or 15 themselves and who gave her a friendly nod. 'And that's the other Annie, Dolly, the two Lils and Ivy the cleaner,' she added, waving to some women who looked very grown-up. They must be in their early twenties at least, thought Gladys.

'That cheeky bugger working on the scrap paper is Alex,' Maisie said, 'and the reel boys are Robbie, Johnny, Barry and Joey – he's that sweet one over there who's lame in one leg. A word of advice – don't get stuck behind a reel with Robbie or you'll find his hands wandering where they shouldn't.'

'Oh no they won't,' said Gladys confidently, 'or he'll get a clout from me.' Inwardly she felt relieved that there were some lads here she could have a laugh with, amid all the glamour girls. She had grown up with four brothers, and most of her friends in Plaistow were male.

Gladys soon discovered that working in the Blue Room was far from strenuous, and after twenty minutes or so she began to realise that the hardest thing about it was keeping her concentration. She found it was perfectly possible to take her eyes off the job for several minutes at a time and look around for something more entertaining to do – as long as she turned back quickly enough when Julie McTaggart came past on patrol, or Miss Smith appeared on her daily round. Since the other girls appeared to be terrified of Miss Smith, a shout of 'The Dragon's coming!' went up from the person nearest the door as soon as she approached, and the warning was quickly passed around the floor.

The best opportunity for fun came from the reel boys who, working on a floor full of girls, were in a permanent good mood. When Barry went past with a reel of paper, Gladys fell into easy conversation with him. 'They left you room to grow in that, have they?' he teased, pointing to her outfit.

'Oi you, don't be cheeky,' she retorted. 'I'm not so skinny I couldn't lift one of those reels of yours.'

'Nah, girls can't do it. That's why you need us strong men around,' he joked.

'Oh yeah?' she said. 'Pass me one then, and let's see.'

As she turned towards him, away from her machine, Gladys felt something tugging at the back of her right thigh. Maisie's warning about Robbie's wandering hands flashed into her head, and she quickly looked over her shoulder, her fist clenched in readiness to deliver the promised clout.

To her surprise, there was no one there. Instead, she looked down with horror to see that the machine was giving her dungarees the alteration they so desperately required, wrapping the baggy material round and round a spindle and making them increasingly tight.

'Barry, help me!' Gladys said, turning back to him while frantically clutching at her behind.

'Oh, so you've changed your mind now, have you?' he joked. 'You girls do need my help after all?'

'No, you don't understand – I'm being sucked into the machine!' she cried, pulling at the material with all her might and feeling it slip, bit by bit, through her fingers.

'Yeah, nice try,' laughed Barry, turning away with his reel.

'It's cutting off my blood flow!' Gladys hollered, her face bright red with the effort of resisting the machine. Her right trouser leg was now at least as figure-hugging as those of the other Blue Room girls, and it was getting tighter by the second. She could feel a creeping numbness at the top of her thigh.

Barry dropped the reel he was holding, which went careering along the floor leaving reams of paper in its wake, and grabbed her around the waist. 'Let's pull at the same time,' he said. 'Maybe we can rip the material.'

Gladys nodded.

'Ready? One … two … three!'

They both yanked as hard as they could, but the factory-issue dungarees were sturdy. Gladys herself was now pressed right up against the machine. 'It's going to swallow me,' she gulped.

Other girls ran over to see what the commotion was about and one of them began to scream.

'Turn off the machine!' shouted Barry.

'But we can't – we're not allowed,' said Maisie, flustered.

'Turn it off now!' screamed Gladys, silencing them all.

One of the other reel boys ran round to where a big red button waited, ready for the unthinkable act. He slammed his hand down hard and the machine whirred briefly before coming to a final, juddering halt. The spindle gave up its claim on Gladys's trouser leg and she pulled it free, feeling the blood rushing back all the way down to her foot. She gave the machine a heartfelt kick of retaliation.

'What do you think you're doing?' Julie McTaggart shouted, rushing out of the office. 'And how dare you turn off this machine!'

Gladys opened her mouth to protest, but Julie didn't give her a chance to answer.

'Get to Miss Smith's office immediately,' she told her.

The other girls stared at Gladys as if she had just been handed a death sentence.

'Good luck,' whispered Maisie, anxiously.

'The rest of you, back to work,' snapped Julie, and they all hurried off to their machines.

Inside the Personnel Office the two Betties were typing away, but there was no sign of Miss Smith.

'Oh, hello,' said Betty Phillips. 'We didn't expect to see you again so soon.'

'I couldn't stay away,' quipped Gladys, bitterly.

Miss Smith marched into the room and took her seat behind the desk, leaving Gladys standing awkwardly before her. 'So what have you done? I'm waiting,' she demanded.

'They had to turn off my machine,' Gladys admitted. 'But it weren't my fault! I only looked away for a second, and my trousers got sucked in.'

'You shouldn't have looked away at all,' Miss Smith told her sternly. 'Not only is it extremely dangerous, but if the machine has to be stopped then the company loses money.'

Gladys looked at the floor. 'It would never have happened if they'd given me the right size uniform,' she muttered bitterly.

'I think you've forgotten my fourth rule,' said Miss Smith.

'What's that?' asked Gladys, struggling to recall anything before the life-threatening incident.

'No cheek,' said Miss Smith, firmly.

When Gladys returned to the Blue Room, the girls were astonished to see her. 'We all thought The Dragon was going to sack you,' Maisie whispered. 'How come you're still here?'

'I dunno. Beginner's luck?' shrugged Gladys.

When break time finally came, the girls invited her to come with them for breakfast at the café across the road. 'You don't want to bother with the canteen here, it's too dear,' Maisie told her.

They joined a gaggle all heading across the road, some of them dressed in dungarees and checked shirts like her own but in a lighter blue. 'Those are the Hesser girls,' said Maisie, disdainfully. 'Look at them, they're like navvies!'

As they neared the café they saw two dockers who were about to go in. Hearing the girls' chatter, the men glanced behind them and immediately changed their minds. 'We're not going in here, mate,' said one to the other, as they hurried off. 'Not when it's full of sugar girls.'

Once inside, Gladys could see why. The place rang with the noise of female shift workers laughing, singing, chatting and shrieking, while the café owners ran around like maniacs trying to deal with the breakfast rush.

She looked at the menu. Eggs, bacon, tomatoes, bread and butter … and fried mushrooms! Gladys had never eaten mushrooms before, and after the events of this morning who knew if she'd survive long enough at Tate & Lyle to get another chance to try them?

'I'll have mushrooms on toast,' she said confidently, as if ordering her usual.

The mushrooms arrived, tender and dripping with butter, and Gladys savoured each bite of her exotic treat, while trying not to appear too excited. As she did so, the other girls confided to her the secrets of the Blue Room. Printing was the easiest job in the factory, they told her, so she was very lucky to have been given it. Theirs was one of the smallest departments – much smaller than the Hesser Floor – and therefore far more exclusive. Peggy Burrows, the forelady, took such pride in her machines that every night at the end of the late shift the girls were told to stop work half an hour early to clean them with methylated spirits till they shone.

But the biggest source of pride was the fact that the Blue Room had acquired the unofficial title of the Beauty Shop, thanks to the svelte appearance of the girls. One of their number, Iris – a six-foot stunner – had gone down in legend for running off to Paris to join the Bluebell Girls as a topless dancer. It was beginning to dawn on Gladys that there were standards she was expected to uphold – and that she was rather ill-equipped to do so. Had Miss Smith sent her to the department for her own amusement?

'Why are all your uniforms so tight compared to mine, then?' she asked, butter dribbling down her chin.

'They weren't when we got them,' winked Joanie. 'The trick is, once you get them home, you put a seam up the front and back of the dungarees so they fit more snug. You'll have to take your blouse in, too.'

'Then you'll have to get that turban up a bit higher,' put in Joycie.

'How do you do that?' asked Gladys.

'Knickers,' she said.

'Knickers?'

'Yeah, you wind up the turban with stockings, knickers, socks, whatever you've got. Helps bulk it out a bit. Flo Smith don't like it – a notice went up saying we wasn't to do it no more, but bit by bit we've been sneaking them in again.'

Work finished at two p.m., but Gladys knew she still had a long afternoon ahead of her. She was determined to rein in her unwieldy dungarees before tomorrow, and that meant taking them in by hand – a laborious process, especially given her pitiful needlework skills.

She caught her two buses home and turned the corner into Eclipse Road, where she spotted the group of local lads she usually hung around with, going up the street with a football. Among them was a bespectacled boy called John, whose mother always made him wear a ridiculously short leather sports jacket. 'Oi, Bum Freezer!' Gladys shouted. This was her nickname for him, in return for which he called her 'The Girl with the Lovely Legs', which was guaranteed to annoy a tomboy like Gladys.

'You coming for a kickabout?' he asked her. 'We're going over Beckton Road Park.'

Gladys considered for a moment. She would dearly love the opportunity to give John a good thrashing at football, especially considering how stupid he looked right now in his jacket. But then the image of the glamour girls in the Blue Room floated back into her mind.

She sighed. 'Can't. Got more important things to do now, ain't I?'

On Wednesday, Gladys went into Tate & Lyle with her head held high – very high, in fact. Her turban was now stuffed full of as many of her brothers' socks as she could find, as well as several pairs of knickers and a few stockings for good measure. Her dungarees had been sliced almost in two to fit her skinny frame, and the crotch was now where it belonged.

As she walked into the Blue Room, the girls nodded in approval. 'I like your turban, Gladys,' said Joycie. 'It's even taller than Maisie's!'

'Thanks,' said Gladys, with attempted nonchalance, shoving the enormous bundle back into place as it began to slide down her forehead.

To the girls, Gladys had come top in the day's unofficial fashion stakes, but the boys saw her new headwear as an irresistible challenge – particularly since they knew what must be wrapped up in it. When the coast was clear, Robbie and Joey gave each other a quick wink and Joey walked over to Gladys's machine with a concerned look on his face. 'Oh dear,' he said, frowning as he pointed to the ink duct. 'I think you might be running out of ink.'

'Really?' said Gladys, peering into the duct, unaware of Robbie sneaking up behind her. 'But I only just had it filled up.'

She felt the turban sliding forwards again as she leaned over, and put up a hand to steady it. But before she even reached her brow, Robbie had already flung out an arm and whipped the turban clean off her head, leaving Gladys to grasp at nothing but a handful of ginger curls.

'Oi, give that back, you buggers!' Gladys shouted, spinning round in time to see the checked cloth flying through the air, her assorted underwear cascading out of it as it unravelled. The boys' laughter was so loud it momentarily drowned out the noise of the machines. Then it stopped abruptly.

Gladys followed their gaze and watched as a pair of white knickers finished its graceful flight and landed, with perfect precision, at the toe of a very large ladies' shoe. She looked up at the shoe's owner and found herself meeting the angry stare of Miss Smith, who had arrived on her daily round of the factory.

'Pick up your things immediately,' she barked, as Gladys scrambled to collect the offending items. 'The turbans are for safety, not for making fashion statements.'

Gladys hurried back to her machine, but when Miss Smith had circled the room she stopped by her again. 'I've got my eye on you,' she said, before marching out of the door.

On Thursday morning, Gladys's mother brought her freshly washed uniform up to her room, along with her bowl of bread and milk.

As Gladys pulled on her dungarees, they seemed smaller than she remembered, and she had trouble getting her feet through the leg holes. By the time she had squeezed her thighs and bottom in, the once-baggy dungarees seemed to have become even tighter than any in the Blue Room.

Gladys attempted to sit back down on the bed and felt a sharp pain around the tops of her legs as the material pinched her skin. She ate her breakfast standing up, before hobbling painfully down the stairs.

At work, Maisie regarded her pityingly. 'Oh dear,' she said. 'You didn't take the dungarees in *before* you put them in the laundry, did you? They always shrink the first time you wash them.'

Gladys spent the morning standing rigidly at her machine, trying not to breathe in too deeply and dreading the inevitable moment when Miss Smith would come by on her daily round. When she saw the matronly form entering the room, she rolled her eyes. 'Here we go,' she muttered to herself.

'Gladys Taylor,' said Miss Smith, with undisguised pleasure, 'I know you're intent on making an impression here, but how on earth do you expect to bend over in those?'

By Friday, Gladys was almost beginning to feel at home in the Blue Room. She might not have been as glamorous as the other girls there, but they seemed to have accepted her as the department's token tomboy. She had even proved useful by piercing a few of the girls' ears in the toilets, and at break times she had begun to join the reel boys in a game of football in the yard rather than spending all her time chatting in the café.

After a week of trials and tribulations, she felt she had been well and truly initiated into life at the factory. But the reel boys had other ideas.

Among Tate & Lyle's male workforce, the tradition of initiation rituals was strongly embedded, and usually involved sugar or syrup being poured down the new recruit's trousers. Girls weren't generally subjected to this sort of thing, but Gladys had unwittingly set herself up as fair game. So what was the appropriate initiation for a boyish girl?

Barry, Joey, Johnny and Robbie put their heads together. It couldn't be anything too mean, they reasoned, or they'd look like bullies. But Gladys didn't seem like the kind who'd burst into tears at a bit of good old-fashioned fun, either.

'I've got it,' said Joey, with a sparkle in his eye. 'The telpher.'

The telpher was a large wooden crate which went around the outside of the building on a cable, carrying items from one department to another. It made its journeys a good twenty feet in the air and was most certainly not designed for human cargo.

The others looked at him apprehensively. 'What if she breaks it and falls out?' asked Barry.

'Nah, she won't,' insisted Joey. 'She'll be safe as houses.'

The boys bided their time until after breakfast, when they saw Julie McTaggart go into the office to talk to Peggy Burrows. A quick wink between them signalled the moment, and once again Joey was dispatched to distract the unsuspecting Gladys.

'I think your ink duct needs refilling,' said Joey, struggling to keep a straight face.

'Oh yeah,' said Gladys, raising her eyebrows. 'What are you buggers up to this time?'

She turned and caught sight of Barry and Johnny attempting to sneak up behind her. 'Oh no you don't!' she called, setting off at a sprint across the room. 'You'll have to catch me first!'

The boys gave chase after Gladys, whose years spent playing football in Beckton Road Park had made her a lithe and speedy runner. As she zigzagged in and out of the machines she eli-cited cheers of 'Go, Gladys!' from the other girls. But with four boys to contend with she eventually found herself cornered.

'You won't find nothing in my turban but my brothers' old socks,' Gladys told them.

'Oh no, we've got other ideas for you,' Barry replied, as they scooped her up and carried her to the opening for the telpher.

'You're going on a little trip,' said Joey as they deposited her into the crate.

'Oh am I?' said Gladys. 'Fair enough then. I quite fancied some air!'

She waved as the telpher set off on its jaunty journey and the boys waved back, clutching their sides with laughter. Gladys sat back in the crate, taking in the view of the sky while it made its way along the cable. It wasn't a bad way to get out of work for a while, she thought to herself, although it was probably best not to look down.

Eventually the telpher arrived back where it had started. Gladys scrambled to her feet to alight from the crate. 'Anyone else fancy a ride?' she called cheerily. Then her heart sank.

Waiting for her by the opening was Miss Smith. 'My office,' she commanded. 'Now.'

4

Ethel

Up in the Hesser Floor office, Ethel was settling in well. She was thrilled to have taken her first step up the company ladder, and keen as ever to live up to her mother's high expectations. The office work was dull, but much easier than the physical labour of manning the machines. Her duties included calculating the overall tonnage of sugar packed by the department, checking the time-keeping records for the girls on the factory floor and liaising with the delivery department about how much sugar was ready to be sent out.

There were no typewriters in the office, so all the writing was done by hand. Ethel's friend Joanie Warren, along with two other girls – Iris Lawrence and Beryl Craven – would sit hunched over their desks, scribbling away under the watchful eye of the forelady, Ivy Batchelor. Ethel found she clicked much more naturally with the girls in the office than the rough-and-ready types on the factory floor, and soon started going out with her new friends to the Imperial cinema in Canning Town or to the roller-skating rink at Forest Gate.

But while her social life was improving, Ethel's love life had hit a new obstacle. One by one the boys in her old gang had begun to volunteer for the forces. First Johnny went into the Air Force, then Alf and Lenny signed up with the Army. Ethel knew the inevitable was coming, and sure enough, her beloved Archie soon followed in their footsteps, becoming a private in the Royal West Kent regiment. He was sent to Germany, and from then on the two young lovers only got to see each other every six months, although they wrote to one another devotedly every day.

One evening, Ethel was surprised by a visit from a neighbour – the only resident of Oriental Road who owned a telephone – announcing that there was a young man on the line for her. She rushed next door and grabbed the receiver, thrilled at the prospect of hearing Archie's voice, but terrified that something might be wrong. What was so urgent that it couldn't wait for a letter?

'Arch?' she shouted down the line. 'Is everything all right?'

There was a pause, and then she heard a voice she hadn't expected.

'Um, hello, Et. It's Len here.'

'Oh, Len …' Ethel hadn't seen Lenny Bridges since the boys had all signed up together. 'What are you doing ringing me?'

'I wanted to ask you something,' Lenny replied, hesitantly.

'Yes?'

'Well, I was wondering …' Lenny's voice trailed off.

'What is it?'

'I thought maybe you might like to marry me.'

Ethel was flabbergasted. Lenny knew how devoted she was to Archie, and Archie was one of his best friends. Was it possible that all this time he had been harbouring his own feelings for her?

'No thank you!' she said shrilly, hanging up immediately. She backed away from the phone and rushed out the door.

As soon as she got home, she wrote to Archie, explaining what Lenny had said to her and asking if he could shed any light on the matter. For the next few days she waited anxiously to receive his reply.

When the letter finally came, Ethel couldn't believe it. Far from the angry tirade she had been expecting, Archie's response was calm and philosophical. He told her that he and Lenny had been drifting out of touch anyway, and this only served to make it more final.

Ethel knew that in Archie's shoes she would have responded very differently, but her mind soon turned to another question. Wasn't it a bit odd that Lenny had beaten Archie to a proposal? Ethel had always assumed that they would marry once he came out of the Army, but he had never actually made his intentions clear. Soon she was worrying again, on this new, more troubling score.

Not long after, Joanie Warren invited Ethel over to her house in Canning Town for a party to celebrate her grandfather's birthday. It was a good old-fashioned knees-up, and by the time she arrived the alcohol was flowing freely.

'What'll it be, young lady?' the host demanded, as she entered a room which was full to bursting with people having a good time. Ethel realised that she didn't know how to answer. She wasn't normally the type to go out to dances or parties, and barely ever drank. She dimly remembered her father pouring her mother a port and lemon in the past, so she asked if she could have one of those.

The drink arrived and Ethel discovered it was surprisingly tasty. She knocked it back more quickly than she had expected, and soon asked for another. Apart from anything else, it was a useful way of avoiding joining in with the general singing and dancing going on around her.

But after a while, with her glass constantly refilled, Ethel found she wasn't quite so averse to joining in after all. Before long, she had linked arms with a circle of people and was jigging around the room. She had spent her life always being the sensible one, and this new wildness felt wonderfully liberating. Soon she had lost count of the number of port and lemons she had necked, and was well and truly letting her hair down.

'I wish the party could go on forever!' she announced to a rather surprised Joanie. The evening was beginning to wind down, however, and it was time for people to make their way home.

Ethel's body was not used to alcohol, least of all the impact of innumerable port and lemons – made worse by the fact that she and Joanie had also gobbled a large quantity of sweets, bought using some ration coupons they had found in the street. By the time she got home her stomach had begun to protest, and soon she was hit by an overwhelming wave of nausea. She did her best to ignore the persistent lurching feeling, but it grew worse and worse, so she took one of her mother's buckets out of the scullery and put it within easy reach of her bed. It wasn't long before she was making good use of it.

Every time Ethel was about to drift off to sleep her stomach began to convulse again and she clambered frantically over to the bucket, holding back her dark frizzy hair as she threw her guts up once again. This sorry routine continued all night long and she was retching well after the last of the weekend's excesses had been expelled.

On Monday morning, as the first rays of light began to stream through the curtains, Ethel felt like each one was stabbing right into her brain, and her stomach was still doing somersaults.

'Time to get up!' her mum shouted, at what seemed like a deafening roar.

'Too sick,' Ethel croaked, pulling the bedclothes over her head. Missing a day at Tate & Lyle was almost unthinkable to her, but on this occasion even she had to admit defeat. She spent the rest of the day in bed, and at lunchtime Joanie came to see how she was doing.

The next morning Ethel's stomach was still in a pretty tender state, but she managed to haul herself into work regardless. When she got up to the office, Iris, Joanie and Beryl had their heads buried in their work, and Ivy Batchelor was waiting in the doorway.

'I'm sorry about yesterday,' Ethel said anxiously.

Ivy looked at her with an expression of disappointment. 'You'll be back on the factory floor today, Ethel,' she told her, 'packing on machine number one.'

Ethel was crushed. 'Yes, Ivy,' she said quietly. She went down to take her place on the belt of the machine, trying to avoid making eye contact with any of the girls around her. She was sure they would be having a good laugh at her expense.

The packing was every bit as exhausting as she remembered, and it did nothing for the queasy feeling in her stomach. At the height of summer, it was now desperately hot on the glass-roofed Hesser Floor, and the girls were soon dripping with sweat. A girl from the canteen brought up a jug of so-called Jungle Juice, a concoction specially formulated to replace salts lost from their bodies, but in her delicate state Ethel found it virtually undrinkable.

She also struggled with the rowdy culture on the factory floor, which seemed more raucous than she remembered from her previous stint on the machines. While they were working, the Hesser girls would shout and joke non-stop, and whenever a poor boy was sent to the department to plug a gap in numbers, the teasing would be merciless.

'Come on then, pretty boy!'

'Ooh, get a look at those big, strong arms!'

'Come and give us a cuddle then!'

By the time Ethel left at the end of the day, her uniform was stiff with sugar. She had forgotten how messy the packing could be. The last time she had worked on the machines she had found the whole experience rather exciting, but now it seemed the ultimate humiliation.

When Ethel got home that afternoon she hurriedly took off her sticky clothes. She was dreading having to explain to her mother what had happened at work. All she could think of was how she had reacted when Ethel's friend Gladys had not progressed beyond sweeping the factory floor.

When it came to it, Louise Alleyne was remarkably restrained. Perhaps she could see the distress on Ethel's face, and couldn't bring herself to compound it with criticism.

'Don't worry, love,' she told her daughter, pulling her close. 'You'll be up there again before long. I know my girls.'

It was small consolation for Ethel, who felt she could scarcely sink any lower in her own estimation, let alone her mother's.

It was not long, however, before the family had more serious problems to deal with. Louise had been in poor health for a while, and one night after the evening meal, when Ethel and Dolly were still sitting at the kitchen table and Winnie was playing outside, she posed a troubling question to her two elder daughters.

'If anything happened to me,' she asked, 'would you want Dad to get married again?'

There was an awkward silence while the question hung in the air.

'Well,' Ethel said thoughtfully, trying her best to channel a wisdom that belied her 16 years, 'I suppose so, if that's what Dad wanted.'

They both looked at Dolly to see what her response would be.

'No,' she said, impulsively. 'I wouldn't want him to.'

Of course, Louise's question had not just come out of the blue, and before long the truth was revealed to the children: their mother was dying. She had been suffering with heart trouble for a while now, and when she caught pneumonia the illness left her weaker than ever. The doctor gave her strict instructions to rest, but, despite Ethel's protestations, she insisted on hobbling around the house, busying herself as usual. Soon she had developed dropsy.

After a spell in hospital, Louise was sent home to spend her final days with her family. As she lay in bed upstairs, the sound of a woman shouting in the street outside irritated her greatly. The woman's name was Peggy, and every time Louise heard her voice she would say to her daughters, 'I wish that woman would just be quiet.'

Ethel couldn't quite put her finger on it, but something about Peggy made her dislike her too.

One night, Ethel was woken before dawn by her father. 'Come and say goodbye to your mum,' he whispered, as he led her, Dolly and Winnie along the corridor to their parents' room. Louise was lying there in perfect silence, as though held in a trance, and Ethel felt half bewitched herself as she walked over, kissed her on the cheek and then stumbled back to bed again. The whole thing felt like a strange dream.

It was only in the morning that Ethel understood clearly that her mother had died. The rest of the family spent the day together, dealing with the undertakers and arrangements for the funeral, while Louise's spinster sister, Aunt Ethel, came up from Brighton to help look after the family. But young Ethel insisted on going to the factory as usual. She knew how proud her mother had been of her success at Tate & Lyle.

Following her sister's death, Aunt Ethel harboured hopes that her newly widowed brother-in-law might make her a nice husband, but she was to be disappointed. Not long afterwards, Jim started a relationship with Peggy, the woman whose loud voice Louise had found so distressing. Ethel thought back to what her mother had said when she was dying, and to her question about their father remarrying. Had she already known what was coming, when Ethel was too young and naïve to see it?

Strangely, now that Louise was gone, Ethel and Dolly's reactions to the prospect of a new woman in their father's life had been reversed. For Ethel, the relationship came far too soon, and she still had an instinctive dislike of Peggy. Yet Dolly – who had argued against her dad moving on – quickly hit it off with her.

The schism in the family became so bad that Ethel no longer felt comfortable in her own home, and she started spending her Sunday afternoons visiting Archie's mother up the road. Maude Colquhoun was a widow and was bringing up a ten-year-old daughter called Honour on her own. She worked in a golf-ball factory not far from Tate & Lyle and, like Ethel's father, played piano in the Graving Dock Tavern for a bit of extra money. Maude treated Ethel like a daughter of her own, saving her helpings of plum pie and custard whenever she came round.

Seeing how unhappy her son's sweetheart was at home, and with Archie away in the forces, Maude soon suggested that Ethel move into the Colquhoun household. To Ethel, it was the perfect solution, even though it meant leaving the house where she had spent half of her childhood. She might only be 16, but after all she was a grown-up now, and surely her future lay with Archie.

Ethel quickly grew fond of Archie's little sister Honour, spending her free time taking the little girl to the pictures or out to the park. Back in the Alleyne house, meanwhile, Dolly grew increasingly close to Peggy, and the two would often spend days out together across the river in Woolwich.

On one such occasion they found themselves at the Army barracks, where a dashing young soldier named Paddy took a shine to Dolly's blonde curls. A whirlwind romance ensured, and within less than a year Dolly had married him. Ethel was not invited to the wedding.

Ethel felt that her family had been well and truly torn apart. She hadn't spoken to her father since she had left home, and soon she learned that her youngest sister, Winnie, was now living with their Nanny Potter in East Ham.

That Christmas, Ethel was about to sit down to a dinner of baked rabbit with Maude and Honour, when there was a knock at the door. She opened it and was surprised to find Dolly on the doorstep, kicking the snow from her boots.

'Have you got a paper that Paddy could borrow?' her sister asked her.

Taken aback at the unexpected visit, Ethel didn't know how to respond. 'No, sorry, Dolly,' she told her, 'there's no papers on Christmas day.' Her sister duly went away again.

Only later did Ethel realise that perhaps Dolly had been feeling lonely, and was trying to find an excuse to come and see her.

Soon Dolly discovered the downside of being married to a soldier: long periods apart while her husband was posted abroad. Paddy went away for an 18-month stretch, leaving her to live with her Aunt Liz. He sent money back to his wife regularly, but one day it suddenly stopped.

Dolly couldn't understand it – had her husband forgotten all about her? She and Peggy hurried to the Army barracks in Woolwich to find out what had happened.

'Don't you know?' an unsympathetic record-keeper asked her incredulously. 'Your husband's a deserter. We ain't seen hide nor hair of him for months.'

Paddy did finally show his face again, and he and Dolly did their best to make a go of things. They moved into a flat together in Custom House, and before long Dolly was pregnant.

When Ethel heard that her sister had given birth, she hurried to the hospital, determined to be there for her. Paddy came too, but he refused to go up to see his wife.

'Where's Paddy?' Dolly asked Ethel, as soon as she entered the room.

'He's sitting in the waiting room,' she said awkwardly.

Dolly was distraught. 'I don't understand. Why won't he come up and see me?'

'I don't know, Doll, I'm sorry,' Ethel told her.

Soon Paddy had left Dolly for good, and before long they were divorced.

The problems at home made Ethel throw herself into her work more than ever, and she was keen to rise up again from her position on the factory floor. Hauling bag after bag into perfectly stacked parcels, never allowing the slightest backlog to form, she did everything she could to prove to Ivy Batchelor that she was the best sugar girl the forelady had ever seen.

Sure enough, her determination paid off, and before long she was invited up to the office and offered a second chance at promotion.

Ethel was ecstatic, thinking about how proud her mother would have been. 'Yes, of course, Ivy,' she said. 'I'll start right away.'

Ethel was in charge of the tally count for all the machines on the floor, marking down on a form the number of bags each had packed so that Ivy could see who was pulling their weight. She would scrawl out blocks of five on a rough sheet and then copy the results onto a neat one at the end of the day. Ever efficient, Ethel would save a few precious minutes in the afternoon by estimating the day's count on the neat sheet first thing in the morning, so that it only had to be slightly amended later when the number of bags packed was known.

This system worked a treat, until one day Ethel made a terrible mistake, copying down the whole of the day's actual output in addition to the prediction she had already marked. She thought the sheet looked fuller than usual as she handed it in, but told herself it must have just been a good day.

Of course the truth came out the next morning, when Ivy took her aside and told her she had overbooked the department. Her mistake had led to chaos throughout the factory as thousands of phantom bags of sugar were promised to customers.

Ethel was mortified. 'I'm so sorry, Ivy,' she pleaded, fighting back tears.

Ivy nodded sagely, aware of the poor girl's distress. 'It's all right, Ethel,' she said kindly. She knew that her mother's death had taken a toll on her, and perhaps a few mistakes were to be expected given the circumstances.

'I'm afraid I'm going to have to put you back on the machines,' she continued. 'We'll start you on packing again for now, but perhaps if all goes well you can work your way up to bag filler and maybe even driver in due course.'

Ethel couldn't believe that once again she had sabotaged her own progress with a silly mistake. She felt as if she was playing a perpetual game of Snakes and Ladders, falling backwards again every time she managed to win a promotion.

When Ethel got home, feeling low, Mrs Colquhoun was nowhere to be seen. Honour collared her in the passage. 'Mum's got a letter from Arch,' she told her, 'and as soon as she read it she disappeared into the front room.'

Ethel's heart sank even further – had something terrible happened to Archie? The door to the front room was locked, and when she and Honour put their ears to it all they could hear was the sound of Maude pacing up and down on the wooden floorboards.

'I need you to help with something, Honour,' Ethel told the little girl. 'Can you find out what it says in that letter?'

Honour nodded eagerly, pleased to be trusted with such an important duty. Ethel walked around the block a few times to give the girl a chance to speak to her mother. When she got back, Honour was there in the passageway waiting for her.

'It's about you, Et,' she told her. 'Archie says he's going to marry you!'

Ethel was stunned. She had received her own letter from Archie that very morning, and he had said nothing of the sort. Despite the embarrassing episode of Lenny's phone call, he had never brought up the subject of marriage.

Ethel's next letter to Archie was a model of artless naïvety. She claimed to know nothing of what he had written to his mother, only how Maude had reacted, locking herself in the front room and pacing up and down. What could he possibly have said to disturb her?

Of course, Ethel's feigned innocence smoked out the truth from her boyfriend, and with typical nonchalance he replied by the next post: 'Don't worry about Mum. I just told her I was going to marry you.'

You might have asked me first! Ethel thought to herself. She immediately fired off another letter, accepting Archie's proposal – and castigating him for his cheek.

5

Lilian

Unfortunately for Lilian, who was nervous and accident-prone at the best of times, the can-making department was something of a pet project for refinery director Oliver Lyle. 'Old Ollie', as he was known to the girls, was a man in his mid-fifties with white hair and large black spectacles. He was an eccentric fellow who had once hired four fire hoses and a jet engine in order to test the claim that his newly installed windows could survive a hurricane (they did not). Mr Lyle was a natural obsessive, and prided himself on the intense personal interest that he took in the workings of his factory. Once, during a visit to a refinery in Hungary, he had fallen into a tank of sugar-beet juice, so intent was he on listening to the details of the production process employed there. The Hungarians got him out quickly enough, but his suit – the only one he had brought with him – crystallised on cooling, and was soon as solid as a suit of armour.

Mr Lyle's obsession with the little tins that still bore his grandfather's iconic branding – the lion and bees, above the biblical quotation 'Out of the strong came forth sweetness' – meant that the girls in the can-making department felt particularly proud to be working there. But his frequent, unannounced visits also kept them on their toes. As soon as his white hair was spotted at the door, the message 'Old Ollie's coming!' went round the room in a flash, and everyone stood up a little straighter, adopting an intensely focused attitude.

As each day wore on, the department would get hotter and hotter, and the girls were in the habit of rolling up their dungarees to cool themselves. One morning, when Old Ollie came in on one of his inspections, Lilian was busy daydreaming of her lost love, Reggie, and didn't heed the boss's arrival.

'Pssst!' she heard from behind her.

Lilian turned to see a short, blonde girl with dimples gesticulating wildly. She was mouthing something that looked like 'Uncles'.

Unfortunately, since Lilian generally kept herself to herself, her lip-reading skills were way behind those of most of the other girls. 'What?' she mouthed back.

'Uncles! Uncles!' the other girl repeated.

Lilian suddenly noticed Old Ollie, who was bending over to inspect a syrup tin, and realised to her horror that she still had her dungarees rolled up almost to her knees. She hastily shoved them down to her ankles, realising as she did so what the girl had been trying to say to her.

Old Ollie didn't speak to the girls, but just smiled a benevolent smile. When he had passed her machine, Lilian turned round and gave the other girl a thumbs-up. She winked in reply.

That lunchtime in the canteen, Lilian collected her food and was about to sit down to eat on her own as usual when she spotted the small, blonde girl waving to her. She hesitated for a moment but it was too late to turn back, so she took her tray and walked over to where the girl was sitting.

'Lilian, ain't it?' the girl said in a high-pitched voice, motioning to her to sit down. 'I'm Lilian too, but they call me Little Lil.'

Little Lil turned to a very large, plump girl next to her who had short, curly blonde hair. 'Lilian was flashing her legs at Old Ollie this morning!' she told her.

'I didn't mean to,' Lilian began to protest.

The large girl broke into the heartiest cackle Lilian had ever heard. Several people turned around and looked over to see what the commotion was. As the girl laughed her second chin wobbled merrily, her huge frame heaved and she slapped an enormous hand onto the table.

'Lilian, this is Old Fat Nell,' said Little Lil.

'Hello,' said Old Fat Nell in a deep, rich voice, offering Lilian an enormous hand. Next to Nell, Little Lil looked even smaller and more birdlike than before. They were certainly a bizarre pair.

'What'll we call you, then?' Old Fat Nell said, looking Lilian up and down and taking in her tall, lanky frame. 'We've already got a Little Lil.'

'She can be Big Lil!' squeaked Little Lil, with another bright, dimpled smile.

Big Lil, Little Lil and Old Fat Nell quickly became a firm trio, their matching fair hair but very different figures making them an eye-catching phenomenon around the factory. Lilian had never met such upbeat, cheery people before. Around them she had the distinct feeling of walking into the sunshine after a long, long time in the shade.

Lilian liked the fact that unlike other girls, who wanted to spend their time dressing up and going out to dances to meet boys, her new friends were happy to spend their Friday nights going to the pictures or having a giggle over a pie and mash. Lilian had been burned too badly by her relationship with Reggie to even look at other men, and ever since she had been buried under the rubble at West Ham station she had developed a morbid fear of the dark, which put her off staying out late.

One day, however, Old Fat Nell pleaded with the two Lils to accompany her to the Liverpool Arms in Canning Town. She had heard it was having a musical night and she was keen to get up and have a sing. 'C'mon, Big Lil,' she said. 'We won't stay out late. I'll look after you.'

'You have to hear this girl sing – she's got a better voice than Vera Lynn,' advised Little Lil, looking at Lilian hopefully. It was difficult to say no to Little Lil, and Lilian found herself agreeing.

The three girls met at seven p.m. and headed into the pub together. It took a while for their eyes to become accustomed to the gloom. The place was busy and they struggled to push their way to the bar.

Little Lil stood on her tiptoes and tried to catch the eye of the barman, but after five minutes she was still waiting to be served. Just as it looked as if he was coming over to them, he was distracted by a man with bleached blond hair who was holding out a note.

'It's not fair,' moaned Little Lil. 'I was here before him!'

The man's name was Georgie Nicholls and he was a well-known local 'queer' who had a penchant for wearing make-up. He was nevertheless hard as nails, and if any of the local dockers gave him lip he wouldn't think twice about belting them with a killer right hook. It was said he had developed this fighting instinct because his father had beaten him as a youngster in an attempt to knock the 'bentness' out of him. Evidently, it hadn't succeeded.

However, Georgie's hard-nut reputation didn't deter Old Fat Nell. 'Excuse me,' she said, pushing past a couple of men who instantly got out of her way. She brought her big hand down on the bar. 'Oi,' she called to the barman. 'She was here first!'

Her booming voice carried across the whole room and heads began to turn. The barman shrugged at Georgie apologetically, heading over to Little Lil instead. She smiled her sweetest smile and ordered two gin and limes, and a beer for Old Fat Nell.

The piano started up and they heard a voice at the other end of the room warbling an awkward rendition of 'I Wonder Who's Kissing Her Now'.

'You could do better than that, Nell,' said Little Lil.

When the song came to an end, Lilian watched uneasily as Old Fat Nell gulped down the last of her beer and marched up to the piano. There was a titter somewhere in the crowd and Lilian bit her lip, hoping that they would be kind to her.

'*I'm not too pretty …*' sang Nell.

'You're not kidding!' a man behind them shouted out, followed by a peal of laughter. Oh God, thought Lilian, covering her face with her hands, why did she have to sing that?

'*I know I'm not bright,*' continued Nell, oblivious. '*But I can still dream a man's holding me tight.*'

Her deep, sonorous voice rang out across the pub, and bit by bit the crowd fell silent. Lilian peeked out from behind her fingers and saw that everyone was watching Nell in awe.

'*Why can't anyone see all the good that's in me? And why shouldn't I be in love too?*'

As soon as she finished singing, the crowd burst into applause. Nell pulled an enormous toothy grin and walked back to join her friends.

'You were bleedin' brilliant!' said Little Lil, reaching up on tiptoes to give her a kiss. Lilian offered her congratulations too. Perhaps it was just the gin and lime, but she felt a rush of pride and happiness. She had found a group of people who she belonged to, and who belonged to her. And she hadn't thought about Reggie once all evening.

Back at the factory, the change in Lilian was noticeable. She seemed happier, more upbeat and less scared of making mistakes with her work. As the days and weeks passed without any accidents, Lilian's confidence grew, and she was moved onto a more complex job, making the bodies of the syrup tins.

One day, as she was switching her machine off, the forelady Rosie Hale approached her. 'Lilian,' she said, 'I've been watching you recently, and you're doing very well. I'd like you to go and see Miss Smith in the Personnel Office.' She gave Lilian's arm an encouraging squeeze.

Lilian beamed. She had never come in for praise at school, and after her miserable experience at Plessey's she had thought factory work wasn't for her either. 'Thank you, Rosie,' she said, blushing.

As she was walking over to Personnel, however, she felt a pang of nervousness spear her stomach. What if Miss Smith wanted to move her to another department, away from Little Lil and Old Fat Nell? She almost welled up at the thought. With Lily Middleditch now living in Blackpool, she couldn't bear to lose her Tate & Lyle mates too.

She knocked on the door of the office and the secretary, Betty Harrington, told her to take a seat. 'Miss Smith won't be a minute,' she said.

Lilian looked around her, uneasily. Away from the factory floor she was starting to feel like her old, unconfident self again.

'Lilian Tull, isn't it?' Miss Smith said, charging through the door a few moments later. To Lilian, she looked like a prison officer.

'Yes, Miss,' she replied, nervously.

'I've heard good things about you from Rosie Hale. She tells me you're a hard worker and not the type for chatting or playing about.'

'I try my best –'

'Just the kind,' Miss Smith interrupted, 'that we need around here to set an example to the other girls.'

Set an example? Thinking of her terrible school reports, Lilian almost let out a nervous laugh.

'We'd like to make you a charge-hand,' said Miss Smith, folding her arms and sitting back in her chair. 'What do you say to that?'

Lilian breathed a sigh of relief – at least she hadn't been asked to leave the can-making. She imagined her father's proud reaction when she told him that she had been promoted.

'I'm very grateful, Miss Smith …' she began, before trailing off. An image had popped into her head, of Old Fat Nell, slightly glazed in sweat after her performance at the Liverpool Arms, and Little Lil reaching up to kiss her. She knew that if she became a supervisor it would set her apart from them, and they would no longer feel able to be themselves around her.

'I … I can't,' she stammered.

Storm clouds seemed to gather on Miss Smith's face. She uncrossed her arms and leaned forward, making her broad shoulders seem larger than ever. 'Can't?' she demanded. 'What do you mean, can't?'

'I can't, because …' Lilian panicked. What could she say that didn't sound ridiculous? Then, from somewhere deep inside, came the courage to tell the truth. She cleared her throat and said, quietly, 'I'm sorry, Miss Smith, but I can't take the job because I don't want to lose my friends. Thank you for the offer, but I've got to turn it down.'

She knew if she stayed any longer her nerves would get the better of her, so as soon as she had finished speaking Lilian jumped up from her chair and walked as quickly as she could out of the office – leaving Miss Smith, for once, speechless.

On her way home, Lilian thought about how much her life had changed since joining Tate & Lyle. Not only did she have a proper social life now, but she had found a job she was actually good at and a boss who thought she was worth promoting.

She wondered what she should say to her parents about the job offer. Part of her wanted to let them know how well she had been doing at work, but she was afraid that her father would try to change her mind, and would probably succeed. She was an honest girl, though, and the thought of hiding it from them was uncomfortable.

When she got to Cranley Road, the decision was taken out of her hands: the rest of the family had been distracted by another, more pressing drama. Her sister Edie was waiting in the hall. 'Oh Lil, Harry's been demobbed from the Army – he's coming to see me and baby Brian,' she told her nervously, twisting the corner of her skirt between her hands. Lilian's parents could be heard debating what Harry Snr should say to the married man who had impregnated his daughter.

The conversation came to an abrupt end with the sound of three heavy raps on the front door. 'Oh my God, that's him,' Edie said, rushing over to answer it.

She threw the door open to reveal the man she had been longing to see all throughout her lonely pregnancy in the Salvation Army home in Hackney. 'Harry!' she said, joyfully, about to throw herself into his arms.

Behind her, Harry Snr appeared in the corridor, a look of cold hatred on his face. 'Upstairs – now!' he ordered the young man. Harry opened his mouth but said nothing, and with an apologetic look at Edie allowed himself to be marched up the stairs by her father.

As the muffled voices thrashed out Edie's future upstairs, Lilian and her mum did their best to reassure her. Lilian knew Edie was praying that, now he knew he had fathered a child, Harry would leave his wife to be with her. But her own experience with men didn't give her much reason to be hopeful.

Harry Tull, however, was an effective antidote to errant fathers, and by the time Edie's young man was marched back down the stairs he had agreed to divorce his wife, marry Edie and recognise Brian as his own.

Edie was ecstatic, and before long plans were being made for her and the baby to join Harry in Suffolk to begin their new life. From growing up as an East End girl, Edie was to become a country wife – and her son would have wide open spaces to play in and fresh air to breathe.

With Edie and Brian gone, and Lilian and her brother Harry Jnr in work, there were now fewer mouths to feed and more money coming into the Tull household than ever before. Tentatively, Lilian wondered whether the Tulls had finally turned a corner and left the family curse behind them.

But now that the burden had lifted slightly, something in Lilian's long-suffering mother seemed to give. One morning, as she was getting herself ready to go to the factory, Lilian noticed that Edith wasn't up yet. 'She's just feeling a bit tired, that's all,' said her father, on his way out of the house.

Lilian ran up the stairs to see if her mother needed anything. Edith barely looked up when she entered the room. 'Mum, are you all right?' she asked, worried. 'Dad said you were tired.'

'I'll be fine, love,' said Edith, weakly. 'Just can't seem to get me old bones out of bed this morning. Don't you let me make you late.'

Reluctantly, Lilian left to catch her bus. But that afternoon, when she came home, Edith had still not got out of bed.

Lilian ran up the stairs again. The curtains in the bedroom were still drawn and her mother looked as if she hadn't moved since Lilian had left her, hours earlier.

Alarmed, Lilian asked, 'Mum, what's wrong? Do you feel ill? Should I get a doctor?'

'No love, there's nothing wrong. I'm just … tired.'

There was a strange, hollow look in Edith's eyes, and Lilian reckoned she knew where it came from. Giving birth to nine babies and burying three of them. Devoting more than twenty years of her life to her family, cleaning for them, cooking for them, scrubbing their dirty laundry. Dragging their shopping from Rathbone Market up all those flights of stairs in the flats. All of it had taken a toll on her fragile health.

'Don't worry, Mum,' said Lilian, 'I'll sort out the tea tonight.'

'Thank you, love,' said her mother, closing her eyes.

While Edith was ill, the running of the household fell to Lilian, as the eldest daughter. Each morning she made breakfast for her father, her brothers Harry Jnr, Vic and Leslie, and her sister Sylvie. She worked her eight hours at the factory, then hurried home and made their dinners. On the weekends she shopped, cleaned the house from top to bottom and did the laundry for seven people. She took meals up to her mother, helped wash her, and tried to cheer her up. But as one week followed another, Edith didn't seem to be getting any better.

Little Lil and Old Fat Nell noticed dark rings forming under Lilian's eyes, and were disappointed that she could no longer accompany them on their trips to the pictures or the pie and mash shop. Lilian missed her friends, but she knew that, even if she could have gone out with them, she wouldn't have wanted to. All her energy was taken up with caring for her mother, and her entire focus was on making her well again. Edith Tull had sacrificed her whole life for her children, and Lilian was determined to look after her now in return. Though she didn't admit it to herself, she was also desperate not to lose yet another person she loved.

At work, Lilian's newly acquired confidence and vitality seemed to have drained out of her, and she reverted to the quiet, melancholy girl she had been when she first joined Tate & Lyle. It had all been too good to be true, she thought. Of course it had. The Tull curse was back with a vengeance.

Lilian's fear of the dark intensified, and if she ever found herself having to go out late it was with a trembling heart. Something about the gloom seemed to call to her, as if she belonged to it, and she felt as claustrophobic as she had that day under the rubble at West Ham station.

Finally, Edith Tull seemed to be improving. She began sitting up in bed and talking more, then even found the energy to come downstairs. After a few days she tried to help Lilian with the chores, but her daughter wouldn't let her. 'No, Mum,' she insisted, 'you mustn't make yourself ill again.'

But as Edith's vitality began to return, the toll on her daughter's health was showing. The burden of physical labour and mental worry that the mother had carried all these years trying to keep her family from the brink had now been transferred to the daughter, and Lilian was struggling to cope. She found it hard to get out of bed in the mornings, and ugly red boils began to break out all over her skin. Horrified, Lilian did her best to cover them up, but at work she could sense people staring.

'You're not well, love,' said her mother one morning. 'You should take the day off.'

'No, Mum, I'm fine. Promise you won't worry about me,' Lilian said. She had never missed a day at Tate & Lyle, and the thought of jeopardising the family income after so many years of poverty was unthinkable to her. She struggled on.

But Lilian's poor health had not gone unnoticed at the factory, and soon she found herself called into the Personnel Office for a second time.

'Lilian,' said Miss Smith, her normally booming voice uncharacteristically soft. 'I understand you haven't been feeling well. I want you to know that we can help you.'

Lilian nodded, vaguely. She was thinking about the shopping that needed to be done, the meal she had to prepare that evening. She felt anxious about the time she was wasting just sitting there.

'I'd like you to take some time off,' continued Miss Smith. 'The company will pay. There's a lovely little place in Weston-super-Mare for people who … need some rest and recuperation. A few weeks by the seaside will do you good.'

Lilian was horrified. How could she possibly leave her mother and the rest of the family? 'I can't –' she began, but Miss Smith interrupted her.

'No can'ts this time,' she said, kindly but firmly. 'I'll make the arrangements.'

6

Gladys

After her ride in the telpher, Gladys had been given her biggest dressing-down yet by Miss Smith. From then on, the labour manageress had the red-headed tomboy marked down as a troublemaker, and she kept a closer watch on her than ever.

In the months that followed, Gladys had become an increasingly regular visitor to the Personnel Office. The routine was by now a familiar one: the two Betties would greet her with a chorus of 'Hello again Gladys,' before Miss Smith began her ritual scolding.

One day Gladys was about to enter the office as usual, when she heard an unfamiliar girl's voice coming from inside. 'Well, she was rude to me, so I answered her back,' it announced defiantly. 'And if she'd said any more I'd have hit her!'

Gladys strained her ears to hear how Miss Smith would respond to such an outburst. To her astonishment, she heard what sounded like a chuckle. 'Well, don't hit her too hard, will you?' said Miss Smith.

Gladys pushed the door open a crack to have a peek at the extraordinary girl who had not only stood up to The Dragon but elicited a laugh from her. In the room was a slim, blonde young woman who couldn't have been more than a couple of years older than herself.

Miss Smith was shuffling some papers. 'I'll have to transfer you,' she told the blonde girl. 'How does the Hesser Floor sound? I think you'll find it keeps you busy after the canteen.'

'Oh please, Miss, not the Hesser Floor,' said the girl, suddenly sounding less sure of herself. 'I'm terrible with heights. I'd never make it up all them stairs.'

'Very well then, I'll send you to the Blue Room. I'm sure Julie will keep you in check. Gladys Taylor! Whatever you're doing skulking behind that door, you can come out now and escort Betty Brightmore up to your department.'

Gladys was more than happy to forsake her usual telling-off. She had already warmed to Betty – the only other person she had encountered in the factory who had the nerve to stand up to Miss Smith. Betty had also, it transpired, taken on another of the refinery's most formidable women – Vera, the manageress of the staff canteen – which was the cause of her transfer. 'Well, some people get a bit of power and they think they're God Almighty,' she explained to Gladys, with a giggle.

If Betty Brightmore was immune to authority figures, it was perhaps because in her own home there were none. Like Gladys's family, hers had survived the South Hallsville School disaster by the skin of their teeth, leaving the building because they thought it was too crowded, hours before it was bombed. But just a few years later Betty's mother had died in childbirth, followed 18 months later by her heartbroken father.

With her older brother Jack off in the Navy, it was left to Betty and her sister Mary to bring up their younger siblings, supporting the family by going out to work at Tate & Lyle. Mary had a job in the can-making department, while their Uncle Charlie, a manager in the lorry bay, did his best to keep an eye on the two girls.

Gladys soon discovered Betty to be a giggler, a scatterbrain and, most importantly, a willing accomplice in whatever mischief she was cooking up. Finally, she had found a true friend among the glamour girls of the Blue Room – even if Betty drew the line at kickabouts in the yard.

Betty's presence inevitably made the temptation to evade work stronger than ever, and over time she and Gladys developed a whole repertoire of excuses to get away from their machines. First they made the most of their ten-minute toilet breaks, spending them smoking and nattering in the loos before returning, with a telltale nicotine smell, to their work stations. Such interruptions were frustratingly short, however, and after a while a new strategy was clearly needed.

The two things that they knew for certain would stop the machines were a lack of ink and a lack of paper. Failing to get the paper replenished in time might get the reel boys into trouble, so their only option was to let the ink run dry, a dangerous tactic since keeping an eye on the ink duct was supposed to be one of their main duties. This method had the advantage of requiring the head engineer, a big man named Wally Evans, to come and reset the machines, which could take some time. The plan worked a treat, and the girls were soon skipping off for extended breaks while professing their surprise that the ink could have drained away so quickly.

Julie McTaggart did not take kindly to the girls' apparent carelessness. To have her staff slacking off was difficult enough at the best of times, and right now she was under the cosh. Tate & Lyle had begun a massive propaganda campaign against the Labour government, who in February 1949 had set their sights on nationalising sugar – and the Blue Room had become the front line of the battle. Realising that sugar bags were a better means of getting their message across to ordinary people than any newspaper or billboard, the company's top brass had announced a new scheme for employees: anyone who came up with an anti-nationalisation slogan that was printed on a bag would receive a £10 reward. They got over 500 suggestions.

In addition, one of a number of enterprising new subcommittees had come up with a mascot for the fight: Mr Cube. This little chap, a sugar cube with the arms and legs of a man, appeared in a series of satirical cartoons on the sugar packets, and soon became a national icon. The beleaguered government, facing the prospect of a drubbing at the polls, accused Tate & Lyle of illegal electioneering, and some left-wing shopkeepers refused to stock the 'Tory propaganda'.

The latest bag designs always raised a titter when they arrived in the Blue Room for printing: slogans such as 'Tate not State' and 'Hands off Sugar', or cartoons of Mr Cube with a club in his hands bravely bashing a snake that made up the S of the word 'State'. For Julie McTaggart and the forelady Peggy Burrows, however, the campaign was primarily a personal headache, since it meant that more eyes than usual were on the Blue Room. Such was the success of the propaganda operation that PR specialists, and even the BBC's Richard Dimbleby, were soon touring the factory to find out how it had been accomplished. Miss Smith would bring the parties of visitors to the department, and it was the worst possible time for Julie and Peggy to have to cope with girls slacking off or misbehaving.

Julie was a shrewd woman, and it was obvious to her that Gladys and Betty were chancing their luck, so she decided to teach them a lesson. If they refused to pull their weight in the Blue Room, she would send them somewhere else instead.

They were dispatched temporarily to join Betty's sister Mary in the can-making department.

Imagining a jolly time spent with Mary, and the prospect of a fresh set of young men to mess about with, the pair arrived on the floor with grins on their faces. These soon turned to frowns, however, when the girls were asked to carry around great sheets of tin, ready for printing with the Lyle's Golden Syrup logo before they were cut and shaped into cans. After the Blue Room it was heavy, hot work, and the sides of the tin were so sharp that Betty cut her hand and had to be taken to the factory's surgery. There, Dr Akawalla, a small fat man with a moustache, bandaged her up, tutting as he did so.

Visiting the surgery, however, highlighted for the girls the possibilities it offered for skiving. The factory's medical facilities were open 24 hours a day and were surprisingly well equipped, with a dentist, eye doctor and chiropodist. Staff were vaccinated against polio, X-rayed every year and given annual check-ups if they were under 18. The surgery dealt with 3,400 cases a month and was one reason that Tate & Lyle was considered such a good employer. For the company, it meant that any minor injuries could be attended to quickly and staff sent back to work as soon as possible.

The surgery also had its own ambulance, since the nature of work at the refinery meant that much more serious accidents sometimes occurred. Stories abounded of girls losing fingers, and on occasion entire arms, to the machines, of young boys being knocked over in the warehouse by forklift trucks skidding on the sugary floor – even of a man who fell into the raw sugar silo and drowned, and another who was roasted alive in the charhouse. It was no surprise that rumours of ghosts were rife – over at the Thames Refinery workers talked in hushed tones of a man in an old-fashioned foreman's uniform who stalked around with an umbrella and walking stick.

As well as Dr Akawalla, a kindly nurse called Hester worked in the surgery, and was known for her sweet tea and sympathy. Any girl who claimed to be suffering period pain could rely on Hester to give her an aspirin, a hot water bottle and an hour tucked up in bed on full pay, something Gladys and her friends made sure to use to their advantage.

But the best get-out of all came when notices went up calling for blood donors. Some girls were horrified at the idea of voluntarily going near a needle – but not a tomboy like Gladys. She was determined to profit from her lack of squeamishness and, as ever, convinced Betty to join her. Officially the girls were under the legal age to give blood, but Miss Smith seemed willing to turn a blind eye when a noble act of duty was involved. Julie McTaggart had no choice but to reluctantly wave them off to the surgery, where they lingered far longer than was necessary, enjoying the tea and biscuits.

While Gladys was generally the instigator of any mischief, there was one area in which Betty was a less than positive influence. Discovering they were both Plaistow girls, she suggested that Gladys should call for her in the mornings, so that they could get the bus to work together. Betty lived in Egham Road, just three streets up the Beckton Road from Gladys, who duly set off early the next morning to knock for her friend. But when she rapped on the door of the little house that Betty shared with her sisters, there was no reply.

She put her hand through the letterbox and, just as she expected, felt a string with a key dangling at the end of it. In an area where everyone knew each other and there was nothing worth stealing, this was common practice.

Pulling the key through the letterbox, she let herself into the house. She could hear snoring coming from upstairs and, following the noise, discovered Betty lying fast asleep in bed. Her friend could only be woken with a series of very vigorous shakes, and by the time she was finally up and dressed they had both missed the bus.

From then on, it was down to Gladys to drag her friend out of bed every morning, and the two of them lost at least a quarter of an hour's pay each day through lateness, a fact that didn't go unnoticed by Gladys's mother Rose, who took half her daughter's wages each week for housekeeping. 'Don't expect me to charge you less just because you've lost pay,' she warned her. With her husband Amos working in the docks, where the men seemed to be constantly on strike, she couldn't afford to be indulgent.

Rose did give Gladys extra money to buy breakfast, but most of it ended up in the hands of the tobacconist on the North Woolwich Road. Since pay day was on Friday, by Thursday morning Betty and Gladys would ask the shopkeeper to sell them individual cigarettes because they didn't have enough money for a packet, and, with no money left for the bus, they would have to walk to and from work.

The girls soon discovered a cost-free method of transport: thumbing down one of the many lorries that trundled past the factory gates. The practice was all the more attractive to Gladys because she knew how much Miss Smith disapproved of it. The Personnel department had recently relocated to a new office block at the front of the refinery, where a grand Portland stone entrance now stood in place of the old factory gate. This meant that The Dragon had the perfect vantage point from which to catch her girls hitchhiking, and as soon as she appeared thumbs would hastily be thrust back into pockets. But try as she might, she couldn't put a stop to the practice.

As the belle of the 'Beauty Shop', Maisie was particularly skilled at stopping traffic, especially with one hand on her hip and her eyelashes fluttering. One morning, a couple of lorry drivers were so taken with her that they begged her to accompany them for the entire day. One was heading for Hitchin, the other for Bury St Edmunds, and they both tried their best to convince her of the delights of their respective destinations. Maisie deliberated for a while, before choosing Bury St Edmunds, on the condition that Gladys and Betty were allowed to accompany her. Betty declined the invitation, scared that Uncle Charlie would notice her absence, but Gladys jumped at the chance to play truant, despite the loss of a day's pay, and spent a happy eight hours out in the countryside.

The next day, Betty and Gladys were trying to thumb a lift home when a lorry carrying sand drew up next to them. They congratulated themselves, thinking that the driver was about to let them on, only for him to lean out of the window and offer a lift to Maisie, who was standing a few feet away.

Before Maisie had a chance to reply, Gladys shouted, 'Cheers, mate!' She yanked open the door of the cab and jumped in next to him, dragging Betty up after her.

'What about me?' wailed Maisie from the pavement.

'Sorry, love, looks like you've been beaten to it. You're welcome to hop on the back, though,' said the man, with a disappointed shrug.

Maisie emitted a loud sigh and stomped off towards the back of the lorry, where she clambered onto the tailboard. 'Ooh, she won't like that,' giggled Betty, as she and Gladys made themselves comfortable.

The lorry made its way over the viaduct, out of Silvertown and towards Canning Town. It was a windy day, and in the wing mirror they could see small clouds of sand blowing off the vehicle each time a gust went over it.

They turned right onto the Barking Road and approached Trinity Church. 'You can let us off here, mate,' Gladys told the driver. She and Betty hopped out of the cab, shut the door and ran round to get Maisie.

Down from the back of the lorry stepped a figure that was almost unrecognisable. Whilst they had been sheltered in the cab, the wind had been blowing the sand from the truck all over the unfortunate girl, turning her once blue uniform a dirty yellow. Every strand of her beautiful blonde hair had been individually coated, lending it the appearance of a stringy, mop-like wig, while her angry face looked as if it had been given the heaviest powdering of its life. Worst of all, her long fake eyelashes were full of the particles, which sprinkled down her cheeks each time she blinked.

'Ooh, Maisie,' giggled Betty, 'you do look a sight!'

With a hoot of laughter she and Gladys legged it up the Beckton Road, before Maisie could get her revenge.

For Gladys, having a close female friend was a new experience. She had always hung around with boys before, kicking a ball about in the park with John ('Bum Freezer') and his gang of local lads. But they had now all gone off to do their military service, and Betty – who lived in a house full of giggling girls – was encouraging her to follow new pursuits.

One week, she persuaded Gladys to go out with her to the Tate Institute, the company's social club opposite the Thames Refinery. Every Friday the turbans in the Blue Room would tower a little higher than usual, since all the girls were wearing rollers underneath them in preparation for the weekend, and many hours would be dedicated to getting ready for the ensuing night out.

Gladys didn't own any rollers, nor any cosmetics to speak of, and she had learned the hard way that getting ready in her own house was perilous. One time, she had applied tea bags to her legs to make it look as if she was wearing stockings. As she had walked down the stairs towards the front door, her father had burst out laughing and shouted, 'What's that shit you've got on your legs?' before hurling a cup of cold water over them, causing the tea to run and ruining the effect.

Fortunately, Betty invited Gladys to get ready at her house, where there were no parents around to interfere. 'I've got some new curling tongs we can use on your hair,' she told her excitedly.

Gladys turned up in Egham Road at the appointed hour, wearing a white, spotted calf-length dress with a flowery border. It was the girliest thing she owned.

When Betty opened the door to let her in, she looked suitably impressed. 'This is going to be so much fun!' she said, as she ushered Gladys into the front room. There, her sister Mary was already getting dolled up in front of the only mirror in the house.

'I haven't brought anything with me,' whispered Gladys.

'Don't worry, all we need is a good lippy,' said her friend, grabbing a lipstick tube from her sister. To Gladys's horror it was bright cherry red and a peculiar, stubby shape.

'Now stand still and say "Ooo",' said Betty.

Gladys distorted her mouth into the necessary shape and Betty set about drawing on her lips with a look of intense concentration.

'Not too much,' she attempted to say with her mouth still open.

'Don't move or you'll spoil it,' replied Betty. 'It's got to look full-lipped. Right, now for the next step.'

She began smearing the lipstick all over her fingertips and reached out her hand towards Gladys's face.

'What do you think you're doing?' Gladys yelled, pulling away.

'Your rouge, silly,' said Betty. 'Stay still.'

Betty rubbed her fingers in a circular motion on each of Gladys's cheeks, before standing back to admire her work.

'Ain't you going to do her eyebrows?' asked Mary, frowning.

'She hasn't got any,' said Betty. Gladys was so fair that her brows were non-existent. 'Maybe a bit of mascara?'

Gladys put her foot down. 'No way are you putting that stick anywhere near my eyeball.'

'All right then,' laughed Betty. 'Now for your hair.'

She put her new metal curling tongs on the stove to heat up. When they were ready, she made Gladys sit on a chair while she stood behind her. Gladys could feel her yanking great clumps of hair onto the tongs and rolling them up painfully tight, holding them for what seemed an eternity while they emitted a sizzling sound. After a while a sulphurous odour filled the room.

'Betty, is it meant to smell like that?' asked Gladys anxiously.

'Yeah, it just means your hair's heating up,' said Betty. 'Don't worry, it'll soon go away.'

After a good twenty minutes Gladys could bear the stench no longer. 'That's it, I've had enough,' she said, jumping out of the chair. 'Let's see what it looks like.'

Bracing herself, she walked towards the mirror to see the results of Betty's makeover.

She was surprised at how plump her lips looked – so full that they were literally spilling over into the surrounding face. Coupled with the shiny red orbs of her cheeks, she almost appeared to be on fire.

Her hair certainly matched the look. There were singed ginger curls sticking up in some places, straight bits hanging down limply in others, and a number of gaps where the hair had burnt off completely and fallen out. Her head reeked of burnt hair fibres.

'Betty!' she screeched. 'You've burnt me hair!'

Betty came to join her at the mirror. 'Gawd, I have, haven't I?' she said, clapping a hand over her mouth and beginning to giggle. 'Oh Gladys, it's burnt to a crisp!'

'Yeah, thanks, I can see that,' said Gladys, looking bitterly at her reflection.

Mary came running over to get a look too, and also collapsed into giggles.

'Don't worry,' said Betty, attempting to get a grip on her laughter. 'I'm sure once we're at the Institute it'll be too dark for anyone to notice.'

Situated on the corner of Wythes Road and Albert Road, the Institute, built by Henry Tate in 1887, was a red-brick building with a pointed, gabled roof. A queue had formed outside, and Gladys and Betty walked over to join it, Gladys keeping her head down as much as possible so as not to attract attention.

'Hey, Betty – over here!' came a shout from further up the queue. There was Maisie, looking every inch the film star, her blonde hair in glossy waves. Gladys reluctantly followed Betty over to where she stood. 'Oh my Lord,' said Maisie, taking one look at Gladys, 'what's happened to you?'

'Betty done it, the dopey cow,' replied Gladys.

'I was doing me best!' Betty protested, beginning to giggle again.

'It's a bit whiffy,' said Maisie, wrinkling her perfect little nose.

At last they reached the front of the queue and walked into the building. They went past a huge ornate mirror, which Gladys did her best to avoid, and into the dance hall. It was like nothing she had ever seen before – a grand room with imposing pillars running along the sides and a big revolving mirror ball in the centre throwing out spots of light. On a stage at one end a band was playing a waltz, while on the floor a hundred or so couples were dancing in time to the music, moving in a circular motion around the room.

Suddenly the dizzying scene came to a halt. A man stepped up to a microphone on the stage. 'You pull me up in the morning and pull me down at bedtime, but whatever you do, don't get me in a twist,' he said mysteriously.

There was much excited chattering before a woman in a yellow dress shrieked, 'Got it!' Waving a pair of knickers in the air, she bustled through the crowd and made her way up to the stage, dragging her sheepish-looking partner behind her. Once there she presented the knickers to the compère.

'Well done!' the man grinned. 'And she hasn't even got them in a twist! What's your name, sweetheart?'

'Jean,' she beamed, squinting under the lights.

'Jean has just earned herself and her bloke two free drinks at the bar – give them a round of applause,' he said, as everyone began clapping. 'I'd better give these to you for safe keeping, mate,' he winked, handing the knickers to the woman's embarrassed boyfriend, as the music started up again.

'Er, let's sit this one out,' said Gladys, heading for some tables at the edge of the room, where lots of young girls were sitting gossiping and pointing at boys. Gladys, Betty and Maisie installed themselves on some chairs nearby with glasses of lemonade, and watched as more unlikely items were brought up onto the stage in return for prizes. Maisie spotted Joycie, Joanie and Rita from the Blue Room, who had just arrived, and waved to them.

'Oh my God, Gladys, what happened to your hair?' asked Joanie, as she plopped down in a chair next to them.

'Ask Betty Brightmore!' said Gladys, glaring at Betty, who looked guiltily down into her lemonade and emitted a snort of laughter.

When the dance came to an end the crowd applauded, and then there was a lull as everybody dispersed to get drinks. As soon as the next number was announced all the single men in the room, who had been hovering at a safe distance from the lines of seated women, made their way over and began asking them to dance. Maisie was soon snapped up by a cheeky blond man who looked as if all his Christmases had come at once.

Meanwhile Gladys noticed the gossiping girls suddenly fall silent as a tall black man approached them. He was the only non-white person in the room and stood out like a sore thumb. 'Would you like to dance?' he asked, smiling at one of the girls and holding out his hand.

'No, ta,' she said, looking down at her feet.

He moved along to her friend. 'How about you, Miss?'

'No, thanks,' she said, turning her head away.

A third girl feigned an interest in her fingernails, and the man retreated to stand in the corner. He looked downcast, and something about his expression made Gladys think that he was used to standing on the sidelines.

To Gladys, who had spent her early childhood living in Draughtboard Alley, the girls' reactions were downright ridiculous. 'Right, that's it,' she said, standing up and putting down her lemonade.

'Gladys, what are you doing?' asked Betty, clutching at her arm.

Gladys brushed Betty off, swept her frazzled red hair out of her face and marched over to where the man stood.

'I'll dance with you, mate,' she announced, enjoying the surprised expressions of the three girls who had rejected him.

The man gave her a grateful smile and quickly took her hand.

Once on the dance floor, his confidence seemed to return. The number was a quickstep, and Gladys's partner was a nifty dancer. She felt heads turn towards them as they glided around the room, but remembering her singed hair she tried not to make eye contact with anyone.

When the music stopped, she was keen to get out of the spotlight. 'See you then,' she told the man, hurrying over to her chair and thirstily grabbing her lemonade.

'C'mon, Gladys, you can't sit this one out,' called Betty, who by this point had found a partner of her own. 'It's a jive!'

Maisie had swapped her blond for a tall, dark, handsome stranger and was also heading onto the dance floor, as were

Joanie, Joycie and Rita. Out of the corner of her eye, Gladys saw her former partner approaching her again. 'Would you like another dance?' he asked her.

She turned to see his hopeful face and realised every other girl nearby had done a swift vanishing act, leaving her, once again, as his only option.

'Oh, go on then,' she said. 'Just one more.'

Four dances later, despite sending beseeching looks to her friends, Gladys had still not managed to shake him off. Clearly her act of charity was destined to last all night long. Doesn't this bloke ever get tired? she thought to herself.

When the next number was called she acted quickly. 'Oi you,' she whispered to Betty, 'you owe me a favour. Sorry, mate,' she said, turning to the man, 'I'm going to have to dance with poor Bets because she doesn't have a partner.'

Before he could answer, she had whisked the surprised Betty onto the dance floor and they were whizzing away across the room.

7

Ethel

Ever since she and Archie had fixed a date for the wedding, Ethel had been counting down the days until she became an official member of the Colquhoun family. As if 14 April wasn't already engraved on her heart, Freddie James, one of the engineers on the Hesser Floor, had been chalking up the number of days remaining on a beam overhead. Every morning he would greet her excitedly when she came into work, bellowing across the floor, 'Only fifteen days to go, Ethel!' or 'Only ten days left now!'

At last the week of the wedding was upon her. Archie was scheduled to arrive home on Wednesday night, giving them a couple of days to get things ready before the big event on Saturday, and Ethel was determined that it should go absolutely perfectly. Archie was only coming home from the Army for his usual three weeks of leave, but she had been told that they could get a special licence to get married more quickly than would otherwise be possible.

When she arrived at the town hall to put in for it, however, she found that not everyone was as keen to make the special day a success as she was.

'Sorry, no can do,' an official informed her breezily from behind his desk. 'You both need to apply in person at least three days before the wedding.'

'We can't,' Ethel replied. 'My fiancé won't be home until Wednesday night, so the earliest he could come in is Thursday.'

'Oh dear,' the man responded, leaning back in his chair and sucking in his cheeks. 'Looks like you won't be getting married after all, then.'

'But it's all been booked,' said Ethel, who was sure she had organised everything down to a T. 'My aunt's lending us her caravan for the honeymoon!'

He tut-tutted. 'You can't just turn up out of the blue and expect to get married, you know. We do have procedures for a reason.'

'I understand that,' Ethel replied, as calmly as possible, 'but the date can't be moved.'

'Well, I think you'd better have a word with your fiancé then, and see if he can't get home a bit quicker.'

But if the official had thought Ethel would simply give up and go away, he had picked the wrong woman.

'Look,' she said, planting her hands firmly on the desk, 'he can't come home any earlier because he's in the Army. Or do you think I should call them up and see if they can spare him so that you can have an extra day's notice?'

The man squirmed in his seat. 'Well, if it's the Army,' he muttered, 'maybe we can make a special exception.'

Ethel wasn't a girl for a big white wedding, so the nuptials were a simple affair at the registry office on West Ham Lane. She wore a beige suit with brown shoes and a brown hat, and Archie was in his Army uniform. The ceremony itself went off flawlessly, just as she had hoped.

The only sadness for Ethel was that neither of her parents was there to see it. She hadn't seen her father since their falling out after her mother's death. Archie's mum laid on a beautiful wedding spread, but there were only 13 people at the table.

The couple were due to head off to her aunt's caravan in Shoeburyness afterwards, but Archie asked Ethel if she would mind popping to the off-licence to buy him a drink before they went. She agreed, and Archie began to write down a list of beverages before giving her some money.

When Ethel got to the shop she was surprised to see how many drinks were on the list, but shrugged her shoulders and bought them anyway.

It was only when she got back that she realised what the drinks were for: a surprise party. Ethel was not going to be allowed to leave for her honeymoon without a good send-off.

'Here you are Ethel, drink this!' her aunt told her, offering her a glass. She was determined to get the normally sober girl tipsy on her wedding day.

'Thanks,' Ethel said, smiling. She had already raised the glass to her mouth before she spotted what was in it: a port and lemon.

'Don't drink that,' said Archie, with a chuckle. Ethel was only too happy to let him take the glass off her.

After the honeymoon, Ethel returned to the Hesser Floor, relieved that – unlike in many other departments – there was no rule there against girls staying on once they were married.

Archie, meanwhile, went back to Germany. Now more than ever he regretted the commitment he had made to the Army, and he spent his final year in the forces miserably counting the days until he could leave. The letters that Ethel received from him had lost their old good humour, and one day he sent her a complaint: 'When I first went away you used to write to me every day,' he told her, 'and now we're married I go for weeks without hearing anything.'

Ethel was astonished, and hurt by the accusation. She had done her best to continue writing every day, and after all, it was he, not she, who had signed up for so many years of separation. Calmly, she wrote Archie a letter, reassuring him that she was still writing as much as she possibly could, and that she looked forward to his return as much as he did.

A few days later, Archie's apology arrived in the post. On returning from manoeuvres, he had discovered a great tower of previously undelivered mail, and had devoured dozens of Ethel's misplaced missives in a single sitting. 'I'm sorry, Et, I shouldn't have doubted you,' he wrote back immediately. 'When I get home I'll be the happiest man in England.'

At long last, Archie came out of the Army, taking a job at the ICI sodaworks in Silvertown. Ethel was ecstatic to have him back permanently, after so many years of only seeing him for three weeks every six months. She was keen to organise the next phase of their life together and sort out a home for them to live in. As kind as his mother Maude had been to her, she couldn't wait to have her own household to run.

Ethel approached a builder who lived nearby and who helped manage a number of properties, asking if he could find them a flat. One night, Archie was working the late shift at ICI and Ethel and his younger sister Honour were talking in the kitchen, when the builder came knocking on the door.

'I've got the perfect place for you, just up the road,' he said. 'Only you'll have to come quick, or it'll be gone.'

'Fine,' Ethel said briskly, grabbing her coat. 'Come on, Honour.' She grabbed a torch from the passageway and strode out into the street. They followed the neighbour to a house at the far end of Oriental Road.

'Upstairs or downstairs?' Ethel asked him.

'Both,' he replied.

'I only asked about a flat,' Ethel remonstrated.

'Look,' he told her, 'why don't you take a butcher's inside? There's no flats coming up for a while, and I'm sure you'd like to get moving, a married woman and all.' He nodded approvingly at the ring on her finger.

'All right then, I'll have a look,' Ethel agreed, and she and Honour followed him inside.

It was a good job they had brought a torch, because the electricity had been disconnected. As they made their way from room to room, casting the feeble light around them, Ethel could see that the house was a bit run down and in need of a good spring clean. The wallpaper was peeling in one corner of the front room, and there seemed to be some junk littering the passageway. But it was nothing a little sprucing up wouldn't fix, she reasoned, and they would be getting a lot more space than they had expected.

'What do you reckon, then?' the neighbour asked her as they returned to the front door.

'I'd better ask my husband first,' said Ethel. 'Can I let you know tomorrow?'

'It'll be gone by then,' said the man, shaking his head, 'what with the rent only being 18 shillings.'

Eighteen shillings – for a whole house? Ethel couldn't believe it. She had assumed that she and Archie would only be able to afford a flat, but 18 shillings was well within their means.

'I'll take it,' she said. Archie would just have to lump it.

The next morning, returning with her husband, Ethel realised what a rash decision she had made. The junk she had noticed in the passageway seemed to be everywhere else too, and they kept tripping over it as she tried to show Archie around. In the back yard they discovered numerous dead chickens, whose feathers and blood littered the ground. The peeling wallpaper needed stripping completely, and when they began to remove it they found another, equally disgusting layer beneath it, and another beneath that, until, several hours later, the shredded remains of nine separate layers were piled up in the middle of the floor.

Such problems were soon forgotten, however, once Ethel saw the state of the outside toilet. The moment she opened the door the rank stench assaulted her nostrils and it was days before she even dared to go near it. Archie's mum grew increasingly puzzled as to why Ethel kept dropping round 'just for a chat' and heading straight for the loo.

When Ethel finally got up the courage to clean the toilet, she scrubbed like a woman possessed, determined not to let a bit of muck defeat her, however putrid and repulsive that muck might be. Meanwhile, Archie spent every evening repainting and re-wallpapering the little house until well after midnight.

In time their persistence won through, and the dilapidated wreck was transformed into the home-sweet-home Ethel so desperately longed for, complete with the most modern of conveniences: a gas boiler.

Not long after they had moved in, Ethel's Nanny Potter sent for her. 'I'm getting old now,' she said. 'You'll have to start thinking about your sister Winnie.'

Ethel considered her grandmother's words. She was now married, with a house of her own. For the first time she was in a position to offer the teenage Winnie a home.

'I tell you what,' she said. 'If Archie agrees, I'll have her with me.'

Archie's permission was willingly given, and Winnie moved into the spare bedroom upstairs. For Ethel, who had not spoken to her father since she'd left home, it felt wonderful to have part of her old family back together. She took to the mothering role like a duck to water, and in time she even got her little sister a job in the syrup-filling department at Tate & Lyle, so that they could walk in to work together.

* * *

On the Hesser Floor, gossip generally travelled fast. One day, when Ethel arrived to start up her machine, she found a group of girls huddled around in intense conversation.

'What's going on?' she asked them.

'Word is the bosses are sending a Hesser machine to the Ideal Home Exhibition,' she was told. 'They want some of us to go and demonstrate the sugar-packing.'

Ethel had heard of the Ideal Home Exhibition, which was held at Olympia in Kensington and featured the latest domestic design and technology innovations. She knew Tate & Lyle had participated before, but this was the first she'd heard of taking a Hesser machine along.

'Who are they sending?' she asked, urgently.

'They're picking the best workers to go,' one of the girls said.

Ethel was elated. In the last few months she had worked her way up through the roles on her machine – from packing to filling, and now driving – and she knew she was one of the best girls on the floor. Surely if she pushed herself even harder for the next week or so, Ivy Batchelor couldn't fail to include her in the team.

All that week, Ethel worked like a Trojan, but to her surprise the forelady didn't approach her about the exhibition. Another week went by and the event was drawing near, yet still she found she hadn't been summoned. Ethel couldn't understand it. Who was a more devoted sugar girl than she was?

The next time she saw Ivy Batchelor she confronted her. 'Why haven't I been picked for the Ideal Home?' she demanded. 'I was told the best workers were going.'

'Don't worry, Ethel,' the forelady replied, reassuringly. 'I think there might be something better in store for you.'

Ethel returned to her machine, disappointed at missing out on the trip to Kensington, but wondering what Ivy's cryptic remark might mean. What 'something better' did she have in mind for her?

Seeing how dejected Ethel looked, her friend Beryl Craven from the office tried to console her. 'I've been given two free tickets to the Ideal Home,' she said. 'Do you want to come with me on Saturday?'

Ethel was still smarting from the rejection, but she was too curious about the Hesser machine demonstration to say no. That Saturday, after she had finished her morning's work at the factory, she and Beryl took the Tube together to Kensington.

Tate & Lyle had really gone to town on the event, and the two young women were astounded by what they saw. As the crowds snaked through the great glass-ceilinged hall towards the Tate & Lyle exhibit they were greeted by a life-size version of Mr Cube with state-of-the-art animatronic lips. The mascot had proved so popular during the company's anti-nationalisation campaign that his services had been retained even now that the battle had been won.

Mr Cube was locked in banal conversation with Daphne Tarsey, a 15-year-old warehouse girl from the Thames Refinery, who had been hand-picked for the role from the factory's amateur dramatics society.

'Did you know, Daphne, that in moderation sugar can actually aid slimming?' Mr Cube demanded mechanically.

'No, Mr Cube, I didn't,' the poor teenager replied, mugging desperately at the crowd.

Beryl was transfixed by the bizarre spectacle, but Ethel was only interested in one thing: the Hesser demonstration. 'Come on,' she said, pulling Beryl away.

They passed through an area where a crowd of visitors sat watching a film about the sugar-harvesting process in the colonies, while a black Trinidadian worker stood on hand to answer any questions. 'No time for this,' muttered Ethel, dragging Beryl up a flight of metal stairs onto a balcony, drawn like a moth to a flame towards the familiar hum and rattle of the Hesser machine. Sure enough, there it was below them, installed and working just as it would have been at the factory.

At either end of the machine stood a woman supervising, and taking the occasional question from the crowd. One was

Daisy Lewis, who had worked on the Hesser Floor since before the war. The other woman, however, was Betty Phillips, Miss Smith's right-hand woman from the Personnel Office. 'I don't know what she's doing here,' Ethel commented angrily. 'What does she know about Hesser machines?'

She was also shocked to see that the women working on the machine itself were all pretty, young girls who had been made up to the nines, with the foundation, powder, lipstick, rouge and mascara of Hollywood starlets – scarcely representative of workers in a hot sugar factory. Had they been chosen for their looks rather than their ability? Poor Ethel felt utterly disillusioned.

On Monday morning, Ethel arrived at work to yet another surprise. When she got to the Hesser Floor, the girls were once again talking in hushed tones.

'What's going on?' she asked. 'Is everything all right?'

'It's Ivy Batchelor,' one of the girls said. 'She's gone.'

'What do you mean gone?' asked Ethel, taken aback.

'Up and left at the end of last week. Apparently she's gone to the other factory.'

Another girl chipped in urgently. 'They've got her packing the sugar, back on the factory floor!'

Ethel couldn't believe it. 'Why?'

'Nobody knows.'

In fact, unbeknown to Ethel, a rumour had already begun to spread around the factory to account for the forelady's sudden departure. The story went that she had been having an affair with one of the managers – some said a member of the Lyle family itself. When the romance had finally been broken off, she had been conveniently dumped out of the way at the Thames Refinery, on a menial job, as though her 25 years' service counted for nothing.

The girls didn't have to wait long to find out who was going to replace her. A notice went up on the departmental board announcing that former charge-hand Mary Doherty would be taking over as forelady immediately. To Ethel's surprise, Mary came up to her machine a little while later and asked if she could have a word.

'Of course,' Ethel replied, a little anxiously.

'Ivy left me some instructions about you,' Mary said.

Ethel held her breath, waiting for the other woman to continue.

'I think congratulations are in order. You're to be made a charge-hand – the youngest this company has ever seen.'

8

Lilian

By the time Lilian was put on the coach to the convalescent home in Weston-super-Mare, she had given up trying to argue that the trip was unnecessary. All the darkness and bleakness of life that she had struggled to hold at bay seemed to have risen up like a tidal wave, crashing over her and leaving her aware of nothing else.

On the coach, there were around a dozen other girls from both Tate & Lyle's Silvertown factories, but Lilian barely took them in. Nor did she take much notice of the view out of the window as they left the East End behind and headed out of London into the countryside.

Many hours later, the coach pulled up outside a limestone building that looked like a grand hotel, standing on a hill overlooking the bay. Lilian felt so drained that she doubted whether she could even find the energy to get off the bus, pick up her bag and climb the steps, but somehow she managed it. Inside, a middle-aged woman with a clipboard marked her name off and assigned her a room number. 'Back downstairs at five p.m. in the Sun Room, please,' she told her, but Lilian was too tired to reply, and headed straight to bed.

A few hours later she was woken by a loud knock on her door, and groggily went to open it. A large girl with glasses stood before her. 'They sent me to fetch you down to the Sun Room,' she said.

Something about the weary, resigned look on the girl's face reminded Lilian of herself. Silently, she slipped on her shoes and followed her downstairs.

In the Sun Room, the Tate & Lyle contingent had been joined by another dozen girls from a number of other factories, including several from a biscuit company in the North. The middle-aged woman with the clipboard was in the midst of giving a welcome speech. 'In between meals, your time is your own,' she said, 'but remember, you have come here because you're not well, so we expect early nights, please. Curfew is at eight p.m. sharp.'

Lilian looked around the room. None of the others looked obviously sick or disabled. Could they be there for the same reason she was – that they were simply sick of life?

The convalescent home was the closest thing to luxury Lilian had ever encountered, and usually she would have been marvelling at every detail. But that evening eating in the dining room was just too overwhelming. The courses came and went, and Lilian's plates returned to the kitchen almost exactly as they had arrived. As soon as she could, she excused herself and went to bed again, sleeping for 12 hours straight.

When she awoke the next morning, the long rest seemed to have turned the bleak, desperate feeling inside her into something less sharp. At breakfast she managed to drink a cup of tea, keeping her head down as the other girls chatted around her. Some of them were planning a trip down to The Sands, but Lilian didn't want to get involved, so when they set off she tried to sneak back to her room.

The woman with the clipboard caught her at the bottom of the stairs. 'Off you go,' she said briskly, with a shepherding motion. 'A bit of fresh air will do you good.'

Reluctantly, Lilian trailed behind the others as they headed down to the bay. After a while she noticed that the large girl with glasses who had knocked on her door earlier had dropped back from the rest of the group too.

'Still tired?' the girl asked.

'I reckon I've just about woken up, thanks,' Lilian replied, aware that her voice sounded flat.

'Ain't I seen you at Plaistow Wharf?'

'Yes,' she replied. 'My name's Lilian Tull.'

'I'm Molly – Molly Humphries,' said the other girl.

'Humphries is my gran's single name,' said Lilian with a slight smile.

'Oh, do you reckon we're related then?' asked Molly. 'Maybe it runs in the family!'

'What does?' Lilian asked.

'Breakdowns.'

'I ain't had a breakdown!' said Lilian, shocked.

The girl looked at her blankly. 'Ain't that why we're all here?'

It was high summer, and every day on their walk to The Sands the girls were confronted with the vibrant atmosphere of a seaside resort in full swing. Children ran into the waves, splashing joyfully, or dug earnestly at the muddy sand with their spades. Couples strolled hand in hand along the promenade eating chips out of newspaper cones, and by the Grand Pier the sound of excited screams could be heard from the wooden rollercoaster in the amusement park.

Fun, laughter, sunshine – all of it was impossible to avoid here, and bit by bit Lilian felt it wheedling its way into her heart. It was having a similar effect on the other girls, too. They were starting to look a bit more like any other group of friends on an outing to the coast, hitching up their skirts for a paddle and eating melting ice creams in the sun.

After a while they even began to spend some of their afternoons in the pub, sneaking back just before the eight p.m. curfew and trying not to make it too obvious where they had been.

When Lilian was with Molly and the other girls, the life she had left behind her in the East End seemed a million miles away. But whenever she was alone in her room a nagging feeling of guilt came over her, and she thought again of her mother. An anxious knot would form in her stomach as she remembered the desperate sense of responsibility she had felt to keep the Tull family from plunging yet again into crisis.

One day at breakfast Lilian received a letter from home. She recognised her brother Harry's handwriting on the envelope, and immediately panicked. What terrible thing could have happened to prompt him to write, rather than her parents? She rushed upstairs to read the letter in private.

'Lilian,' it read, '*I just wanted to say, you deserve to look after yourself for a change. No one could have done more to take care of us all than you have. I hope you have a good time at the seaside.*'

The words brought tears of relief to Lilian's eyes. From then on, she no longer felt guilty about enjoying herself at Weston-super-Mare, and she determined to make the most of her stay.

By the time Lilian got on the coach back to London, the dark shadows under her eyes had faded and the painful blisters on her body were almost completely healed. Instead of sitting quietly on her own, she now sat next to her new friend Molly, and the two young women chatted all the way home.

Back at the factory, once again the change in Lilian didn't go unnoticed. This time, she was approached to become a union rep.

'What does that involve?' Lilian asked hesitantly.

'Oh, you know, just collecting up the money from the other girls,' she was told.

Lilian's natural shyness made her recoil from the idea of demanding money from people, so she declined the offer. But inwardly she glowed with pride that she, Lilian Tull, had been asked to represent the other girls in her department.

Meanwhile, Molly also had a new glow about her, and Lilian couldn't help thinking it was down to more than just the sea air at Weston-super-Mare.

'Lilian,' she said one lunchtime, 'if I tell you a secret, do you promise to keep it?'

'Course.'

'I've met a bloke … and he's got a car!'

'A *car*?' Lilian was speechless. No one she knew had a car. 'Who is he? Where'd he come from?'

'He's one of the engineers here at the factory,' her friend replied, lowering her voice. 'But you mustn't tell a soul. He says he don't want it to come out at work.'

Lilian nodded, but something about it didn't seem right.

Molly had met her new man while waiting for the bus to work on the Barking Road. Drawing up in his bright-red Lagonda alongside the queue of people, Bob had caused quite a stir, and when he rolled down the window and asked Molly if she needed a lift to the factory she was stunned. She followed her gut instinct and said no, but as the car sped off into the distance she felt a stab of regret. Who was this mysterious man with such a smart set of wheels?

The next day the Lagonda reappeared at the bus stop, and this time Molly couldn't resist. Ignoring the stares of the people in the queue, she hopped in beside Bob and together they cruised down the Barking Road.

Soon Molly was being chauffeured to and from work every day, and before long the lifts had progressed into dates.

Despite Bob's insistence that no one should know about the liaison, inevitably word got out at the factory and the gossip soon spread. But when Lilian heard the story repeated, she was surprised to hear a worrying addition to it. 'I heard Molly's bloke's a married man!' one of the other girls told her. Lilian was horrified, and relayed the information to Molly as soon as she saw her.

The next time Molly had Bob captive in the Lagonda, she quizzed him about it.

'No, darlin' – I *was* married,' he told her, 'but I'm not any more. I'm living with me mum and dad off the Barking Road.'

Molly looked at him, doubtfully.

'Tell you what,' he reassured her. 'We'll stop in on them on the way home.'

Molly was promptly taken round to Bob's parents' house, and left convinced of the truth of the tale. The next day at lunch she told Lilian there was nothing to worry about.

That afternoon Lilian was turning off her machine when the forelady Rosie Hale approached her with a grave look on her face. 'I've heard some things from the girls that I had to pass on to Miss Smith,' she told her. 'She wants to see you in her office before you leave today.'

Lilian gulped. Had she done something wrong – made a mistake she wasn't even aware of? As she crossed the factory yard and headed to the Personnel Office, she felt the old familiar anxieties returning.

Miss Smith was waiting for her. 'Take a seat, Lilian,' she commanded. 'You're friends with Molly Humphries, aren't you?'

'Yes, Miss. I met her at Weston-super-Mare.'

'Rosie tells me that Molly's struck up an affair with another employee. Do you know anything about that?'

'She's going out with Bob, Miss,' Lilian said innocently. 'The one with the Lagonda.'

'I see,' said Miss Smith, with a look of concern. 'And you do know he's married?'

Lilian felt as if she were in the dock being cross-examined. 'He was married before, but he's not any more,' she protested, repeating what Molly had told her. 'He's living off the Barking Road with his parents.'

Miss Smith snorted. 'He most certainly is not. He is living with his wife, I can assure you.'

What was it with married men? thought Lilian. First her sister Edie and now Molly had found herself unknowingly caught up with them. Why couldn't they be trusted to keep their rings on their fingers?

'I don't know anything about it,' she blurted out.

Miss Smith nodded. 'Well, perhaps for your friend's sake you could let her know.'

Lilian could see that Miss Smith was genuinely concerned for Molly, but she wanted to get out of there as quickly as possible. 'Is that all, Miss?' she asked.

Miss Smith gave an exasperated sigh. 'Yes, Lilian, I suppose so.'

Lilian hurried away before she changed her mind.

The next time she saw Molly she tried to raise the subject, but her friend didn't seem to want to talk about it, and Lilian didn't feel able to push her. Perhaps Molly knew the truth already, or perhaps she didn't want to know. Either way, she and Bob kept seeing each other.

The two friends grew apart, but some time later Lilian heard that Bob had left his wife and was now living with Molly. She was pleased for Molly, but had already made a mental note for herself: never accept a lift from a stranger with a flashy car.

* * *

The longer Lilian worked at Tate & Lyle, the more she realised that Bob wasn't the only one there who was having an extra-marital affair. With thousands of young men and women working together in the factories, there were abundant opportunities for illicit romance. Two of the canteen workers – both of them married – were widely known to have been carrying on together for years. A foreman and a forelady, meanwhile, were enjoying a furtive romance in a storeroom accessed only by a ladder. They regretted their choice of location one day, when two young men spotted them going up there and promptly removed it.

Some jobs offered more opportunities to stray than others. Dot Cartwright was married when she started working in the post room at the Thames Refinery, but while delivering the mail to the garages she got friendly with a senior engineer called Billy. Her daily rounds gave them ample chance to chat, and soon they were enjoying evenings at the Institute together and having a full-blown affair. When she returned late from a dance one night, her husband had been waiting up for her and told her to leave. She promptly did so, and married Billy instead.

A young man called Dave, another Thames employee, had the perfect job for indulging his love of sugar girls. Tasked with making sure the Hesser floors were well stocked, he spent much of his time chatting to the girls there, and also had the keys to a storeroom in which he could privately entertain them. Dave wasn't the best-looking man in the world but he was a natural talker, and the girls always felt he really listened to them, so he was never short of female attention. In fact, Dave went out with so many Tate & Lyle girls that he struggled to remember their names, but this problem was easily solved by giving them the same pet-name: 'Sparkler'.

It was with the gift of the gab that Dave managed to score with Elsie, a tall girl with auburn hair and very large breasts. She was the belle of the icing-sugar floor, and young men would often wander through the department for the most spurious of reasons just to get a look at her. Elsie was engaged to someone else, and was fully aware of Dave's other liaisons. 'Just tell the last girl when she leaves to make sure all your buttons are done up,' she told him one day in the storeroom. But Dave took one too many risks by going on a date with Elsie outside the factory. Her fiancé found out, and the next time Dave saw her, Elsie was sporting a black eye.

Dave only entertained the ladies during the working day, because in the evenings he dedicated himself to sport. Soon, however, he discovered that there was a demand for his store-room after hours, from male colleagues pursuing extra-marital affairs. Dave was happy to loan them the keys, as long as they were left in an agreed pick-up place ready for him to collect the next morning.

Dave always warned his conquests not to expect a serious relationship, and although the sugar girls claimed to be fine with his no-strings-attached approach to sex, some of them couldn't help trying to change him. One girl named Maggie knew she wasn't the only visitor to the storeroom, but told him that she didn't want to know the details. 'When I'm not with you, it's nothing to do with me,' she said. Taking her at her word, Dave continued the affair. But one day Maggie declared, 'Dave, why don't we just pack our bags, get the first train out of London and be together!'

Dave was taken aback. 'I told you from the beginning I'll never do that,' he replied.

'I know you said that, but now I want to be with you all the time,' the distraught girl cried. 'I don't think I can take this any more!'

Maggie served the week out and quit Tate & Lyle that Friday. Dave saw her at the gate as she was going, and pulled her into a telephone box to kiss her goodbye. 'That's our last kiss,' she told him. 'I'm going to walk over the bridge across the railway tracks, and I'm not going to look back.'

He watched her go – and she didn't look back.

9

Gladys

Despite the unfortunate incident with the curling tongs, Gladys and Betty had been going out to dances together more and more. One night, they were out in Canning Town when they bumped into a young man called Joe, who Betty knew from church. Joe asked if he could bring one of his friends over to meet them, who had just come out of the Army.

'He's a bit of a war hero,' said Joe. 'Almost lost his leg in Normandy, but he don't like to talk about it.'

Betty was intrigued, and told Joe that she'd like to meet the stranger. He duly introduced her to Sid, a stocky man with black hair who seemed far more grown up than any of the boys she had encountered at Tate & Lyle. He had a noticeable chunk missing from one ear which she was dying to ask about, but after what her friend had said she didn't feel she could.

As it turned out, she didn't need to. 'So what happened to your ear, then?' Gladys asked, unashamedly.

There was an awkward silence, before Sid replied, 'I went in for a haircut and the barber's hand slipped.'

'Oh, that's terrible,' gasped Betty, wide-eyed.

In fact, Sid's ear had been shot through by a German bullet during his time serving with the Devonshire Regiment. He was one of the Pegasus Bridge heroes, who had crossed enemy lines at night in gliders to seize two bridges in Normandy as part of Operation Deadstick. Their brave efforts prevented the enemy from sending in reinforcements, helping to pave the way for the D-Day landings the following morning, and their mission was later immortalised in the film *The Longest Day*.

Gladys could see that Betty was impressed with Sid, and wasn't at all surprised when the two started dating. She was happy for her friend, but couldn't help noticing that around him Betty's characteristic giggle was less in evidence.

'He's making a lady out of me,' Betty insisted, proudly. But she also knew that Sid wasn't too keen on Gladys roping her into every mischievous plan she had going.

With Betty busy dating, Gladys threw herself into a love affair of her own: sport. She had always been as fast as the boys when playing football in the park, but at Tate & Lyle she finally had the opportunity to hone her athletic talents.

The company laid huge store by its sports facilities and had established sports centres at each refinery back in the thirties, with Vernon Tate himself running the one at Thames. Between them, the two clubs had bought a sports field on Manor Way, Beckton, where their various teams could practise and where the summer sports day – the highlight of the Tate & Lyle social calendar – was held. Clubs and teams on offer ranged from athletics, football and cricket to archery, judo and rifle shooting. The company also had a wide range of non-sporting organisations, from pet clubs to photography societies.

Gladys was disappointed to discover there was no women's football team, but she decided to join the athletics club and the netball team – which had recently graduated to the first division in the London Business Houses League. She already knew one person on both teams, Miss Smith's secretary Betty Harrington.

On the day of her first netball practice Gladys bolted out of the factory at two p.m. and headed across to the sports field. As she neared the netball court she saw a young man lying on his back, enthusiastically pumping his legs in the air in a cycling action. What a show-off, she thought to herself.

As she walked past him, Gladys noticed that the man's shorts were hanging down loosely around his buttocks, leaving a large gap from which a particularly sweaty body part could be seen. It jangled around grotesquely in time with his exercises, and Gladys quickly looked away, shocked. Surely that wasn't what a grown man's willy looked like? She recalled her father telling her about nurses having to hold old men's private parts while they wee'd, and thanked her lucky stars she had heeded his warning. Nevertheless, she thought it worth making the most of the opportunity for research and, after walking a few feet, turned back to get a second look.

Changing for netball also proved to be a bit of an eye-opener. Like most of the girls, Gladys couldn't afford to buy a bra, and while she wouldn't have had much to put in it anyway, there were some members of the team for whom running and jumping around a netball court could have proved quite a challenge. The trainer, however, had a solution of his own.

'Right, tops off, girls,' he announced, striding into the changing room.

'What's he playing at?' Gladys whispered to Betty Harrington.

'Oh, it's all right, he just wants to wrap our boobs up,' she replied.

Gladys watched, astonished, as all the girls obediently took off their blouses. The man produced a length of bandage and went over to the girl nearest to him, who raised her hands above her head. He then began wrapping the material over her bosom and round her back, securing it tightly so that her breasts were squashed almost flat against her torso.

'Stops them wobbling about,' Betty Harrington whispered.

Gladys could see she was right – there was no way those boobs were going to be bouncing about on the court. When her time came, she too lifted up her arms and allowed the trainer to mummify her, silently thanking her mother for having made her wear a vest.

From then on, Gladys could be found at the sports field every afternoon if she was working the early shift, and every morning if she was working the late one. The place seemed to have a magnetic pull on her, and even if she didn't have a practice to go to she would wander down on her own, hanging around in the hope of finding some lads who might fancy a kickabout. Though she would never have admitted it to Miss Smith, she was becoming quite grateful for her job at Tate & Lyle. First it had provided her with a best friend, and now it had given her a hobby to pursue.

Nevertheless, during factory hours, Gladys was as mischievous as ever. She had now been threatened with the sack more times than she could count, but the warnings would go straight out of her head whenever a fresh opportunity for fun presented itself.

One day, she and Betty had been told off by their charge-hand Julie McTaggart for taking too long on a toilet break.

'It's not fair, we was only ten minutes!' Betty complained, when Julie marched off. 'Why does she have to be so strict?'

'Don't worry, we'll get our own back,' Gladys said, confidently.

Gladys waited until Julie had gone into the glass-fronted office to speak to the forelady, Peggy Burrows. Then she left her machine and wandered over to where Alex, one of the boys, was unloading waste paper into a large bin. Gladys looked at him with a naughty smile on her face, and put a finger to her lips. Alex nodded and carried on with his work as if he hadn't seen her.

Gladys knelt down and peered around the back of the bin, where bits of waste paper frequently got caught against the wall. She poked about gently with her finger until she found what she was looking for: a perfect little nest made of discarded sugar bags, containing a mother mouse and her six sleeping babies. She pulled the nest out of its hiding place, rose to her feet and walked calmly towards the glass-fronted office.

Then she knocked firmly on the window. 'Julie,' she called innocently, 'what do you want me to do with this?'

Julie was leaning over Peggy Burrows's desk, deep in conversation, and turned round with an annoyed look on her face. As she caught sight of the little mouse family – who were beginning to wake up and peer around inquisitively – she was suddenly transformed from sergeant major to terrified schoolgirl, throwing her hands up and shrieking.

Peggy jumped out of her seat and rushed around the desk to see what had prompted the usually implacable Julie to such hysteria. As soon as she saw what was in Gladys's hand, she too looked horrified. The mice, agitated by the noise, were now squiggling around and attempting to escape from the nest, the babies hopping at the sides and falling backwards again onto one another. Meanwhile the office secretaries had also gathered at the glass, and were adding their own shrieks to the commotion.

'Get rid of them! Get rid of them!' Julie shouted frantically, gesturing to the nest.

'What's that? Can't hear you!' Gladys called. 'I said what do you want me to do with *this*.' She shoved the nest right up against the glass, causing the gaggle of women on the other side to take a collective step backwards in terror.

'I think it's safe to have a break now,' Gladys called over her shoulder to the other Blue Room girls.

'Nice one, Gladys!' came the reply, as they gratefully took advantage of their bosses' imprisonment and scampered off for a cheeky fag break.

Later, in Miss Smith's office, Gladys prepared to face the music. Well, she told herself, she couldn't be held responsible for the Blue Room being infested with vermin. Tate & Lyle ought to thank her for being the only girl on the floor brave enough to clean the things up!

'You've really done it this time, Gladys,' whispered Betty Harrington, looking worried.

Suddenly, Gladys was hit with a sickening feeling. If Miss Smith actually did sack her, she could say goodbye to her friends, to the nights out at the Tate Institute and the sports clubs – all the things that had made her decision to join the factory seem like the best she had ever made.

As Miss Smith marched in, the little office seemed to shake with every step. She really did look enormous today, thought

Gladys. Her eyes were burning and her brow was deeply furrowed.

'Gladys Taylor,' she boomed. 'I have given you warning after warning.'

'I was only –' Gladys began.

'Don't you dare interrupt me!' Miss Smith shouted, jabbing a finger towards her. 'I don't want to hear your explanations. I don't want to hear your excuses. You've had your warnings. This time, you're out!'

Gladys felt the rebellious Taylor blood boiling in her veins. All thoughts of the sports clubs, nights out and friendships went clean out of her head, and before she could stop herself she snapped back: 'Please yourself!'

Miss Smith's mouth dropped open and her eyes bulged. Gladys and the two Betties waited with bated breath for her response, the tension mounting with every second that ticked by.

Miss Smith stormed over to the filing cabinet and took out Gladys's file, ready to initiate the dismissal procedure.

'Wait!' squeaked Betty Harrington, suddenly jumping out of her chair. 'You can't sack her!'

Miss Smith's head swivelled towards her young secretary. 'I can sack anybody I like,' she retorted.

'Not Gladys,' Betty exclaimed. 'She's the fastest girl on the relay team. Without her we won't stand a chance at the sports day!'

If there was one thing that pleased Miss Smith above all else, it was seeing her girls triumph over their counterparts at the Thames Refinery. This year Gladys was the athletic team's secret weapon – as their best runner they were planning to keep her until last in order to surprise their opponents.

Miss Smith's mouth twitched for a few seconds, and Gladys and the two Betties waited again, anxiously. Finally she spoke, her voice audibly constrained. 'Gladys Taylor,' she said, 'you can count yourself very, very lucky. Now get back to work.'

Although Gladys's participation in the sports day was now secured, the relay team soon suffered another crisis when a girl went off sick the day before the event. 'We'll never find anyone to replace her at such short notice!' the others wailed.

'I know someone who'll do it,' said Gladys. 'Leave it to me.'

At break time, she approached her friend Betty Brightmore. 'So, you know you're on the relay team tomorrow?' she said breezily.

'You what? I can't run to save me life!' Betty protested.

'I've seen you leg it for the 669 when you want to get home,' replied Gladys. 'We're one girl short, and if you don't help us we won't be able to compete.' She looked Betty squarely in the eyes. 'Or are you too much of a lady these days?'

The next day, Betty and Gladys made their way to the sports field, dressed in identical black shorts and white T-shirts adorned with the Plaistow Wharf logo.

'So what do I do again?' asked Betty.

'You just grab the baton and run as fast as you can!' said Gladys, rolling her eyes. 'You'll be great, I promise.'

Down on the sports field there was barely a patch of grass visible, as hundreds of Tate & Lyle workers and their families milled about the grounds. An enormous crowd of children were gathered around a Punch and Judy stall, while others queued to get a ride in a wooden carriage drawn by a miniature pony. People dressed in their Sunday best took rides along the edge of the grounds on a little steam train, and girls cheered their boyfriends on in a game of tug-of-war. Down on the athletics track a sack race was taking place, with grown men falling over each other, to the whoops and claps of the onlookers.

At one end a large, covered stage had been erected, where some important-looking men in suits were sitting, along with a group of smart ladies. Betty elbowed Gladys. 'Look, there's John Lyle,' she said, pointing to a blond man in his thirties. He was sitting next to his father Oliver, the refinery director. 'Don't he look gorgeous?'

'Not as gorgeous as Derrick,' said Gladys, nodding towards a dark-haired chap. Derrick de Marney, the star of Alfred Hitchcock's *Young and Innocent*, sat smouldering alongside members of the Tate and Lyle families. They always recruited a celebrity to congratulate the sports-day winners and have their photo taken with them. The special guest would also present the 'Inter-Refinery Shield' to whichever factory was the overall winner, and was responsible for judging the beauty contest. In this, De Marney was following in the footsteps of fellow film stars such as Paul Dupuis and Dennis Price, who had recently done their duty for Tate & Lyle.

That day all Gladys's early morning practices and long afternoons at the sports club seemed to pay off. First the netball team thrashed their counterparts from the Thames Refinery. Then, in the women's athletics, Gladys herself scooped gold in the 80 yards sprint, bronze in the high jump, gold in the 80 yards skipping and bronze in the long jump. By the time it came to the relay, she was on such a high that she felt sure they would win. While the men of Plaistow Wharf had already triumphed in their own relay race, the factory had lost in a few other events, and the Inter-Refinery Shield hung in the balance.

The starting pistol sounded and the team got off to a good start on the first and second legs, their girls three or four yards in front of those from Thames. Gladys, as the anchor, was waiting until the final leg, while Betty, the wild card, was in penultimate place. A look of determined concentration was on Betty's face, as if she was about to tackle a complex mathematical equation, not run around a racetrack. 'C'mon, Betty,' shouted Gladys as her friend seized the baton. 'Run for your life!'

Betty hugged the baton tightly to her chest and set off at full pelt. She was several yards ahead by the time the other team's girl started running, and managed to keep her advantage for a good few seconds. Then suddenly a look of horror passed across her face. There in the crowd, staring right at her, was her boyfriend Sid.

Betty became acutely aware of the unladylike sports shorts she was wearing, the wet marks forming under her armpits and the ungraceful lace-up running shoes that were pounding the ground. A feeling of weakness passed through her and her sense of determination seemed to drain away. Gladys saw her falter and almost trip, while the girl behind her began to catch up.

'C'mon Betty! You can do it!' Gladys shouted anxiously as the pair of runners strained towards the line.

Hearing the words, Betty gripped the baton tighter than ever and made a concerted effort to speed up, her eyes pricking with tears as she saw the other girl overtake her.

'I'm sorry, Gladys,' she said breathlessly, as she finally passed her the baton. There was no time for a reply. Gladys snatched it out of Betty's hand and set off, her teeth clenched, determined to make up the lost ground. Her legs cried out in exhaustion from all the day's efforts, but she forced herself on, pushing harder than she ever had before. All the crowds now seemed to be lining the track, Plaistow Wharf workers shouting and egging her on as she gained ground on the other girl. Gladys saw the finishing line approaching and made a final massive effort.

A few yards from the end of the race she overtook the other girl and heard the crowd erupt into cheers. She sailed across the line, and collapsed panting onto the grass.

Her team-mates ran over, pulling her to her feet and holding her arm up in the air. 'We did it!' they cried, as Gladys fought to catch her breath. 'We won every single medal in the athletics!'

Betty stood slightly to one side. 'Sorry, Gladys, I saw Sid in the crowd and me legs went all wobbly,' she said.

'Come here, silly,' said Gladys, pulling her into a hug. 'We couldn't have done it without you.'

With the sporting activities concluded, the crowds began to migrate over to the main stage for the most hotly anticipated event of the day: the beauty contest. The winner was to be the cover girl for the next edition of the company magazine, the *Tate & Lyle Times*, and would have her picture taken wearing the coveted Festival Beauty Queen sash and tiara.

A line of heavily made-up girls in swimming costumes and high heels filed up the stairs onto the stage, and one by one took a walk across the platform to a symphony of wolf whistles. In the last few weeks, Miss Smith had been busy recruiting girls for the event, twisting a few arms here and there to ensure they had the best possible chance of a Plaistow Wharf girl winning. Now Gladys could see her chivvying a couple of nervous-looking contestants up the stairs. Well, she thought mischievously, if she's that desperate for volunteers …

She made her way towards the stage and went to jump over the rope that sectioned it off from the crowd. But still giddy from running, she missed her footing – and fell flat on her face, causing a stir among the onlookers. 'What's that girl doing?' people murmured.

Gladys hauled herself up again, her knees slightly grazed from the fall and her white shirt now decidedly grubby. When she got to the steps at the side of the stage she saw Miss Smith, who had a look of panic on her face. 'Gladys, this is the beauty contest,' she hissed.

'I know,' Gladys replied confidently, marching up the steps close on the heels of a pretty blonde girl, before Miss Smith could stop her.

She strode across the platform, her hands on the hips of her dirty sports kit, and flashed a toothy grin at the crowd, who started laughing and clapping in response. The Tates and the Lyles looked at each other in dismay, while the girls in their bathing costumes exchanged annoyed looks, before shuffling up to let her join their ranks. For Gladys, however, the true triumph was seeing Miss Smith seething in the wings, unable to prevent the embarrassing spectacle.

Derrick de Marney left no one in doubt of his acting talents as he pretended not to notice the unusual attire of the scruffy redhead amid the line-up of perfectly groomed women. After some deliberation, he chose Kathleen Myers, a raven-haired 18-year-old from Plaistow Wharf, as the beauty queen, and while the onlookers applauded he surprised everyone by planting a great big smacker on her lips.

After the girls had tottered off the stage there was a pause in proceedings before the awards ceremony began. The victories of Gladys and her team-mates in the athletics had helped Plaistow Wharf to overall success, and in light of the significant part Gladys had played she was asked to collect the shield on behalf of the factory. The volume of applause was overwhelming as she took the enormous wooden emblem, which was almost as big as she was, and posed for photographs with Derrick de Marney.

'I reckon I was robbed in the beauty contest,' she told him cheekily. Ever the professional, he merely nodded and smiled at the cameras.

After the ceremony, Gladys went to find Betty. 'I think I saw her with Sid,' one of her team-mates told her. 'Looked like they were heading off together.'

'Oh, right,' said Gladys, swallowing her disappointment. 'See you girls in a minute then. I'm just off to get some lemonade.'

She walked away from the group towards a little drinks stall, but when she reached it she decided to keep on going. It had been an incredible day – not only had she held the shield in her arms, but she had cocked a snook at Miss Smith as well – yet suddenly she felt strangely empty.

Gladys carried on walking until she neared the edge of the ground, where she spotted a sight familiar from her childhood: a little red caravan painted with yellow flowers. It belonged to her mother's sister Harriet, who had come to make the most of the sports-day crowds. On the door was a cardboard sign that read 'Gypsy Rose Lee, Fortune Teller'.

Aunt Harriet, at it again, thought Gladys.

Two girls emerged from the caravan. 'Ooh, a tall, dark stranger – don't mind if I do!' said one of them, and they both burst out laughing as they walked off. Their words made Gladys feel even worse.

She knocked at the little wooden door.

'Cross my palm with silver to hear your destiny,' a mysterious, low voice wailed from within.

'Aunt Harriet, it's me,' called Gladys.

'Oh, Gladys,' her aunt replied in a brisk, normal voice, poking her head out of the caravan. 'What are you doing here?'

'Can you tell my fortune?' Gladys asked mournfully.

'Don't be silly, you little cow,' Aunt Harriet said. 'That's for daft girls with more money than sense.'

Gladys couldn't help giggling. 'No tall dark stranger for me, then?'

'How on earth should I know!' said Aunt Harriet, lighting up a fag.

10

Ethel

Ethel was determined to prove herself worthy of having been made the factory's youngest ever charge-hand. At 20, she was only a few years older than most of the girls she was supervising, and considerably younger than a few of the veterans who had been packing sugar since long before the war. Most of them knew her and had seen her wobbly ascent to the top, the string of promotions and demotions that had led to her finally donning the coveted white coat. It was important, therefore, to establish her authority.

She decided that the best approach would be to spend as much time as possible on the factory floor itself, rather than hidden away in the department office. The sight of Ethel pacing around the Hesser Floor, hands clasped tightly behind her back, quickly became a familiar one to the girls, who saw her as a rather bossy, if fair, supervisor who knew the factory rulebook inside out.

Smoking was certainly against the rules, and now when the girls in the toilets heard Ethel's footsteps coming up the corridor they would hastily stub out their cigarettes. Two sugar girls, Betty Foster and Jeanie Pearse, were smoking in the Ladies one day, when they heard the distinctive click-clack getting louder.

'Quick, Ethel's coming!' Betty shouted suddenly.

Jeanie panicked and threw her cigarette away from her, frantically wafting the door of a nearby cubicle in an attempt to dissipate the smoke. But the fag end remained lit as it flew through the air, and just as Ethel poked her head into the room it landed in Betty's front dungaree pocket. Feeling the burning fag scorching a hole through the fabric and beginning to warm her flesh, Betty tried subtly to pat it out. When that didn't work she began furiously beating herself in a desperate attempt to extinguish it, causing both girls to collapse in a fit of giggles.

'What are you two doing?' Ethel asked, bewildered.

'Nothing, Ethel,' they said in unison, before rushing back to the factory floor.

On another occasion the same two girls were drinking tea in the cloakroom – also a prohibited act. Jeanie had just filled their cups from her thermos flask when they heard footsteps approaching at speed. Betty quickly gulped hers down and hid the cup in her pocket, but poor Jeanie panicked at the thought of Ethel's imminent arrival. Spotting a spare pair of boots in an open locker, she poured the steaming contents into one of them and slammed the locker shut.

The girls waited anxiously, their eyes glued to the cloakroom door, but before long the urgent footfalls passed away again, and they breathed a sigh of relief.

'Those are Renie's boots you've ruined,' Betty giggled. 'What's she going to say when you tell her?'

Jeanie shruggled her shoulders, helplessly. 'I didn't know what else to do!' she said.

Ethel's strict adherence to the rules was not always appreciated, and she soon became tired of hearing at second hand that one girl or another had been moaning about something she'd done. Despite her best efforts to navigate the tricky waters of being a boss, it seemed that everyone had something to say about the way she was doing her job.

At night, when she went to bed, Ethel found herself worrying about the Hesser Floor. Every time she was about to drift off, thoughts of work would flit back into her head and stop her from sleeping.

'What's the matter, Et?' Archie asked one night, after she had been tossing and turning for hours as usual.

'Just thinking about Tate & Lyle,' she replied.

'Oh, not again!' he muttered, turning over and going back to sleep.

Before long, Ethel decided that a new, direct strategy was called for: she would summon all the girls with complaints up to the office one by one, and let them tell her exactly what they were unhappy about. Surely, she reasoned, once she had explained her thinking to them, they would have to understand her position.

On the appointed day, Ethel waited in the Hesser Floor office for the complainants to arrive. There was a knock on the door and the first girl shuffled in.

'Have a seat,' said Ethel, motioning to a chair.

The girl sat down and waited.

'Yes?' asked Ethel.

'Every time the machine stops, you always want to know why,' the girl blurted out.

Ethel smiled. 'Well,' she countered sweetly, 'I have to know why it stopped because if one of the managers comes along and asks me, I need to know what to say to him. If I say I don't know, I won't be doing my job, will I?'

The girl seemed to accept this explanation and silently got up and left the room.

That shut her up, thought Ethel.

Next, a check-weigher came in to see her. 'You always want to know when people go outside for a loo break,' she grumbled.

'That's right,' responded Ethel. 'You're only allowed ten minutes outside, and you're supposed to wait for a relief girl to cover you so that there are always two people on the job. If you don't wait for cover, one day someone's going to notice that one girl can manage on her own, and they'll turn it into a one-woman job.' She lowered her voice. 'And then you could be out on your ear.'

One by one, the complainants trickled in, and to each in turn Ethel explained that, while they might not be happy with how things were, there was always a good reason behind her behaviour. At the end of the day she went home utterly exhausted, but convinced she had made some headway with the Hesser girls.

Ethel's next challenge, however, came in the form of an older woman from another department. Walking past the area where the engineers worked, Ethel spotted her sitting down and chatting to them over a cup of tea. Since eating and drinking were strictly forbidden on the floor, she could hardly walk past and let the situation continue. She marched over immediately and told the woman to stop drinking.

The woman left without any trouble, but the male engineers were furious. 'What right does a girl like you have to tell a woman of her age what to do?' demanded one of them. 'It ain't proper!'

'No one's allowed to drink on the factory floor,' Ethel replied coolly. 'It's against the rules.' She walked off, leaving the men seething.

The next day Ethel was called into the office of her foreman, Tony Tunkin. He was a stocky man with bleached blond hair and was known in the department as The Canary, but he did his best to maintain an air of authority nonetheless.

'I've had a complaint about you from one of the engineers, Ethel,' he said. 'What's this about you telling off an older woman from another department?'

'She was drinking tea, Tony,' Ethel explained calmly. 'And it don't matter what department she's from or how old she is, rules is rules. What if one of my girls saw me walk on by without saying anything to her? How would that make them feel?'

Tony sighed. 'Look, just try to stick to your own department, Ethel.'

'I ain't doing no more than my job, Tony. If a rule is good enough for one, it's good enough for all.'

Tony could see he wasn't going to win the argument. 'All right, Ethel, you can go now,' he agreed reluctantly.

With Tony and the other managers, Ethel was becoming known for speaking her mind, and her straight-talking, fair-is-fair approach didn't always go down well with them. One day Tony summoned her to help vet some girls who were being transferred from the Thames Refinery. Ethel went down to the other factory with him, where they interviewed the candidates together. She accepted all of them except one, whose father had many years' service with the company but who Ethel felt wasn't up to the job.

On hearing what had happened, a senior manager at Thames marched into the room to remonstrate with Ethel. 'Why didn't you take her?' he protested. 'She comes from a very good family.'

'Well, I'm not employing her family!' Ethel retorted.

There was nothing the manager could say to that, and the girl was not hired.

Since Ethel prided herself on being a stickler for rules, she couldn't afford to be seen failing to apply the same high standards to herself as she did to others. One day, however, she was caught off guard.

Every week the Hesser department ran a raffle, with the proceeds going to Guide Dogs for the Blind. It was a popular activity, both among the girls, who regularly gambled what little they could spare from their wages, and in the offices, where the little pewter dogs offered by the charity as thanks were displayed with pride.

The top prize in this weekly competition had traditionally been a set of sheets and towels, which meant that whoever was running it had to go shopping every week in Rathbone Market. When Ethel took over she hit upon a time-saving alternative: she would simply give the money for the sheets and towels to the winner as a cash prize. The Hesser girls were delighted, since for many of them buying a new pair of shoes or a dress was infinitely more appealing.

Ethel congratulated herself on a brilliant piece of innovation. Until, that is, she arrived at work one day to find Tony Tunkin waiting outside the department office for her.

'Ethel,' he asked anxiously, 'have you been running a cash prize in your raffle?'

'Yes,' she replied proudly. 'The girls love it.'

'Oh.' His face dropped. 'I think you'd better come inside.'

Tony shut the door. 'The police have just rung,' he said. 'They've heard about your raffle. Apparently it's against the law to have a cash prize!'

Ethel was stunned. 'Why?'

'They said it's basically a lottery,' he replied. 'And those are illegal.'

Ethel didn't know what to say. 'What am I going to do, Tony?' she whispered.

'We'll just have to tell them you didn't know you were doing anything wrong,' Tony said. 'And that it will stop immediately.'

'Of course,' Ethel agreed, quickly.

She went back to the floor feeling mortified. How could she face her girls if they ever found out she was in trouble with the law? Her reputation would be shot to pieces. And what if the police decided to prosecute?

Before long, Ethel saw Tony hurrying over to talk to her. The police had been back on the line.

'Well, I told them it won't happen again,' he said, breathlessly, 'and they're going to let it go – this time.'

'Thank you!' Ethel cried, overwhelmed with relief.

Rules might be rules, but in this instance Ethel was grateful that they hadn't been too stringently enforced.

The next time a worker got into trouble, Ethel was on the side of leniency. An engineer by the name of Frank had been having a particularly difficult day, summoned onto the floor again and again by a sugar girl who just couldn't get her machine to work properly. First the weighing mechanism was miscalibrated, then the bags got stuck going along the belt, then there was a problem with the glue trough. Every time, Frank gritted his teeth as she called him over to attend to the next minor difficulty.

After the seventh or eighth incident that morning, however, Frank's goodwill had dried up completely. 'What is it now?' he demanded, as the girl asked him to look at the machine.

'It's still broken,' she complained. 'Can't you fix it properly?'

Frank had had enough. How dare she complain, when it was he who had to do all the repairs and adjustments and she just sat there having a break?

'Maybe it'd work better if you took a bit more fucking care, you stupid cow,' he muttered under his breath.

'What did you say?' the girl demanded loudly.

Frank immediately apologised for the outburst, but it was too late – the girl was already in floods of tears and complaining about how cruelly she had been treated. She was duly taken away to calm down in the factory surgery, where Ethel heard the whole unfortunate tale.

Frank was waiting outside the surgery, looking penitent. 'I'm sorry about this, Ethel,' he said.

'All right, Frank,' she replied. 'Don't worry about it.'

The next day, when Ethel arrived at work, Frank was nowhere to be seen. When she inquired about what had happened to him, she was told he was on suspension while the management decided what to do with him. A little while later, one of the managers came into the office to speak to Ethel.

'What do you think?' he asked her. 'Do you reckon we should let him go?'

Although swearing on the floor was certainly frowned upon, Ethel couldn't help but feel sorry for poor Frank. After all, he had spoken in the heat of the moment, at the end of a frustrating morning, and had apologised straight away. Surely nothing would really be gained by punishing him.

'No, I don't,' she said firmly.

The manager was taken aback. This wasn't what he had expected from Ethel.

'Why not?' he asked her.

'Well, *she* swears with the other girls,' Ethel pointed out. 'I don't swear, but if a man swore at me and said he was sorry, as far as I'm concerned that's the end of it. Besides, Frank's just getting the hang of those machines, and if we get rid of him we've got to start training someone else up all over again.'

Her reasoning was hard to argue with, and the manager went away, scratching his head.

A few days later, a grateful Frank was back on the job.

Gaining the respect and acceptance of the girls, learning to deal with the higher tiers of management, and knowing when to be strict and when to be lenient wasn't always easy. But after a while it was clear that Ethel's efforts were paying off. Her superiors remarked that whenever she was on the factory floor the amount of sugar packed would noticeably increase.

One afternoon, while Ethel was roaming the department, doing her best to keep the girls in check, a distinguished guest stepped onto the floor. Within seconds a whisper went round the room, and the girls busied themselves intently with their work.

Ethel looked up to see Oliver Lyle approaching. To her surprise he walked straight towards her as if she was the person he had come to see.

'You must be Ethel,' he said, beaming.

'Yes, sir,' she replied, as he shook her by the hand.

'I just wanted to tell you personally that we all know what an excellent job you're doing.'

'Thank you, sir,' she replied, proudly.

That night, much to Archie's relief, Ethel slept blissfully all night long.

11

Lilian

For hard-working factory girls in the East End, the beano – a company-sponsored day out at the seaside – was a highlight of the year. Each company in Silvertown had its own trips, usually to Margate, Southend or Clacton.

At Tate & Lyle every department had a beano, as did each of the sports teams. To transport the merry-makers, coaches were hired and in some cases whole trains commandeered. The *Royal Daffodil*, a twin-funnelled pleasure steamer, was frequently used to ship workers from North Woolwich pier down to Margate and back. The boat had a distinguished history, having previously transported 9,000 people safely home from Dunkirk in a total of seven trips across the Channel.

As each beano approached, male and female workers alike anticipated the opportunity to turn workplace crushes into something more, aided by cheap booze, sea air and an absence of managerial control. 'Who are you going to cop off with?' was the question most heard in the lead-up to a beano. Couples had been known to disappear behind the bushes during a pit stop on the way back from the seaside, emerging grass-stained and grinning before boarding the coach once again. Thankfully, a 'what happens on beano stays on beano' mentality prevailed.

One young man called Alan, however, seemed unaware of this golden rule. A husband and father of two, he got off with a female colleague who was also married. But on the journey home neither of them felt like returning to reality. Instead, they booked into a hotel that night, and never went back to their spouses again.

As the can-making department's beano to Margate loomed, the girls on Lilian's floor were in a flurry of excitement as usual. Since she had managed to avoid all the previous trips, Old Fat Nell and Little Lil were determined to make sure she came this time.

'C'mon, Big Lil, we've never all been on a beano together,' begged Little Lil, looking up at her with beseeching eyes.

'Think of all the fish and chips,' added Old Fat Nell.

Lilian was about to plead family commitments, but then memories of Weston-super-Mare popped into her head. The walks along the promenade, the feeling of the sun on her face, the laughter of the other girls – she had discovered a lighter side of life on that trip. Why shouldn't she have another taste of it now?

'I'm in!' she told them.

The can-making girls met their coach at eight-thirty a.m. outside Trinity Church on the Barking Road. By the time Lilian got there, the luggage hold was already being loaded up with crates of beer. 'Oh, were we meant to bring some?' she asked nervously. 'I didn't know.'

'I brought something far more useful,' a girl next to her said, blasting her ear with the noise of an accordion. 'No beano's complete without a bit of music, eh?'

Lilian got on the coach, sitting next to Little Lil, while Old Fat Nell spread out across two seats behind them. As the vehicle drew away, a gaggle of little boys ran after them shouting, 'Chuck out your mouldies! Chuck out your mouldies!' Purses were obligingly taken out and coppers rained down on the excited children, who scrabbled around picking them up.

The accordion was put to immediate use, accompanying a few rounds of 'Knees Up, Mother Brown', 'Roll out the Barrel' and 'Maybe It's Because I'm a Londoner', sung at an astonishing volume which caused the coach driver, Dave, to grimace. Lilian sang along quietly; if the girls were this noisy at eight-thirty, she thought, what would they be like after the crates of beer were cracked open?

The singing stopped abruptly, however, when the passengers spotted a coach driving past that was packed full of young men. Windows were wound down, this time for some less child-friendly behaviour. 'Oi, give us a mooner!' the shout went up, and a few of the boys willingly turned round and dropped their trousers.

An hour or so later the girls were ecstatic when the other coach pulled in at the same pub as theirs for a pit stop. Looking harrowed already, Dave promptly hit the bar, while his passengers set about getting to know the young men, who came from Pinchin Johnson's paint factory. Lilian, Little Lil and Old Fat Nell concentrated on their drinks. Lilian had no intention of getting entangled with some boy she would most likely never see again. From what she had so far seen of men, he would probably turn out to have a wife and kids at home.

Eventually Dave marched the girls back onto the coach, and the boys waved them off with calls of 'See you in Margate!'

The crates in the hold were raided for the second leg of the journey, and by the time they finally reached their destination the singing had become even louder. They drew into an enormous car park full of coaches just like their own, but the girls soon spotted the one with their boys on it, and hurried off to find them. 'Meet back at the coach at six p.m. sharp or you'll be spending the night here!' shouted Dave. He shook his head, knowing from experience that at least one person would fail to heed the warning.

Towering overhead was the train track of the great Scenic Railway, the centrepiece of Dreamland amusement park. The park was the big draw in Margate, and with their posse of paint factory boys now in tow to pay for all their rides, the girls intended to make the most of it.

A crowd of people surged through the archway into the park, many of them families with children but a good number, from the looks of them, on beanos too. Rows of girls in their best dresses, arm in arm, hitched up their skirts as they danced and sang, eyed up by gangs of lads smoking cigarettes and trying to look cool.

Inside, an aroma of candyfloss and onions immediately hit Lilian's nostrils. 'Hot dogs!' said Old Fat Nell, sniffing the air and dragging them towards a small stand. Lilian and some of the other girls opted for candyfloss instead, which they washed down with the last of the drinks they had brought from the coach. She was already starting to feel pleasantly tipsy.

The next essential item was a paper hat, printed with the requisite seaside slogan. Little Lil opted for 'Too Young to Be in Love' which, combined with her diminutive height, was unlikely to do her any favours with the boys. Lilian surveyed the other options. She had no desire to broadcast commands such as 'Kiss Me Quick' or 'Take Me Home for Luck', so she opted for 'Drunk Again', hoping that it didn't sound too maudlin. Old Fat Nell was finishing off Lilian's candyfloss for her, underneath a hat that read: 'My Resistance is Low'.

The trio followed the other can-making girls towards the rides. 'It really is like a dreamland, ain't it?' said Little Lil, surveying the scene with wide eyes. A Ferris wheel soared into the sky in front of them, while a little further off the long arms of The Octopus spun wildly, whizzing green-looking people through the air. Young men shouted and laughed as they smashed into each other on the dodgems, while children bobbed up and down on merry-go-round horses, or begged their parents for rides on real ones in the little paddock.

The paint factory boys herded the girls towards one ride in particular: The Caterpillar. As they walked towards the ticket booth, Lilian and her friends looked up to see the creature's face staring down at them, with its enormous eyebrows, thick lips and huge antennae. 'What do they want to go on that thing for?' said Little Lil, crumpling up her face in disgust. But the boys were already buying everyone tickets.

They stepped into the little two-seater carriages, mostly with a boy and a girl in each, but with Lilian and Little Lil together and Old Fat Nell on her own. The carriages formed a train that began to undulate around a circular track, at first in the open air and then diving underneath a canopy. As they were plunged into darkness, Lilian heard delighted shrieks and giggles from the other carriages, as the boys seized the moment and went in for a kiss and a cuddle. Each time they returned to daylight the pairs would hastily draw apart and wipe their mouths on their sleeves, before puckering up as the canopy came over them again.

When The Caterpillar came to a stop, the boys hastily dragged the girls over to the River Cave, where little boats waited to waft them through a series of decorative caverns. Once again the ride had been chosen on the basis that it took place in semi-darkness, and most of the group were too busy snogging to notice the magical scenes lit up before them. 'It's enough to make you sick, ain't it?' said Old Fat Nell. 'Oi, mate, you're dribbling!' she shouted at a boy in front, splashing water over him and the girl he was kissing. She and Little Lil burst out laughing and Lilian soon joined in, although a part of her couldn't help imagining what it might have been like sailing through the River Cave with her lost love Reggie.

Once they'd exhausted most of the snogging opportunities, the boys turned their attentions to the Scenic Railway. Despite its benign name, the one-mile rollercoaster had some fairly terrifying drops, and screams could be heard coming from it all day long. 'Let's see if they can keep kissing on *that*!' said Old Fat Nell as she marched over to the ticket booth. Lilian and Little Lil looked at each other apprehensively before following her.

They stepped into their seats and sat down as the rollercoaster set off at a gentle pace. 'This ain't so bad,' said Lilian, as they climbed the first peak, taking in a panoramic view of the seafront. As the train neared the top, a large sign instructed the occupants to ensure they were seated, and Lilian clutched the bar in front of her tightly in preparation. Nevertheless, the sensation of dropping through the air caught her completely off guard. She felt as if she were soaring upwards, completely weightless, far away from everything down on earth. Around her she could hear the screams of the other girls and, a few notes higher than the rest of them, the piercing tones of Little

Lil. But to her surprise she didn't feel like screaming too. Instead she found herself laughing and laughing, until tears streamed down her face. The sense of release was wonderful.

As soon as the ride stopped, Lilian begged her friends to go again. They looked at her, confused – this wasn't like shy old Lilian. 'You sure you're feeling all right?' asked Little Lil.

'That girl ain't,' said Old Fat Nell, pointing towards one of the others, who was puking up a sticky mixture of candyfloss and beer. The boy who had been kissing her in the River Cave did his best not to look.

Once the girl's queasiness wore off, they all headed down to the seafront in search of lunch, and the paint factory boys bought them little paper tubs of cockles and winkles, which they ate with toothpicks. The beach was even more crowded than Dreamland, with hardly an inch of sand visible between the deckchairs, so they soon decided to hit the pub instead. There they whiled away the last few hours of the day, getting increasingly merry, until it got dangerously close to six p.m.

'We're going to miss the bus!' one girl shouted suddenly, slamming her drink down. The others hurriedly followed suit and abandoned their half-full glasses, grabbing their belongings and making for the door.

'Hey, where are you going?' the boys from the paint factory protested.

'We've got to leave. See ya!' said the girls as they flew out the door.

'Wait!' one of the boys called after them. 'We've spent all that money on you and now you're just buggering off?'

'Looks like it, mate,' said Old Fat Nell, finishing off a couple of the drinks that had been left behind, before following the others out.

Back in the car park, Dave the driver counted the girls as they stumbled drunkenly back onto the coach. 'Two missing,' he said. 'Anyone know where they are?'

'Maybe they've had a better offer!' someone shouted, and the whole bus erupted into laughter. Dave shook his head before pulling out of the car park.

The journey home was always the part he dreaded the most, especially when his passengers were women. Sure enough, less than 20 minutes in, the first requests for a toilet stop were made. Dave obligingly pulled over and waited while some of his passengers relieved themselves and others stood at the side of the road clutching their stomachs and throwing up.

The calls came again 20 minutes later, and then another 20 minutes after that.

'I can't keep stopping the coach!' Dave said, exasperated. 'Can't you hold it in?'

After the large amounts of alcohol consumed over the course of the day, however, this was nigh on impossible, and by the time the coach pulled in for a pit stop at a pub called the Black Prince there were several wet seats.

Another coach was parked alongside theirs, which the girls soon learned belonged to a group of lads from the Spitals gas company in Stratford, who were also on their way back from a beano. With all thoughts of their paint factory boys now long gone, the girls were soon enjoying drinks with the new lads, and singing and dancing with almost as much energy as they had on the outward journey.

Emboldened by the alcohol, Lilian was heartily joining the others in a chorus of 'My Old Man', and barely noticed that a young bloke with ginger hair was watching her intently. By the end of the song she was laughing and gasping for breath, and when she looked up he was smiling at her.

'Drunk again, eh?' he said.

Lilian was about to take offence, when she remembered the paper hat she was wearing.

'You can't talk,' she laughed, pointing to a hat on his head which read 'One Drink and I'm Yours'. 'What are you wearing that for?'

'I thought I might get a free drink out of it,' he quipped. Then, suddenly realising that Lilian might take his joke the wrong way, he blurted out, 'Oh no, I didn't mean … I mean, can I buy *you* a drink?'

Lilian giggled, and the young man looked thrilled to have made her laugh. 'Go on then,' she said, and he ran off eagerly to the bar.

By the time he returned another song was well underway and, once he had handed Lilian her drink, they both joined in. It wasn't long, however, before Dave the driver was rounding up his drunken flock for the last leg of the journey, and as they were leaving, Lilian lost the young man in the crowd.

She went to the back of the coach and found two empty seats, where she lay down, smiling to herself. All day she had watched the other girls being chased around by boys and had counted herself lucky to have avoided their attentions. But she had to admit that for once she had enjoyed getting a little bit of notice from someone, even if it was only for five minutes. She closed her eyes and settled down happily into the seat.

'Do you mind if I sit here?'

Lilian opened her eyes to see the ginger-haired young man with the silly hat standing in the aisle, looking at her hopefully.

'What are you doing here?' she asked in astonishment, sitting up abruptly.

'I wanted to see you home,' he said, as if it were the most natural thing in the world.

'You don't know where I live!' said Lilian, laughing.

The young man squeezed into the seat next to her. 'Where do you live?'

'Cranley Road, Plaistow. Where do you live?'

'Stratford.'

'That's a long walk!'

He smiled. 'It's no trouble. I'm Alec, by the way.'

As the coach finally neared Trinity Church, the girls began singing 'For He's a Jolly Good Fellow', in honour of their long-suffering driver, and a paper hat stuffed full of notes was sent up to the front of the coach for him.

'You lot take care of yourselves,' said Dave, with a weary smile, as he dropped them off and gratefully drove away.

They had arrived back later than planned, and night was beginning to fall. Lilian could feel the old fear of the dark tugging at her once more, and suddenly hoped that Alec had meant what he'd said about walking her home.

As soon as Old Fat Nell and Little Lil had said their good-byes, Alec held out his arm for Lilian to take. He looked so earnest as he made the gesture that she couldn't help giggling a little, but she took it and they began to walk along the Beckton Road together.

On the way Alec asked her so many questions about herself, and seemed so fascinated by everything she had to say, that for once in her life Lilian found she barely stopped talking. She discovered much less about him, but did learn that he was a gas fitter, that he lived with his mum, sister and brother-in-law in Stratford, and that he was four years younger than she was.

Lilian knew it was an hour's walk from her house to where Alec lived, so at each turn she expected him to drop her off and head home, leaving her to walk the rest of the way by herself. But to her surprise he escorted her right up to the gate of her house in Cranley Road. What a gentleman, she thought to herself.

'Well, thank you for walking me home,' she said, giving him a friendly smile and turning to the door.

As she got the key into the lock, the young man cried, 'Wait!'

Lilian turned round in surprise.

'Can I see you again next Saturday?' he asked.

She studied him. His face was so open and honest that he looked as if he couldn't hurt a fly. But then she remembered Reggie, and how he had broken her heart. She couldn't risk falling in love again, especially not with a boy four years younger than herself.

'No, sorry, I can't,' she said, hastily pushing the door open. 'Nice to meet you – bye.'

But her hesitation had given him hope.

'Look, I'll come and knock for you next Saturday, all right?' he called, as she closed the door on him.

Old Fat Nell and Little Lil pounced on Lilian as soon as she got to the factory on Monday.

'What happened? Did you snog him? Are you going to see him again?'

'Keep your hair on!' Lilian said, laughing. 'He wants to take me out on Saturday.'

'Hooray!' said Little Lil.

Old Fat Nell looked at Lilian suspiciously. 'You said no, didn't you?'

Lilian nodded.

'Oh no!' squeaked Little Lil. 'But why? He's nice, ain't he?'

'Yeah,' said Lilian, 'but I'm older than him.'

'That don't matter,' said Old Fat Nell, confidently. 'A bloke likes a proper woman to show him what's what.'

By the time Saturday came round, Lilian was still in two minds about whether to go on the date. She took out her old picture of Reggie and looked at it, as she had done so many times before. Even now, long after any hopes of hearing from him had vanished, it cut her to the quick to see his face. It wasn't just that she didn't want to have her heart broken again, she realised. She just didn't believe she was capable of falling in love like that a second time.

But did that mean she should spend the rest of her life alone? Never marry, never leave her strict father's house? Alec seemed like a real gentleman. Who knew when another one of those would come her way?

Lilian looked at herself in the mirror. 'Grab a hold of him, girl,' she told her reflection.

12

Gladys

The Blue Room had recently moved to the top of a new building at the eastern edge of the factory – strictly speaking it wasn't blue any more, but the old name had stuck. The girls now had to climb many flights of stairs every day to reach their department. On the plus side, a new set of toilets had been installed, and they came with some intriguing additions: a row of bidets.

'What are those sinks doing all the way down there?' Gladys asked when she first spotted the unfamiliar objects.

'Don't know,' replied Betty. 'They must be for washing your feet in.'

'Why do they think our feet need washing?' asked Maisie, a little insulted, as she took a seat on one of the bidets and lit up a fag. Several girls followed her example.

'It's quite comfy like this actually,' said one of them as she straddled the porcelain basin.

As the others chatted away, Gladys crept stealthily up behind them on her tiptoes. Then, in a flash, she ran along the back of the row, flicking the taps on full blast.

Maisie and the other girls leapt to their feet screaming, while Gladys legged it, crying with laughter, back to the Blue Room, where her friends spent the rest of the day attempting to hide the wet patches on their bottoms.

As well as extra equipment in the lavatories, the new Blue Room also afforded quite a view – of the stinking mountain of animal carcasses in the yard of John Knight's soap works next door. From their vantage point on the top floor, the Blue Room girls could see the swarm of over-fed bluebottles that buzzed constantly around the rotting pile. Every so often, the poor men would appear whose job it was to shift the putrid mound, and as they shovelled away, rats measuring at least a foot long would come scurrying out, only to be chopped in half by the men and added to the top of the pile.

The first time the inhabitants of the Beauty Shop witnessed this event there were screams of horror, cries of 'I'm going to be sick' and at least two near-fainting fits. 'Get away from that window at once,' commanded Julie McTaggart.

'I'm never using soap again!' declared Maisie. 'Me neither,' said Betty, wiping her brow.

But for Gladys the spectacle held a grotesque fascination, and thereafter she kept an eye out for the men and their shovels. 'Quick, they're chopping up rats again!' she would shout to the reel boys, who like her found it morbidly fascinating.

With the new Blue Room came a number of new workers. While Gladys's friend Betty had an uncle and a sister at the factory, fresh recruit Eva Browning seemed to have her entire family there. When Eva joined the Blue Room she became the fifth Browning to work at Plaistow Wharf – her father was in the offices, her younger sister Rosie in syrup-filling, another younger sister Jean in can-making and her brother Danny on the lorry bank.

Eva had tried her best to avoid the family firm. Determined to go into dressmaking, she had been excited to land a job as a machinist in an Oxford Street workshop. When she brought home her first pitiful week's pay, however, she realised she had made a mistake.

'No more arguments,' said her mother. 'Your dad's got you a job down Tate & Lyle paying twice that, plus bonuses. You start at six a.m. tomorrow.'

Like thousands before her, Eva had to admit that Tate & Lyle was the best-paying employer around, and duly donned her dungarees.

Unlike Gladys, Eva immediately felt at home in the so-called Beauty Shop. At the end of each shift she would whisk off her turban and shake out her bouffant blonde hair, which, combined with her sparkling blue eyes, ensured that she caused quite a stir among the reel boys. Her status in the department was further enhanced by the fact that her family lived in East Ham, and were therefore considered rather posh.

Maisie, however, was none too pleased to find herself with a rival for the unofficial title of Blue Room beauty queen. Although Eva was naturally shy, the reel boys were soon looking for excuses to stop by her machine for a chat, and in response Maisie began flirting more and more outrageously with Alex by the waste paper.

'Maisie hates me like the devil hates holy water,' Eva complained to Gladys in the café one morning.

'Nah, she don't really,' Gladys assured her. 'She's just never met anyone with hair as big as yours.'

After a while, Eva decided to play Maisie at her own game. For every button that Maisie undid on her blouse, Eva would ensure that one of her own came magically undone. Half an hour later, Maisie would respond by showing a little bit more cleavage herself, and, sure as anything, Eva would soon follow suit.

'What's the matter, beauty queens? Is it too hot in here for you?' Gladys asked one day, prompting a contemptuous flick of the hair from Maisie, and a giggle from Eva.

Gladys, Betty and Eva quickly became a trio, and Gladys was pleased to have a new friend around to spend time with whenever Betty was busy with her boyfriend Sid. The three girls soon discovered a new hangout, an Italian café on the Barking Road near Gladys and Betty's bus stop. Bianchi's was run by a little old man named Horace, and had the misfortune of still being open when the girls were coming back from their late shift. After they had been chained to their machines for eight hours, the last thing the three of them felt like doing was going home to bed, and if it was midweek a good natter over a cup of tea was just the ticket. Unfortunately, caffeine tended to enhance the girls' manic energy rather than dampen it, and one cup of tea could often prompt an hour or more of hysterical laughter while poor Horace wiped his brow behind the counter and prayed for the night to end.

After a couple of these encounters, Horace began to keep a lookout for the telltale checked turbans through the windows of the bus as Gladys, Betty and Eva drew up at Trinity Church each evening. As soon as he saw them, he would spring from behind his counter and hobble as fast as his little legs would carry him towards the door, attempting to slam it shut and lock it before the girls could reach him. 'I am closing! Go home! I am closing!' he would shout, as the three of them hurled themselves at the door, giggling and demanding 'just one cup of tea for us hard-working sugar girls!'

Their late-night tormenting of Horace led unintentionally to the suffering of someone else, however. Not long before Eva had joined the Blue Room, a young man called John Rodwell had returned to Tate & Lyle from his national service. John had just come back from Egypt and was sporting quite a tan. The sun had made his blond hair even lighter than usual, and the effect was very striking – at least in the eyes of the Blue Room girls, who got a good look at him when he came in one day on an errand.

John only had eyes for the one person in the room whose blonde hair was even more brilliant than his own: Eva. One night, he spotted her getting off the 669 at Trinity Church and heading to Bianchi's with Gladys and Betty. Unaware that she actually lived in East Ham, he assumed this was her regular route home and decided to hang around outside Bianchi's after work the next day to ask her out, rather than risk humiliation in front of the entire Blue Room.

Poor John waited in vain outside the café every day for a fortnight, hoping to catch sight of her, while inside, old Horace wondered what the lovelorn youth was doing there. In the end John realised his error and the golden couple finally got together.

Like his new girlfriend, however, John came from a Tate & Lyle family, which meant it was virtually impossible to have a love life without all his relations finding out. Eva already knew his cousin Hester, the kind nurse in the factory surgery. A more formidable problem was his mother, who was a charge-hand in the syrup-filling department, where Eva's sister Rosie also worked. 'Dozy Rosie', as she was known in the family, unthinkingly blabbed to some of her colleagues that her big sister was going out with the boss's son, and before long the news had reached John's mother. Mrs Rodwell promptly decided to take herself up to the Blue Room in order to assess her son's new sweetheart.

One afternoon, Eva was standing at her machine when she saw a middle-aged woman in a white coat fixing her with a penetrating gaze. Eva's first thought was to hope she hadn't inadvertently broken a Tate & Lyle rule in case her own father heard about it in the offices, so she was relieved when the strange woman left the department without even coming over to speak to her. Mrs Rodwell evidently approved of what she saw, because the workplace romance was allowed to continue – albeit under the watchful eye of both families.

Eva wasn't the only new girl in the Blue Room. Another fresh recruit was Irene, a girl who, like Betty, had lost both her parents. One Monday at break time Irene and Eva got chatting, and she told Eva it was her birthday.

'Will you come for a quick drink in the Rec with me to celebrate?' she asked.

'Oh sorry, I'm not allowed to drink,' Eva replied. 'My Dad works here, and if he found out he'd kill me.' Mr Browning had warned her and her sisters to steer clear of the Recreation Room, where he and his fellow workers spent many of their lunch breaks. In any case, Eva was too young to buy alcohol and he had assured her that if she so much as tried to get served there one of his moles around the factory would soon let him hear of it.

'Well, you're not doing anything wrong if you're just sitting there,' reasoned Irene. 'Go on, I'll only have time for one.'

Eva had to admit that the other girl had a point, and reluctantly followed her over to the canteen and up the stairs to the Rec. She looked over her shoulder constantly as she went, checking to see that she wasn't being spotted by a fellow Browning, but they managed to reach the bar undetected.

'What'll you have, love?' the barman asked Irene.

'I don't know – whatever those men over there are having. With a straw.'

The barman placed a bottle of cider on the bar, pushing a stripey straw down its neck.

Eva dragged Irene over to some seats in the corner and sat with one elbow on the table, so she could shield her face with her hand in case a family member came through the door.

With the help of the straw, Irene surprised herself by finishing the whole bottle of cider in a matter of minutes. 'Just like drinking lemonade, really, ain't it?' she said.

'Right, let's go then,' said Eva, jumping up.

'Hang about, we've still got twenty minutes,' replied Irene, whose cheeks were beginning to glow. 'I can easily have another one and get back in time.'

Irene headed to the bar again before Eva could stop her, and the second drink went down as quickly as the first, ending with a little hiccup.

'We've really got to go now,' said Eva, peering anxiously through her fingers to check that her father was still not in the room.

But a young man who was passing spotted Irene's empty cider bottle and offered to replace it. 'Aw – thank you!' she said. 'Everyone's really, really nice here, aren't they?'

At some point during the course of the third bottle, Irene lost the ability to sit up straight and, in a fit of giggles, began to fall off her stool. Eva rushed forward to catch her, and managed to pull her to her feet. She put her arm round Irene's shoulders and led her towards the door.

As they reached the entrance, she paused to let a group of men file in. The last of them stopped dead in his tracks. Eva looked up into the face of her father.

'Eva Browning, what the hell do you think you're playing at?' he demanded. 'What did I tell you about drinking on the job?'

'I didn't drink a thing, Dad, I promise!' Eva protested, struggling to keep the hiccupping Irene upright. 'She just kept ordering more and more cider and I couldn't get her to leave.'

'Well, never mind that now,' said her father, relenting a little at his daughter's obvious distress. 'You'd better get your friend back to the Blue Room, or you'll both be in trouble for being late.'

With great difficulty, Eva managed to escort Irene back to their department. 'Maybe we should tell Julie you're not feeling well,' she said, looking at her dubiously. 'I'm not sure you should be on the machines.'

'You can't do that, I'll lose me job!' the other girl wailed. 'Promise you won't tell her, Eva?'

'Oh, all right,' said Eva, wishing to heaven that she hadn't agreed to go to the Rec.

As they started back on the machines poor Irene did her best to attend to her duties, but out of the corner of her eye Eva could see her stumbling around clumsily. Finally, Irene knocked over a barrel of ink, and when Eva looked over she was horrified to see that her face and clothes were covered in the dark-blue liquid.

Julie McTaggart was furious. 'Somebody take this girl down to the surgery!' she barked.

'I'll do it,' said Eva quickly, feeling guilty for having let Irene go back on her machine.

Down at the surgery, Eva and Nurse Hester stripped Irene of her ink-splattered clothes and did their best to wash her down, before she was sent home in the company ambulance. At least Irene had no parents to read her the riot act, Eva thought to herself, knowing her own father would probably give her another ticking-off when she got home. To make matters worse, since Hester was her boyfriend John's cousin, she knew there was no way of hiding the story from his family, either.

The next day Irene returned to work rather the worse for wear, and in the Blue Room the girls were convinced that it was only a matter of time before she was sacked by Miss Smith. But to their surprise The Dragon came by on her daily round and didn't say a word to her.

The following day, and another, passed without any action from Miss Smith, and each time Irene saw her she became more jumpy. 'I bet old Flo's stringing it out on purpose to scare her,' remarked Gladys.

By the end of the week the anticipation had reached fever pitch, and poor Irene was a nervous wreck. On Friday afternoon the girls were just shutting down their machines when Miss Smith appeared in the doorway.

'Irene!' Her deep voice echoed across the floor.

Irene froze, and all the girls' hearts began beating in sympathetic terror.

'Yes, Miss Smith?' she replied meekly, stepping forward.

'I believe you were drunk on the job on Monday. Is that correct?'

Irene nodded, silently. Her cheeks were even redder than they had been in the Rec.

'It goes without saying that I cannot tolerate that kind of behaviour in the factory.'

'No, Miss,' Irene said quietly. She hung her head, braced for the much-anticipated dismissal.

But there was a long pause, and Miss Smith seemed to be wrestling with herself over what to say next.

'I trust you have learned your lesson?' she asked, eventually.

Irene looked up in surprise. Could this mean what she thought it did?

'Yes, Miss,' she said, quickly. 'Of course, Miss.'

'Good. Then don't let me see you covered in ink next week,' said Miss Smith, turning on her heel and walking out of the room.

As soon as she had gone, the girls all gathered round Irene, hugging and congratulating her. Gladys could scarcely believe that the girl had got off so lightly – and if she was honest, she felt a little bit annoyed about it. True, Irene had been subjected to a very public warning, but Miss Smith had not even threatened her with the sack, much less gone through with it. Gladys had had that threat dangled over her constantly ever since she started at the factory.

'You know Irene don't have no family,' said Betty, when Gladys told her what she was thinking. 'Maybe that's why Miss Smith went easy on her.'

The following week at work, the Blue Room girls were excitedly planning for an upcoming beano to Southend. 'I know what we'll need,' said Gladys. 'Paper hats!'

'Oh, we can buy them when we get there,' replied Eva.

'Why wait?' Gladys said. Checking that Julie McTaggart was out of sight, she grabbed a freshly printed sheet of paper. 'We can make our own.'

She folded the paper up until she had something vaguely resembling a hat. Nervously, the other girls followed her example, knowing that if they were caught they would be in big trouble for wasting good paper.

'Now we need something to write on 'em,' said Gladys.

'I've got a pen,' said Maisie, and began adding the time-honoured phrase 'Kiss Me Quick' across the front of hers.

'That's too boring,' said Gladys, grabbing the pen with a mischievous smile. She leant over and began scribbling on her own hat, then put it on her head and turned to the others, hands on her hips. 'Like it?' she asked.

In large letters were the words 'Do Me Quick'.

To her surprise the other girls hastily looked away and tended to their machines, crumpling up their hats and stuffing them into their pockets.

'Well, don't take offence!' Gladys said, rather put out. She turned round grumpily to her own machine, her hat still on, and came face to face with Miss Smith.

The labour manageress's eyes flicked over the words on Gladys's forehead. Then she reached over and whisked the hat off, crushing it in one large hand.

'I am shocked at you …' she began, fixing Gladys with her familiar, penetrating stare. Then she stopped and narrowed her eyes. 'No, come to think of it, I'm not shocked,' she said, turning to go. 'It's exactly the sort of thing I expect from you.'

Was that it, thought Gladys – no punishment? Not even the ritual summons to the Personnel Office?

As Miss Smith left the room, Gladys gave a careless laugh. 'Maybe she's keeping the hat for herself,' she joked to the other girls.

She knew she ought to be pleased that Miss Smith had gone easy on her, but she couldn't help feeling disappointed. For the first time, her naughtiness had not provoked a reaction.

13

Ethel

The winter of 1952 was bitterly cold, and families everywhere were throwing as much coal on the fire as they could afford. The timing could not have been worse. On Friday 5 December, an anticyclone settled over London, and combined with the cold weather it created a lid of warm air, under which an unliftable yellow-black smog began to form. The East Enders were used to pea-soupers, but this was on a scale never experienced before, and on Silvertown's Sugar Mile, where the factories belched out their own smoke hour after hour, visibility was reduced to a mere foot.

That morning the buses crawled the streets as slowly and carefully as they could, conductors carrying lanterns out in front in a desperate attempt to see through the smog. At the Plaistow Wharf Refinery, workers arrived in dribs and drabs, and even by midday less than half of the machines were fully staffed. In a rare act of generosity towards latecomers, the management announced that anyone who had made it in at all, however late, would be paid for the full day. Those who had stayed at home would be docked pay accordingly.

Dave Price, who worked on the raw sugar landing, spent most of his morning stuck on the Woolwich Ferry. Halfway across the Thames, the captain of the paddle steamer lost his way, and the passengers were ordered to line the sides of the boat as lookouts, to warn of any incoming vessels. They endured a near miss from a petrol tanker and collided with a barge, before the captain decided it was best to stay where they were. Four hours later they were rescued by a police boat.

When Dave finally made it in to work, his supervisor demanded to know where he had been.

'I've been marooned,' he told him, 'in the middle of the river!'

'Oh well, you better go straight home again,' his boss responded. 'There's no work on the landing today anyway.'

The sugar girls had no such luck, since the Hesser Floor was still running. When the day came to an end they struggled as best they could to find their way home, stumbling from street to street and relying largely on memory to guide them. By the time one poor girl found her way back to Argyle Street, she had walked around St Luke's Square four times. She got home to find that not only her dungarees but her underclothes had been blackened by the smog.

Ethel had less distance to travel home from work than most, but she found it a challenge nonetheless. It was as if a velvety cloth had fallen upon Silvertown, smothering everyone and everything beneath it, and even the familiar sounds of the area seemed muffled.

In the market at Smithfields, livestock were dying of suffocation, and they weren't the only ones to perish. In the following weeks, the human casualties of the Great Smog reached 12,000.

That weekend most families stayed indoors, and by the following week there was still little sign of improvement. On

Tuesday the shop steward cornered Ethel to request that a girl with a particularly tough commute be allowed to leave early.

'You've got to do something about Lucy Humphries,' the woman pleaded. 'She's got to go all the way to Basildon. It ain't right making her struggle through the smog for hours.'

'I'm not sure,' Ethel responded, fearful of making an exception for one girl that might set a bad example to the others. Rules were rules, after all – wasn't that what she had always told herself?

'Come on, Ethel,' the other woman continued. 'You can't see your own two feet out there.'

'All right then,' Ethel relented. 'She can leave a couple of hours early.'

Lucy was grateful to be able to pack up and begin the long, blind trudge home. She had not been gone ten minutes, however, when a light wind began to blow. It grew and grew in strength, until before long the dank stillness that had descended on the city had lifted, and the smog started to clear.

Just my luck, thought Ethel to herself – I sent that girl home early, and now she gets two hours off work for nothing!

* * *

The festive period was always a special time at Tate & Lyle. At the Plaistow Wharf Refinery Oliver Lyle and his family toured the various departments, wishing the workers a merry Christmas. Parties were laid on for the employees' children, featuring pantomimes performed by enthusiastic members of staff, with regular wags like Soupy Edwards from the Thames Refinery canteen dolled up in drag as the dames. The kids would be invited to compete for prizes in a carol-singing competition, and all of them would leave with a present from Father Christmas. For parents who often struggled to make ends meet at such an expensive time of year, it offered an opportunity to give their children an added treat.

But the generosity of the management was as nothing to that of the workers who, despite their own lack of means, would dig deep in their pockets for the various collections and raffles that were held for deserving causes throughout the festive period. At Plaistow Wharf, a giant Christmas tree in the office entrance hall was soon festooned with presents – toy cars, dolls, footballs, knitted animals and games, many of them home-made – to be donated to the orphans of Dr Barnardo's children's homes. Such was the quantity of gifts supplied that within a week extension tables had to be added at the base of the tree to hold them all. By the time the presents were delivered to the orphanages on 19 December, many hundreds of pounds' worth of toys had been donated, by one of the poorest communities in the country.

The orphans offered thanks by performing carols around the tree, which were piped throughout the factory over the tannoy. Up on the Hesser Floor, Betty Holder, one of Ethel's girls, would listen with tears in her eyes. On her way home she would pop into the offices to watch the children, still singing away. She always paid for two of the orphans to attend the company Christmas party, and she liked to keep a lookout for the kids she had sponsored the year before. This year, though, one of the orphans she had sponsored was missing – a little black boy who had stood out from the crowd, not just because of his race but for his beautiful high-pitched singing voice. Betty asked the children's guardian if she knew why he was absent.

'I'm sorry, love,' replied the other woman, shaking her head. 'He was out on a bike he'd been given, and got hit by a lorry. Poor little thing never stood a chance.'

Despite the season of goodwill, Christmas cheer was not universal at the factory, as Ethel soon discovered. Over the past few weeks she had been helping the foreman Tony Tunkin order in the sugar for the Hesser Floor, with quantities carefully worked out according to the number of bags packed the previous week. This involved a trip to the main office block one morning a week, where the clerical workers would take down the relevant figures and phone through the requests.

While Ethel learned the ropes, Tony was by her side, talking her through the instructions she was to give to the office workers. The staff were always courteous and friendly, offering their guests comfortable chairs and cups of tea while they went through the figures. Ethel arranged with Tony that she could take her break mid-morning rather than at lunchtime, so she could have a cooked breakfast in the canteen after the meetings.

The run-up to Christmas was a busy time, and Tony decided that Ethel was now capable of putting in the sugar order without his help. She jumped at the chance of a bit of extra responsibility, and headed to the office with the paperwork as usual. But this time the atmosphere there was completely different. The men in the room barely looked up from their desks when she said hello, and they acted as if they didn't know her.

'Yes?' a chubby woman behind a desk demanded coldly.

'I've come to do the sugar order,' Ethel replied.

The woman sighed. 'All right then, go ahead.'

Ethel was shocked. The woman hadn't even offered her a chair, much less a cup of tea. Struggling to mask her surprise, she laid the documents out on the desk and began going through the sums. The secretary merely nodded as she noted down each figure, never once looking up throughout Ethel's long speech, and leaving her standing throughout.

'Fine,' she snapped, as Ethel came to the last of the figures. 'I'll see the details are phoned through. You can go now.'

'All right,' Ethel said awkwardly, turning to leave. Had she done something wrong? She couldn't understand why things were so different to how they had been before.

As she went to leave the room, she heard a whisper behind her, and froze with her fingers on the door handle. 'Come up from the factory floor, you know,' a male office worker muttered to his colleagues, one of whom laughed contemptuously. Ethel tried not to bristle as she pulled the door open and walked out.

'How did you get on?' Tony Tunkin asked her when she returned to the Hesser Floor.

'The woman in there treated me like a school kid!' Ethel told him. 'She sat there while I ordered the sugar, and didn't even let me sit down. Who does she think she is? I could do her job standing on me head, but I'd like to see her try and run around the Hesser Floor like I do.'

Tony nodded quietly at Ethel's words, and she went away, still seething.

But the next time she went to the office to do the sugar order, she found that the chubby woman was nowhere to be seen, and a new man had been put in her place. She must have been given the push, Ethel thought to herself, with satisfaction. Clearly Tony had taken what she said seriously.

Just as last time, the other men in the office treated Ethel as if she was beneath their notice. But to her pleasure, the new man had obviously been given careful instructions. He offered Ethel a chair to sit in, and was kind and courteous as they went through the figures.

'Thanks for your help,' she said cheerily, when they had finished their sums. 'Now I'm off to the canteen for my cooked breakfast.'

'Ooh, that sounds good,' the man said. 'I could murder a bacon sarnie.'

Ethel smiled at him and left the room. But on her way to the canteen she decided she would make a point of acknowledging his politeness in front of his rude colleagues. She ate her own breakfast as usual, but before going back to the Hesser Floor she asked for a bacon sandwich wrapped in brown paper to take away with her.

A few minutes later she was back in the office. 'Here you are,' she said loudly, placing the package on the nice man's desk. 'I bought you a Christmas present!'

The man eagerly unwrapped the brown paper to reveal the piping hot bacon sandwich inside, and its aroma quickly filled the room.

'Ethel, you're an angel!' he exclaimed. 'Thank you.'

'*You're* very welcome,' Ethel said pointedly, glancing at the other office workers, who looked on hungrily as he sank his teeth into the sandwich.

Although Ethel had worked at the factory for several years before finding herself on the receiving end of such snobbery, it was far from a rare phenomenon at Tate & Lyle. Class was ingrained in every aspect of day-to-day life, from the timetable – with office staff coming in at nine and factory-floor day-workers at eight – to the crockery. Senior managers took their tea on trays with bone china cups, individual milk jugs and silver sugar bowls, while the rank and file drank from mugs straight off the tea trolley. The office staff enjoyed silver service in an upstairs restaurant, but floor workers had to rush to the canteen in their break to queue up, swallow their food and get back to work in under half an hour.

Sometimes this arrangement had unfortunate consequences for families. When a girl called Barbara Bailey started work in the costing office she found that her father was not allowed to join her for lunch in the restaurant, despite having worked for the company for 30 years. Nor was she supposed to show her face in the workers' canteen. Meanwhile the directors' private dining room was off limits to all but the top brass and their privileged guests, and was rumoured to be a plushly carpeted affair with leather chairs and an enormous table.

One young woman who was constantly reminded of the class distinctions inherent in the company was Joan Adams. A waitress in the staff restaurant at the Thames Refinery, like Ethel she was Silvertown born and bred. From the moment she arrived at Tate & Lyle, Joan was acutely aware of the gulf that existed between workers who lived locally and those who commuted across the Thames from Woolwich. As she wheeled her tea trolley along to the offices, Joan would hear the girls joking about how they were 'slumming it' by coming to work across the water, loudly wondering how people could possibly live in Silvertown.

As a waitress, Joan had been told never to answer back to her betters. But despite growing up in relative poverty, she believed that she was equal to anyone. One day the snide comments from the office girls got too much, and she retorted, 'It can't be that bad – else why do you lot come to work here?' Before they could answer she had trundled off, leaving them open-mouthed.

Despite having joined the supervisor class herself, Ethel was determined not to let her sugar girls be looked down on. She was quick to remind anyone in the offices who made disparaging remarks that without the girls to pack the sugar there would be no job for them to do. And when one of the managers commented wearily, 'Oh those kids – they drive me mad at Christmas,' Ethel promptly replied, 'They're not kids, they're young ladies, so don't you go calling them that.'

Christmas, as it turned out, presented Ethel with a new reason to stand up for her girls. Of all the festive traditions at the factory, perhaps none was as legendary as that which took place at lunchtime on Christmas Eve. The sugar girls, knowing that only a few hours of work stood between them and the much-anticipated holiday, would head not for the canteen but for the Rec, where they would knock back as much alcohol as was physically possible in a 30-minute period.

Not even the terrifying figure of Miss Smith could prevent the inevitable, although she did try her best. Every year, without fail, she would instruct the womenfolk of the factory to remember their modesty and take care not to drink more than they could handle. But she knew such entreaties fell on deaf ears, and as long as the girls were back at work on the dot, there was little she could do. In the years before health and safety had permeated workplace culture, they were entitled to do as they pleased with their free time, and, after all, the bar was open during the working day.

Of course, if the girls failed to report back to their machines on time, then Miss Smith was ready to pounce. One year, when a group of tardy syrup-fillers failed to return from their break, she turned the factory upside down searching for them. Holed up in the Jubilee pub across the road they thought they were safe, but before long the door was thrown open. 'Look out, girls, it's the guv'nor,' joked the landlord Eric Bowden, before Miss Smith marched in and dragged them back to the factory.

At the Thames Refinery, forelady Rosie Bennett was once so shocked at the state of her Hesser girls on Christmas Eve that she ordered them to be shut in the 'cage' where the paper bags were stored, instructing the men to keep them there until they quietened down. It worked out pretty well for the girls in question, since they were paid for the rest of the day without having to lift a finger, and the only lasting consequence was the hangovers they woke up with the following morning.

Understandably, Ethel was nervous at the prospect of her girls hitting the Rec for the traditional lunchtime booze-up, but she was well aware that there was nothing she could do to dissuade them. She ate her own lunch hurriedly, and without alcoholic accompaniment, before anxiously returning to the floor. To her horror she saw that some girls from the office block, who normally visited the department once a week to check the tally figures and to calculate the weight of sugar wastage, had arrived uncharacteristically early – and it didn't take much guessing to work out why. They had obviously heard the legends of the intoxicated sugar girls and had come to catch their walk of shame back onto the floor. No doubt it would be highly diverting to see their 'inferiors' fall arse over tit as they struggled back to their machines, and would provide a good joke to share with everyone else back in the office.

Not on my watch, Ethel told herself. She went to wait in the cloakroom for the girls to return, determined to intercept them before they got back to the floor.

Meanwhile, in the Rec, the party was in full swing. It was a raucous enough place at the best of times, but never more so than now. Workers were laughing and singing together as they knocked back drink after drink. The poor barmen and women on duty were struggling to keep up with all the orders, not helped by the fact that one of their number was chasing a group of boys around the room who were playing a game of football with her wig. 'Give it back!' she shouted. 'You'll get it all filthy!'

As their half-hour break neared an end, the Hesser girls reluctantly swigged the last of their drinks and staggered out of the Rec.

When they barrelled into the cloakroom of the Hesser Floor, Ethel leapt to her feet.

'We're not late, Ethel!' one of them protested.

'It's not that,' she replied, urgently. 'There's something that I thought you'd want to know before you go back on the floor.'

At this even the most bleary eyes attempted to focus on her.

'Listen,' Ethel continued, 'there are some office girls in there right now, and I know what they're up to. They're waiting to see how you act when you come in, so they can go back and have a good old laugh with them upstairs about how you carried on.'

There was a moment's pause as the girls' befuddled minds processed the information. Once it had sunk in, outraged comments about the 'stuck-up pigs from the office' went round the group.

'All right, thanks Ethel,' one girl said. 'Yeah, thanks Ethel,' the rest echoed.

'I'll walk you back in,' she replied. 'Ready?'

Ethel watched as they drew themselves up to their full height and fixed their faces in an expression of the utmost sobriety. Then she led the way through the double doors onto the floor, with her head held high like a proud mother duck followed by her ducklings.

The sugar girls walked calmly and carefully to their machines and began to start them up, all without a murmur passing between them. The girls from the office stood watching in astonishment at this picture of sober professionalism. An engineer did his best not to laugh as their faces turned from haughty amusement to embarrassed disappointment, and they quickly shuffled off to do their work.

That afternoon, Ethel's sugar girls gave her a big box of chocolates to say thank you – and she, in turn, persuaded the foreman to let them all go home early.

14

Joan

On Saturday 31 January 1953, with the Christmas decorations all tidied away for another year, an unusual combination of high tides and a severe windstorm coming from the North Sea conspired to blast the east coast of England with a devastating storm tide. By sunset, sea walls were giving way along the coast and the water was rushing inland, leaving a trail of destruction and ruin in its wake.

At one a.m. the watchman at North Woolwich Pier reported that the Thames had reached a dangerous level. Less than an hour later, six feet of surplus water was spilling out of the Royal Docks and onto the streets of Silvertown, where it was flushed into the local sewers and back up into the lower-lying neighbourhoods of Custom House and Tidal Basin. The public hall at Canning Town was converted into a control and rest centre, and was soon home to nearly 200 displaced local people. Refugees began to arrive from further afield, including many from Canvey Island, which had been completely submerged in water with the loss of 58 lives. The locals had fared much better, with only one fatality recorded – William Hayward, a night-watchman at William Ritchie & Son in Tidal Basin, who had escaped the flood waters only to be gassed thanks to a damaged pipe. Across Europe the total death toll was over 2,000.

By Monday morning, after much pumping from the local fire brigade, the waters had receded. But they left a carpet of thick black mud on the streets, and in the downstairs rooms of many people's houses. The local residents mopped their ruined homes down and dragged what little furniture they owned out onto the streets, rinsing it with buckets of water and trying to avoid the rats that had been washed up from the sewers.

Although both Tate & Lyle factories escaped any serious damage, not all the girls who worked in them were as lucky. A young can-tester from Plaistow Wharf had been forced to flee upstairs when the water completely flooded the ground floor of her family's house. The Salvation Army came round in a rubber dinghy mid-morning, passing tea and biscuits through their window. But it was many hours before the Army proper arrived with a rescue boat and they were evacuated to Canning Town Public Hall, and several days before their belongings were free of the black mud.

Not everyone, though, saw the flood in such grim terms. While most people were doing their best to stay safe and dry, one girl, Joan Cook, was rushing headlong into the water for a swim.

'What do you think you're doing?' her mother cried, running after her as she waded in. But it was no use. The girl was already diving into the bracingly cold water, and emerged a few moments later, laughing and holding aloft an old boot.

'Mum! Look what I found down here!' she shouted.

'Put it back, Joan,' her mother said urgently. 'You don't know where it's been!'

'Nah, it's all right, Mum,' she replied. 'The water's washed it clean.' She tossed the boot back into the murky depths and flipped onto her back for a few strokes.

Fortunately it was February, and no girl, however bold, could spend more than a few minutes in such cold water. Joan soon hauled herself out and staggered back towards her mother, her clothes clinging to her goose-pimpled flesh.

Mrs Cook took off her own coat and hastily threw it round her daughter, covering as much of her slippery wet body as she could manage. She hurried the dripping girl back into the house, quickly pulling the door closed behind them.

'What were you thinking, Joan?' she exclaimed frantically, towelling down the long blonde hair, now grown sticky and dull with the dirty water. 'What will the neighbours say?'

'Just felt like a dip, that's all,' Joan replied. 'It ain't every day there's a swimming pool in the street.'

Joan lived in Otley Road, a stone's throw from the old West Ham Stadium, where crowds of more than 50,000 gathered several times a week for the motorcycle speedway and greyhound racing. When there was a race on, half the neighbourhood seemed to pass by her front door, and she would rush outside to watch the great saloon cars chauffeuring the speedway riders past.

Joan's father, and his mother who lived downstairs, both kept greyhounds and whippets, and raced them at the track. Nanny Cook was well known in the neighbourhood for lending money to those who found themselves a few bob short. She was also thick as thieves with the local fairground community, the Bolesworths, whose young boys she regularly took in while the adults were touring around the country. The travellers' gratitude was evidenced in the old woman's sideboard, proudly stuffed with silverware they had presented her with over the years.

Joan herself had never got on with Nanny Cook, who she felt favoured her younger brother John. But the appeal of the fairground connection was not lost on her. She adored the bright lights, the swirling waltzers, the colourful prizes on offer and the smell of candyfloss and popcorn, and was never happier than when the fairground folk allowed her to help out with manning one of their stalls.

Her mother, on the other hand, was not so keen. 'I don't know what your old mum sees in that lot,' she would tell her husband, John. 'And I don't want our Joan getting mixed up with them.'

Mrs Cook, who had named her daughter Joan after herself, was a woman with aspirations for her family. Although an East Ender born and bred, she would assume the accent and demeanour of a middle-class lady when it suited her. Joan found it excruciating getting onto the trolleybus with her mother and hearing her ask the conductor for 'two singles, if you would be so kind'.

Nevertheless, Joan adored her mother, whose warm and cheerful personality ensured she was beloved by everyone she met. And Mrs Cook's desire for respectability had not come from nowhere. Her own mother, Nanny Polly, was a former ship's scrubber who had worked hard all her life, and had often been forced to pawn family jewellery in order to make ends meet. She valued such small luxuries as she could afford, like a sparkling white tablecloth and a set of china teacups, which would be whipped out at the drop of a hat for visitors. But despite this positive example, not all her progeny had taken such a refined approach to life as Mrs Cook had, and some of their in-laws were rather less salubrious than the two of them would have liked.

Mrs Cook's brother George had married a woman who already had two children from a previous marriage. To make matters worse, she was the madam in a brothel, where her daughter was employed as a maid. Their son had spent time in prison after using his own vehicle as the getaway car in a robbery, and was later found dead on a bridge near Portsmouth, on his way back from a trip to buy bootleg cigarettes.

Meanwhile, Mrs Cook's brother Peter had a new young wife called Iris, who had produced her first baby alarmingly soon after their wedding. 'Probably hooked him,' Joan heard her mother mutter one time when they were round visiting the couple, who unfortunately lived upstairs from Nanny Polly and were therefore rather hard to avoid.

As ever, Mrs Cook's anxieties about Iris had served to have the opposite effect on her daughter. Joan was in awe of the attractive young woman, who was only ten years her senior. Iris wore a red chiffon headscarf and worked at the local cinema, and to Joan she exuded pure glamour. Best of all was Iris's bedroom, where the mantelpiece was piled high with all the latest make-up. Every weekend, when Joan and her mum went to visit Nanny Polly, she would dash straight upstairs to see if Iris was in, and her mum would have a job dragging her back downstairs to see the rest of the family.

'I'm sure your aunt is very busy,' Mrs Cook would call up hopefully. 'Why don't you come and say hello to Nanny?'

'It's all right, love,' Iris would shout back from her room. 'I'm just showing Joan how to do her mascara.'

Equally trying for Mrs Cook was Joan's choice of best friend at school, Peggy, who came from a local Irish family. On the face of it, the two households had a lot in common: Peggy's dad worked in the docks, just as Joan's did, and her mum was a ship's scrubber, just as Joan's grandmother had been. But Peggy's family were poorer, and their tastes were rather different.

'Can I have a fried-egg sandwich?' Joan had asked her mum one day when she came back from a visit to Peggy's.

'A fried-egg sandwich?' her mother asked her, incredulously. 'What on earth do you mean by that?'

'Well, you fry an egg, put it on some bread, add a bit of brown sauce, put another piece of bread on top and then chop it in half,' Joan replied, innocently.

'And where did you hear about this?' Mrs Cook enquired.

'Down Peggy's,' came the expected response.

No more was said on the matter, but from then on Joan made sure to get her egg sandwiches at her friend's house rather than asking her mum to provide them.

Fortunately for Joan's mother, in joining the Cook clan she had married into money, which made keeping her own house as nice and proper as she liked that bit easier. Whether it came from cash-rich Nanny Cook or from his own hard work, her husband was somehow able to make sure that the family never wanted for anything. They were the most well-off people in their neighbourhood by a long shot, and the tally man didn't even bother knocking on their door since they could afford whatever they wanted without hire purchase. Mrs Cook had fur collars on her coats and they always had the latest mod-cons, paid for up-front in cash. Mr Cook was the proud owner of a motorbike, and his children bundled into the little sidecar for regular days out. Later, he even splashed out on an old black

Ford 10. When domestic fridges came on the market, the Cooks were the first in the area to buy one, and Joan did good business selling ice cubes to kids in the street.

Most extravagant of all was the family's holiday home, a caravan near Burnham-on-Crouch, complete with a fully fitted miniature kitchen and net curtains on all the windows. Joan lost count of the number of weekends and summer holidays she spent cooped up there with her parents and little brother, with no one her own age to have fun with. To her mother's dismay, she dreamed of joining the other boys and girls from Otley Road, who went hop-picking for six weeks of the year and returned with romantic-sounding stories of sing-songs around open fires and gazing up at the stars.

After much badgering, Mrs Cook decided that the best way to knock this notion on the head was to go along with it, and agreed to let her daughter head off with the neighbours instead of accompanying the rest of the family to the caravan.

Once there, Joan realised she had made a terrible mistake. Spending all day stripping the bines was exhausting, and she hated the bitter taste of the hops, not to mention the mud and dirt – and sleeping every night in a tin hut. When her mother came to visit her, she cried and begged to come home.

'All right, love,' Mrs Cook laughed, affectionately. 'Perhaps now you'll realise how lucky you are.'

The Cooks fancied themselves a cut above the rest in other ways, too. Joan's parents didn't drink – unlike their neighbours, the aptly named Dances, who would stagger down the road every weekend singing on their way back from the pub. They had never smoked, not even when Mrs Cook was working at a cigarette factory. They wouldn't dream of swearing, either out in public or within their own walls.

In June 1953, when the coronation of the new Queen Elizabeth turned the East End into one big street party, the Cooks declined to RSVP. Otley Road had been chosen as one of 70 'roads of revelry' hosting festivities in West Ham, and the 60 local kids were joined by a contingent from a nearby children's home for a fancy-dress parade, while neighbours vied with each other to put up the most bunting and flags. Mr and Mrs Cook, however, did not decorate their house, nor did they take their places at the long row of tables lining the centre of the road, where the inhabitants of every other house were eagerly eating, drinking, laughing and singing. Instead, they watched discreetly from their doorway.

Although they projected a picture of respectability, the Cook family hid an ugly secret, one that sadly was all too common at the time. The outwardly affable Mr Cook had a temper that often bubbled over into violence, and while the kids were fortunate enough to be spared his blows poor Mrs Cook bore them frequently.

Each evening, mother and children would quake with fear when Dad came home from work, waiting to find out what mood he was in. Joan and her brother John would do their best to protect their mum, jumping on top of her and trying to shield every inch of her body from his blows. But sometimes Mr Cook was too quick for them. Watching the beatings night after night, Joan grew determined that no one would ever make a victim out of her.

The source of Mr Cook's anger was hard to fathom, but his own life had not been an easy one. Perhaps feeling displaced in his mother's affections by the fairground children had left him with a burning resentment. Perhaps the trauma of more recent experiences had poisoned his personality. A crane driver in the docks, he had accidentally killed a man by dropping a load of coal on top of him. On a single day he had been forced to attend two inquests at the same coroner's court – one for the victim and another for his own father, who had died in his sleep just a few days before.

Whatever the reason, Mr Cook also struggled to express affection for his children, and Joan could not remember a time in all her life when he had so much as put his arm around her. He was, however, very attached to his whippets, which he had blessed with human names: Peter and Poppy.

By the time Joan left school at the age of 15 – the leaving age having now been raised by a year – her mother had already made up her mind what to do with her. Although no one would have known it, Mrs Cook had spent her own early life working at various factories, including Tate & Lyle's Thames Refinery, and she was determined that her children would not follow in her footsteps. 'My daughter is no factory fodder,' she would say. 'I'm getting her a job in an office.'

This was easier said than done, since Joan's academic record was less than stellar. She had been placed solidly at the bottom of almost every class at school, where the only talent anyone had discerned in her was a remarkable capacity for rhyming. From a young age, Joan had talked to her friends in rhyme, firing back rapid, perfectly sensible responses to whatever they said, and turning every exchange into a couplet.

The nuns who taught her at school found it rather exasperating. 'Write the answer on the board,' they would tell her, only to hear in reply, 'Yes, Miss, let us praise the Lord' – which they couldn't really argue with. It was an unusual ability, to be sure, but it didn't really lend itself to gainful employment.

Joan did have one skill useful for office work – like her mother, she was an excellent mimic. When Mrs Cook secured her an interview for an office job at CWS Flour Mills in Silvertown, she reminded Joan to follow her example. 'Talk proper,' she told her. 'None of your ain'ts and fings!'

Putting on her plummiest accent, Joan sailed through the interview and soon found herself operating their switchboard. 'Good afternoon, may I transfer you?' she would ask demurely, before pushing the little wooden sliders up and down to connect the calls to the relevant offices. It was fun to begin with, but after many months in the job, with only a few old fogies for company, Joan was desperate for something more exciting.

Her friend Peggy, whose parents could ill afford Joan's mother's prejudices about factory labour, had taken a job on the Hesser Floor at Tate & Lyle, and the more Joan heard from her friend about the life there, the more she felt convinced it was for her. 'So you go out every weekend,' she quizzed her, 'and the company has its own parties?'

'Yeah,' Peggy replied proudly. 'And the pay's brilliant, what with the bonuses and all.'

In the end, Joan chucked in the job at the flour mill without asking her parents' permission. 'Oh, Joan, what have you done?' her mother wailed when she heard the news. But it was too late. Her daughter had already gone to the Personnel Office at Plaistow Wharf and got herself a position on the Hesser Floor, where an early and late shift were now running in addition to day-work.

Joan couldn't have been happier – she had found a lively, vibrant place to work, where she was surrounded by people her own age. Every day she left home with a spring in her step, eager to spend time with the other sugar girls. Her colleagues even seemed to appreciate her little rhyming poems, which she scribbled away in a notebook during her breaks. Once they realised what she was up to, they began to put in requests.

'Can you write one about me, Joan?' Peggy asked one morning, while a group of girls were gathered round smoking in the toilets.

'All right then,' Joan replied, happy for the challenge. She thought for a moment.

'*Peggy O's a charming lass, her smile so full of grace / But if you pinch her on the ass, she'll smack you round the face.*'

'You cheeky cow!' Peggy squealed, between fits of giggles.

Another girl on the floor was desperate for a ditty about Miss Smith, who had just given her a particularly humiliating telling-off. Joan was happy to oblige.

'*Fear The Dragon at the door, her presence signals death / But it isn't flames she breathes, it's just her stinking breath.*'

Before long, half Joan's colleagues were challenging her to come up with witty couplets and limericks, on every topic under the sun. One man approached her for some help with his best man's speech for a friend's wedding. 'I need something funny to start off with,' he told her, 'like one of your little rhymes.'

'What's the bloke's name?' Joan asked him.

'Buck,' the young man replied.

Joan laughed. 'Well, you don't need me to tell you what rhymes with that!'

'I know,' he replied, 'but I can't say fuck at a wedding, Joan!'

'All right, let me have a think.' She considered awhile, chewing on the end of her pencil. 'I've got it,' she said, standing up confidently.

'I know a word that rhymes with Buck, but use it I may not /
Because I fear that if I did, I surely would get shot.'

'Cheers, Joan,' the young man replied. 'You're a genius!'

Unfortunately, not everyone's opinion of Joan's rhymes was
quite so enthusiastic. One day she was picking a bag of sugar off
the belt to check its weight when she was tapped on the shoulder by a charge-hand.

'Is this one of yours?' the older woman demanded, holding
out a little slip of paper. Joan read the words scrawled upon it.

> There was a young fella called Lyles,
> Who suffered from terrible piles.
> He'd sit scratching his bum,
> Looking gloomy and glum,
> And no one would come within miles.

The ditty about the refinery director's son, John Lyle, did have a
shred of truth to it – he had attracted ridicule on the Hesser Floor
for his habit of scratching his bottom when he thought no one
was looking. And Joan felt rather proud of her handiwork. 'Yeah,
I wrote it,' she replied boldly. 'But how did you get hold of it?'

The woman looked genuinely surprised. 'You mean you
didn't put it there?' she asked.

'Put it where?'

'In one of the sugar bags – it arrived by post this morning,
along with a complaint from an angry customer.'

Joan suppressed the urge to giggle. 'Well, someone must
have nicked it then,' she said. 'Pinched it out of me notebook
and put it in there to get me in trouble.'

There was a long pause while the woman stared at Joan, obviously trying to work out whether she was lying. But Joan was not the sort for deception, and her natural honesty was clear for all to see.

'All right,' the charge-hand replied. She smiled, despite herself, as she passed the poem back to Joan. 'We won't ask Mr Lyle what he thinks of your writing. But in future you'd better keep that little book of yours better hidden.'

'I will,' Joan replied, gratefully.

As soon as the shift ended, she rushed straight to the cloak-room and grabbed her notebook. In a hasty scrawl she wrote:

> *Cheeky rhymes in sugar bags may lead to a complaint,*
> *But who's to say a sugar girl should always be a saint?*

15

Lilian

Lilian may have shut the door on Alec, the ginger-haired young man she had met on the beano, but the following Saturday he turned up at her house nonetheless. When he knocked she was already waiting for him, and dressed in her best outfit. She took his arm and together they set off to the Imperial cinema in Canning Town.

The next Saturday the knock came again, at exactly the same time. And then the next Saturday, and the next. Each time they set off for the cinema just as before, and each time Alec walked Lilian home afterwards, right up to the gate. She hadn't told him about her fear of the dark, but somehow he seemed to know instinctively.

One day Alec would bring Lilian a Terry's Chocolate Orange, another time a gift of silk stockings. It wouldn't have mattered if he'd offered her a bag of potato peelings – no one had ever bought Lilian a present before, and she felt like the Queen of Sheba.

After a while, Alec started to be invited into the house at Cranley Road. Lilian's father, who had once watched her like a hawk through her brother's toy telescope, had to admit that he couldn't find fault with the young man's manners and quickly warmed to him. Her mother, who had begun to fear her daughter's heart would never be mended after Reggie, welcomed Alec with open arms.

Meanwhile, Alec's family introduced Lilian to a different way of seeing the world. While the Tulls had always been a quiet family, doing their best to muddle through, the Clarks seemed to grab life with both hands and shake as much fun out of it as they could. Alec had two older brothers, George and Jim, who adored their 'little bruv' and always insisted that he and Lilian come out to socials with them. Soon Lilian was going out so much she felt she was barely ever at home, and to her astonishment, as long as she was with Alec, her normally strict father didn't seem to mind.

However, it was Alec's relationship with his mum that intrigued Lilian the most. 'You can always tell what a man's like by the way he treats his mother,' Old Fat Nell had advised her, but Lilian still hadn't met Mrs Clark. Every time she hinted she would like to be invited round for tea, Alec took her to Romford, to the house of one of his brothers, instead.

'Why don't you ever take me home to your mum's?' Lilian asked eventually.

'Well,' said Alec, looking sheepish, 'it's a bit posher in Romford.'

'I don't care about that,' she said, squeezing his hand.

Lilian was duly taken round to the family home in Stratford and presented to Mrs Clark, who opened the door in her pinny, looking every inch the East End mother. 'Good old Mum!' Alec cried, throwing his arms around her. Then, to Lilian's surprise, he pinched each of her rounded cheeks between a thumb and forefinger, and waggled them affectionately. The old woman beamed in delight at what was obviously a regular ritual. Alec's father had been killed in the Second World War, and it was clear that the youngest son had become the apple of his mother's eye.

Mrs Clark's second biggest love in life was Guinness, and Alec was proud to be the one tasked with going to the off-licence to get it. Lilian noticed a brown stain on the pocket of the old woman's pinny that hinted Guinness wasn't all Mrs Clark was getting from the offy: it was keeping her in half-ounces of Wilson's snuff too.

Lilian also discovered that Alec's sister and her husband, who lived upstairs, were fond of having a drink and then a row with each other. Their arguments would evaporate the next day and they would be seen walking up the road arm in arm as if nothing had happened. Lilian was beginning to see why Alec might have preferred to take her to Romford, but he needn't have worried. He had passed Old Fat Nell's test with flying colours – he was certainly a mummy's boy.

One day Alec turned up at Cranley Road with a gift as usual, but this time, instead of chocolates, the box he carried contained a sapphire engagement ring. Lilian stared at it, feeling his hopeful eyes on her.

Alec was good to her, she knew – too good. Everyone said what a lovely man he was, and it was true. He was the kindest person she had ever known, and he had even won over her father. In the months since they had met she had genuinely come to love him, but in her heart of hearts she knew that she was not *in love* with him, and never would be. He didn't stir in her the kind of all-consuming passion that Reggie had done.

Perhaps, she thought, you only get to fall in love once.

But you can love again, in a different way.

She held out her hand and let Alec slip the ring on.

Lilian's friends were thrilled when they heard the news, and Little Lil squealed in delight at the sight of the ring. 'So where are you two going to live when you get married?' she asked. 'Say you'll stay nearby.'

The question prompted a pang of guilt for Lilian. The Tulls had always had a hard life, but they had stuck together. Getting married would mean leaving the family home – and leaving her poor old mum to run it on her own. What would happen if she got sick again?

'Well, you and Alec can live with us,' her father had said matter-of-factly when the engagement was announced, and Lilian immediately felt overcome with a sense of suffocation. Though Harry Tull was beginning to mellow a little as he got older, he was still the strictest dad she knew. The thought of being unable to get away from him, and of Alec having to live under his roof too, was unbearable.

'Alec,' she said, 'we need to start saving. Fast.'

Over the coming months, Lilian and Alec scrimped and saved like mad to get a deposit together, and soon a flat came up for rent in Cecil Road, Plaistow, three doors down from one of his brothers. It was about half an hour's walk from Cranley Road, a safe distance away from Lilian's father but not so far that she wouldn't be able to visit her mother if she needed help.

The flat was small, and just about within their price range. 'We'll take it!' said Lilian, ecstatic.

Edith Tull offered to go round a few days later to help her daughter clean the place, in preparation for the move. 'What this needs is a good swill of bleach,' she said, rubbing her hands together at the prospect of thoroughly disinfecting and scrubbing the toilet.

Lilian smiled. 'You always kept the cleanest house in the street, Mum,' she said. 'No one ever had a whiter step than you.'

'Too right,' said her mother, proudly.

'Will you be all right without me, Mum?' asked Lilian, blinking back tears.

'Course I will, love,' her mother replied, rolling up her sleeves. 'Don't you worry about me.'

Although the flat had been sorted out, Lilian and Alec had yet to furnish it, and one day he surprised her with a trip to Olympia to see the Ideal Home Exhibition.

'We won't be able to afford anything here!' Lilian protested.

'My future wife deserves the best,' Alec replied, stroking her hair fondly. 'Anyway, it can't hurt to have a look, can it?'

They wandered through a show village of shiny new houses and marvelled at miniature Baby Belling cookers and Kenwood food mixers. The ultra-modern furniture included seats that unfolded into cocktail cabinets and sofas that turned into beds.

'Oh Alec, look!' said Lilian. Inside one show house was the most beautiful bedroom suite she had ever seen: a double bed, an enormous wardrobe with a big golden key, a big dressing table and matching his-and-hers bedside tables.

'You want it, don't you?' he said, smiling at her.

Lilian couldn't recall her parents ever going out to buy furniture, and she thought back with a sense of guilt to the time when the only item in their front room was the little marble washstand that her father had used for Charlie's gravestone.

'Maybe in another life,' she told Alec.

'No, in this one,' he said, pressing her hand.

'But –'

'We'll manage,' Alec said firmly.

In the can-making department female workers had to leave their jobs when they got married, and as her wedding loomed, so too did Lilian's last day at the factory. Her happiness about the one was tinged with sadness at the other.

Tate & Lyle had been the first place where Lilian had felt she was really good at something, and although she had turned down the offer of promotion she had never forgotten the sense of pride she had felt when the forelady, Rosie Hale, had expressed confidence in her. It was also the place where she had found true friendship with Old Fat Nell and Little Lil, and rediscovered her own capacity to have fun again, after the heartbreak of Reggie and the bleakness of life at home. The thought of losing all that brought a lump to her throat.

But Old Fat Nell and Little Lil weren't going to let her leave without something to remember them by, and when Lilian came in telling them about the new bedroom suite she and Alec were buying, they winked at each other. A collection was soon started and all the girls, including the forelady, pitched in.

When Lilian came in on her very last day, a present was waiting by her machine. She blushed as everyone crowded round to watch her undo the ribbon and lift the lid off the box.

Inside, resting on a bed of white tissue paper, was a sparkling trinket set in pink glass, with a tray, a pair of trinket dishes, a powder box and two candle holders. Lilian gasped at the beauty of it.

'For your new dressing table,' said Little Lil, smiling up at her. 'You'll need something to put on it, won't you?'

Married life, Lilian discovered, was surprisingly simple with Alec. As long as he had a home-cooked meal on the table when he got in, his clothes set out ready for him in the morning, and enough money for his smokes, he was satisfied. He was a hard worker, didn't drink too much, and lived only to make her happy. After her Victorian father, Lilian couldn't quite believe how laid-back a husband could be.

'Why was my old dad so strict?' she asked Alec. 'He didn't need to be like that.'

'Well, Lil,' he replied, looking at her admiringly, 'it never did you any harm.'

He was the perfect husband, thought Lilian. But still she couldn't bring herself to throw out the photograph of Reggie, and kept it squirrelled away in a locked drawer where Alec wouldn't find it. It was a secret she would just have to keep throughout their marriage.

With her Tate & Lyle job gone, Lilian looked for work elsewhere, and she soon found a position in the laundry room of the school of nursing at the London Hospital, Whitechapel. There were over 300 student nurses there, kitted out in the traditional uniform of big puffed sleeves, white aprons and caps, all of which Lilian had to wash, starch and iron. The student quarters were presided over by an elderly Sister who kept a strict eye on her young charges, creeping up behind any hapless girl who so much as dropped her hanky, and startling her by shouting 'Nurse!' in her ear. The students, Lilian discovered, liked to get their own back on Sister by leaving imitation turds on the floor of the bathroom.

It was hard work in the laundry, and as she spent her days scrubbing away, Lilian was reminded of her poor mother doing the washing for the whole family every Monday when she was a child. But she was content, and soon she and Alec had moved to a nicer flat in Warwick Road, Stratford, 15 minutes from their previous one.

Her siblings were all getting married now and starting families of their own, and she and Alec spent many happy evenings playing bingo at West Ham Lane with her sister Sylvie and her new husband Tom. One night, to her astonishment, Lilian scooped the jackpot. It was more money than she had ever seen in one place before, and as soon as she got home she threw all the notes up in the air for the sheer joy of watching them flutter down around her. My luck really has changed, she thought.

But Luck is a tricky lady, and with Lilian's reversal in fortune came a corresponding one for her mother. Edith Tull's health was once again deteriorating rapidly. First climbing the stairs left her breathless and weak, then walking anywhere became a trial, and finally she was more or less housebound. Despite being a married woman now, Lilian was still the eldest Tull daughter, and once again the responsibility of caring for her invalided mother fell to her.

After exhausting days in the laundry Lilian would rush back to Cranley Road to tend to Edith, cook the dinner for her father and clean the old house. She began to feel the familiar tiredness and sense of foreboding creeping back into her bones, just as it had the last time her mother was ill and Lilian had suffered her breakdown at Tate & Lyle. This time, however, she had Alec in her life, and the thought of him made her determined not to go down that road again. She asked the London

Hospital for a leave of absence, so that she could care for her mother properly.

Lilian devoted herself utterly to Edith's care, but all the love and attention in the world couldn't bring her mother's fragile body back to health. At 62, Edith Tull was already an old lady, worn out and weary from all that life had thrown at her. One day, her heart simply gave up beating.

Harry Tull fell to his knees, lifted his wife's tired head from the carpet where she lay dead, and cradled her in his arms. 'That's the girl I married,' he said, looking into her face, devastated. 'That's the girl I married.'

Lilian had always thought of her father as a strong, even formidable man, but with the death of his wife something in Harry Tull seemed to crumble. He was now living alone in the house at Cranley Road, where Lilian and her sister Sylvie visited him frequently.

'Your mum used to like this wallpaper,' he would mutter wistfully, as he opened the door and led them in. 'Your mum loved this table.'

'Yes, Dad, she did,' Lilian would reply gently.

Not long after they had buried Edith, the Tulls had another worry on their minds. Harry Jnr, the great hope of the family – who had passed his exams and elevated himself to an office job at his father's old firm – had left the East End and was living in Harold Hill, Essex, with his wife and their two little girls. One day, taking the train into London, Harry Jnr collapsed and was rushed to Westminster Hospital.

Harry Tull Snr was beside himself at the news, and insisted on going up to visit him immediately.

'Let me come with you, Dad,' said Lilian, worried about her father's state of mind.

At the hospital, Harry Jnr was stable, but the doctor drew Lilian and her father to one side. 'I'm afraid it's his heart,' he said, gravely. 'Do you have any history of heart trouble in your family?'

'No,' Mr Tull replied confidently.

But Lilian couldn't help thinking back to the time her brother had been rejected from the Air Force during the war because of an irregular heartbeat, and of little Charlie and the baby twin boys who had died so suddenly. Could the Tull curse be returning?

A few days later, just three months after his mother, Harry Jnr was dead.

Losing his golden boy so quickly after his beloved wife plunged Mr Tull into new depths of despair, and he was inconsolable. 'You don't bring children into this world to see them go before you,' he cried, shaking his head. 'It's not right.'

Lilian and Sylvie increased their regular visits to Cranley Road, but they could see that their father was in a hole so deep he was at risk of never coming out.

One day, Harry Tull went to the corner shop on Cranley Road and bought a newspaper. 'Can I have the change in shillings?' he asked the woman behind the counter. 'For the gas meter.'

When Sylvie came round that evening to check on her father as usual, there was no reply to her knock on the door. She put her key in the lock, but for some reason the door wouldn't open.

When she finally managed to fight her way inside, she discovered her father's body on the floor. Harry Tull had gassed himself.

Next to him lay a letter, addressed to his eldest daughter, Lilian.

Later that day, Lilian trembled as she held it in her hand. 'For what I'm about to do, I shall be happy,' it read. 'I'll be with Mum and Harry.'

At the coroner's inquest in Poplar, Lilian and the rest of the family were determined not to have their father's death recorded as suicide. Apart from the shame the word still carried at the time, after all the years that Harry Tull had toiled to keep his family going it seemed like an insult to suggest that he had somehow given up.

Lilian pleaded with the coroner. 'His mind was warped,' she said, 'losing his wife and son like he did.'

But once the suicide note was produced, there could be no doubt. 'He must have known what he was going to do, because he left you a letter,' she was told.

The remaining Tulls did what they did best: carried on in the face of tragedy. Two years later, Lilian's youngest brother Leslie's heart stopped beating. The doctors opened it up and got it going again, but shortly afterwards he dropped dead on holiday in Dorset, leaving a wife and two children.

The doctors asked Lilian and her remaining siblings to have themselves checked out at the hospital. There, on the screen, the real Tull curse was revealed: a genetic flaw in the wall of the heart. Everyone in the family had inherited it, except for Lilian and her brother Victor.

So I'm the lucky one, after all, she thought.

Over the years, Lilian watched her sisters Edie and Sylvie die before their time too. Gradually nieces and nephews were also diagnosed with the heart condition. As ever, Lilian took on the role of carer, looking after them when they were sick and being there for everyone when they needed her.

But Lilian herself never went under again. In the past few years she had discovered a brighter side to life, thanks to Alec and to her friends at the factory. She had been fortunate enough to be given a chance that so many members of her family had been denied, and she certainly wasn't going to waste it.

16

Gladys

For all her fearsome reputation, Miss Smith seemed to have a genuine soft spot for any sugar girl who she discovered was an orphan. First she had shown mercy to Eva's friend Irene, choosing not to fire her when she got drunk on the job, and soon she was extending her care towards Gladys's friend Betty as well.

Gladys had recently noticed that Betty was becoming thinner, and her usually giggly personality seemed to have been dampened. Miss Smith must have spotted it too, because every time she came on her daily round she would stop by Betty's machine and ask, 'How are you today?' – to Gladys's perpetual surprise. 'I'm fine, thanks, Miss Smith,' Betty would reply weakly.

Betty started to go off work sick, and Miss Smith went to her house to see if she needed anything.

'You'd better watch out,' the reel boys told her with a nudge when she returned to work. 'Flo Smith's quite partial to Betties. She's already got two of them in her office.'

With her close-cropped hair and broad shoulders, Miss Smith was widely rumoured to be a 'dyke', and there was speculation that she was in a relationship with one of the Betties. Some even claimed that they lived together.

Poor Betty Brightmore, however, was either too depressed or too innocent to get the joke. It seemed the loss of her parents and the struggle she and her siblings had gone through to support themselves had finally caught up with her.

Gladys and Eva tried to cheer her up with trips to Bianchi's and nights out at dances, while her boyfriend Sid did his best to look after her. But nothing seemed to revive her spirits, and she was getting thinner than ever.

One day, Miss Smith stopped to talk to Betty as usual, but on her way out added, 'Come and see me later in my office.'

'It's usually me she says that to,' joked Gladys, though privately she was worried about what The Dragon might have to say.

When Betty returned from the meeting, however, there was a flicker of hope in her eyes. 'Miss Smith's given me two weeks' paid leave, at the convalescent home in Weston-super-Mare,' she told her friends. 'She said she thought I needed a holiday.'

When Betty came back to London a fortnight later, the colour was beginning to return to her cheeks. Sid had proved his worth during her time there, travelling up to see her and reporting back on her progress. It was no surprise to the rest of the girls when the two of them became engaged.

Gladys was genuinely astonished, however, when word got round that Maisie had hooked up with Alex on the waste paper. 'But they were always taking the piss out of each other!' she said, confused.

Betty and Eva gave her a knowing look.

'Oh right, so everyone got that except me?' she stropped.

The Blue Room had always been a jokey, flirty place to work, but for some reason love was in the air now more than usual.

Gladys could hardly stand the constant stream of suggestive remarks and the silly, giggly laughs they prompted.

Worse, every Monday morning a new couple seemed to have got together over the weekend. The reel boys were doing very well – Barry had hooked up with Rita, Joey with the bad leg had coupled up with Joycie, and even Robbie with the groping hands had got himself a girlfriend. 'What is this, a factory or a bleedin' dating agency?' wailed Gladys.

Meanwhile, Eva's relationship with her blond-haired boyfriend John from the Hesser Floor was going stronger than ever, despite the watchful eye of their ever-present families.

To Gladys's annoyance, as soon as a girl became coupled up, it seemed they instantly wanted her to be coupled up too. She lost count of the times she was asked, 'When are you going to get a bloke, Gladys?' or 'Why don't I set you up with my brother?'

One afternoon, feeling exasperated, she went down to the sports ground after her shift finished, to see if there was anyone there who wanted to have a kickabout. As she neared the field she spotted a small group of lads playing football. They looked so happy and carefree in the afternoon sun, and normally Gladys would have run straight over and tackled them for the ball, the way she had in the old days with Bum Freezer and his mates at Beckton Park. But now that she was here, she realised that she just didn't feel like it. Instead, she sat down and watched the group of boys, idly picking at the grass beside her. Gladys had been a tomboy all her life, but now she felt the world was trying to force her in a different direction, and to be always swimming against the stream was becoming tiring. There was nothing for it, she decided, but to get a boyfriend.

The solution came in the form of Eric Piggott, a young man she had met at a dance who had been pursuing her relentlessly ever since, despite repeated brush-offs. Eric was quite a bit shorter than Gladys, and she didn't find him the least bit attractive, but he did have the advantage of being in the Air Force, which meant he was away for long periods of time.

Despite Gladys's lukewarm opinion of him, Eric's ardour was more than enough for the pair of them, and he was thrilled to finally have her on his arm. He beamed up at her in adoration, and no amount of frosty goodbyes at the end of the night, or cinema trips spent sitting at the very front of the auditorium, could dissuade him from the belief that the sun shone out of Gladys's backside. His whole family seemed very happy about the relationship too, and treated Gladys like their own daughter, a fact that led her to avoid their house as much as possible.

Now at least when the Blue Room girls were gossiping excitedly about their boyfriends in the café at lunchtimes, Gladys no longer had to put up with their attempts to set her up with any available single men. 'Me and Eric are doing fine, ta,' she would say, happily tucking into her food.

This bought Gladys some time, but inevitably the new question she had to face was, 'When are you bringing Eric out to meet us?' For a while, Gladys found it easy enough to explain away her boyfriend's absence. 'Oh, he's gone off again with the Air Force,' she would tell the other girls, who accepted this with understanding nods. But as time went on she started getting the inevitable jokes about whether Eric really existed.

It was clear that, sooner or later, Gladys was going to have to introduce her boyfriend to the others, but whenever she pictured the meeting in her head she recoiled from the thought of it. Deep down she knew that the reason she was putting it off was that she was embarrassed of him.

In the end, Eric resolved the situation for her. Exasperated by Gladys's unavailability, he turned up at the 669 bus stop outside Trinity Church one evening, determined to catch her on her way home from work.

On the bus, Gladys was laughing about with Betty when she caught sight of Eric's hopeful face looking up at the window. 'Oh, Christ,' she cried. 'What's *he* doing here?'

'What's the matter, Gladys?' asked Betty.

'Well, you wanted to meet Eric, didn't you?' Gladys said, pointing. 'There he is!'

After a quick glance in Eric's direction, Betty gave Gladys a shove. 'Very funny,' she said, laughing. Then her expression changed as she realised Gladys wasn't joking.

As they descended from the bus, Eric immediately gave Gladys a kiss on the cheek. 'This is my mate, Betty Brightmore,' she said, pushing him off.

'Eric Piggott. Good to meet you,' he said, shaking Betty's hand. Though Betty tried her best to smile back, it was clear from the look on her face that she wasn't too impressed with Gladys's new beau.

Gladys may have introduced Eric to Betty, but she was damned if she was going to start bringing him out with her every Saturday night. Eric, however, had been granted a particularly long period of leave, and it became harder and harder to keep him at arm's length. One night, just as Gladys was about to go out with her friends, the doorbell rang and her heart sank as she heard the sound of Eric's voice.

'Good evening, Mrs Taylor. Is Gladys in?' he asked politely.

'Of course, Eric. Why don't you come in?' her mother said, studiously ignoring Gladys hissing, 'I'm not here, I'm not here!' from the top of the stairs.

'Oh hi, Eric,' Gladys said, through gritted teeth. 'I'm just on my way out.'

'You can't go out – Eric's on leave!' her mother replied, ushering him into the room. Rose was greatly relieved her daughter had finally brought home a man, and as far as she was concerned he wouldn't be going anywhere unless it was over her dead body.

Behind both their backs, Gladys's mischievous father could be heard whispering to her, 'Go on! Go out if you want to – have a dance!'

The devil and the angel on her shoulders tugged at Gladys's conscience until she gave in and spent the evening with Eric.

Betty was keen for Gladys to come out with her and Sid, so one week she suggested they go for a double date at Sid's favourite hangout, the British Legion.

'Eric won't be able to make it,' lied Gladys.

'That's a shame,' Betty lied back, and promptly invited Joe instead, the friend from church who had set her and Sid up in the first place.

The idea of inviting Joe got Gladys thinking, and by the time she met the others on the Barking Road she had decided that if she had to have a boyfriend he would be a far better choice than Eric. If the evening went well and he seemed interested, she would end it with Eric and cross her fingers that Joe asked her out instead.

As she walked up to Betty and the two men, Gladys pushed her red hair behind her ears and did her best to give Joe an alluring smile. The four of them had just started walking up the road when Gladys experienced a sudden jolt of recognition. There, on the other side of the street, was Eric.

She quickly turned her face away, towards Betty. 'That's a nice dress, Bets. Where did you get it from?' she asked, a little unconvincingly.

Betty looked at Gladys suspiciously. Behind her, she could see a man waving on the other side of the road.

'Oi, Gladys,' she said, 'isn't that –'

'Shh!' said Gladys, trying to silence her. But it was too late – Eric had already started to cross the road, and he looked very pleased at having found his sweetheart. Gladys silently cursed her mother, who she felt sure must have told him where she was going.

'Hi, Eric,' she said ruefully as he bounded up to the group. 'Sid, Joe, this is my, er, boyfriend – Eric Piggott.'

Gladys watched with a sense of resignation as the two men shook Eric's hand. Joe was never going to be interested in her now.

'You lot enjoy your drink,' she told Betty. 'I'll see you later.' As the three of them disappeared into the distance, she reluctantly took Eric's arm.

Rather than simply dumping Eric, Gladys soon found herself more entangled than ever. Like Betty, the other Blue Room girls were fast acquiring engagement rings, and break times were now filled with excited squeals and gushing comments about the latest rock on a girl's finger. Before long, Barry and

Rita, Joey and Joycie, and now Eva and John were all betrothed.

'They're dropping like flies,' Gladys complained, unwisely, to her mother.

Sure enough, the next time she was out with Eric he came to a sudden stop outside a jewellers' shop. 'Gladys,' he said, 'do you think we should choose a ring?'

Gladys felt her mouth open in protest, but as she looked at the sparkling jewels in the window, somehow no noise came out.

'I thought maybe this one,' said Eric, pointing to a particularly expensive-looking ring.

'Eric, that'll cost a fortune!' Gladys protested.

Eric looked suitably gratified.

Well, she reasoned, he *was* about to go off on another tour of duty. Maybe it would be kindest just to go along with it for now. She would have plenty of time to work out what she really wanted once he was gone.

The next day, it was Gladys's ring the girls were gushing and squealing about in the café at break time. But once they got back to the Blue Room, the reel boys rather ruined the moment.

'You know what this means, don't you?' one of them said, loudly. 'You're going to be Mr and Mrs Piggott – and your kids will be little piglets!'

17

Joan

Joan had joined Tate & Lyle expressly for the social life, and she was determined to make the most of it. She could see that her old friend Peggy already had an established group of her own among the sugar girls, so she set about building a new set of friends. It wasn't difficult for Joan, whose cheerful self-confidence, natural chattiness and naughty sense of humour acted as a magnet to those around her.

She had soon found a best friend in Kathy, a shy, sweet-natured girl who was the perfect complement to Joan's big personality. Kathy came from a local factory-working family: her sister was at Tate & Lyle too, and her father spent his days getting his hands stained black at an ink works. She was a decent-looking girl but remarkably thin, which she considered a personal disaster. To disguise this perceived flaw she always wore high collars, fixed with a brooch. 'Why can't I look like Lana Turner or Jane Russell?' she would moan.

Kathy and Joan could often be found at Mrs Olley's pie and mash shop on Rathbone Street, or at Chan's Chinese restaurant, one of the few places you could get dinner after the cafés and fish and chip shops closed. Kathy would eat as much as she possibly could, but invariably stayed as skinny as a rake.

Another of Joan's new friends was Rosie. She had a little chubby face and came from a family who, unlike Joan's own parents, knew how to party. Many was the night that Joan and Rosie would collapse exhausted onto the put-me-up in Rosie's front room after roller-skating all evening at the Forest Gate rink – only for her brothers to carry on partying around them as they slept.

A sugar girl called Doris, meanwhile, shared Joan's passion for shopping. Unlike most girls at Tate & Lyle, Joan didn't have to pay 'housekeeping' because her family were so well off, so she could dedicate every last penny of her wages to fashion. She would get paid on a Thursday, and by Saturday the money had usually evaporated.

Joan and Doris's favourite haunt was the market at Green Street, Upton Park, where they had dresses made in imitation of the film stars they had seen at the cinema the week before. If they were feeling really flush, they went to Blooms in Canning Town, where the bright new colours and fabrics dangled tantalisingly in the window.

But it was at Queen Bee's in Green Gate that Joan truly fell in love. There, in the display, were the first half-cup bras she had ever seen in her life.

'Cor, Doris – look at those!' she said, her face pressed to the window. 'They must be what the actresses wear.'

'You'd fall right out of them,' her friend protested.

'Yeah, that's the point!' she replied, already adding up in her head the number of weeks' pay it would take to buy the whole lot.

Every Friday thereafter, Joan visited Queen Bee's and handed over as much of her hard-earned cash as she could afford. Week after week she returned, until the whole window display was safely in her underwear drawer at home.

When no one else was around, she tried on the exotic new items in front of the mirror. She had no particular use for fancy lingerie – not yet at least – but the sheer glamour made her feel like a million dollars.

Like all good consumers, however, Joan quickly tired of her latest purchases and was soon aching for new ones. Not long after the bras had been triumphantly attained, she set her sights on a fresh target: an exquisite green suede coat that she had seen in the window at Blooms.

'I've got to have it,' she wailed to Doris, 'but I've spent this week's wages already!'

'We've got a bonus coming next Thursday,' her friend reminded her. 'You could blow that.'

'But how can I wait that long, knowing it's there?' asked Joan, reluctantly allowing herself to be led away from the shop.

The following week, Joan made sure to plan a big night out with the girls, to show off the new coat she was intending to buy. After they had picked up their pay packets on Thursday afternoon, she and Doris got the bus to Canning Town, Doris paying the bus fare on the way there and Joan promising to pay it on the way back, as was their usual arrangement.

They headed to Ideal Hairdressers, where they could be found every Thursday, having their hair curled and set in preparation for the weekend. 'Do it like Grace Kelly in *Dial M for Murder*,' instructed Joan, scrunching her hair up at the sides to demonstrate.

As the hairdressers bustled around them, the two girls chatted about the outfits they were going to wear on Saturday night and where they would go. Doris favoured the Lotus

Ballroom at Forest Gate, but Joan had her heart set on the Ilford Palais.

They were still debating the question half an hour later when they got to the bus stop. As she mounted the bus, Joan reached into her bag for her purse to pay both their fares as agreed. She and Doris were both carrying large open bags, which were not only trendy but handy for stuffing any last-minute buys into on the way home.

'Where's me darn purse?' Joan said, scrabbling around inside. 'I can never find anything in this huge bloody thing.'

'Get a wiggle on, love,' said the man behind them in the queue.

Joan had to admit defeat, and she and her friend pushed back past the queue of annoyed people onto the pavement, where they promptly tipped the huge bag upside down. But the purse was nowhere to be seen.

'My whole bonus was in there!' Joan cried. 'Someone must have nicked it.'

'Well, it ain't difficult to do with bags like these,' reasoned Doris, 'but let's get back to the hairdressers and see if it's turned up there.'

The two girls legged it back to Ideal Hairdressers, but the purse had not been seen.

'How am I going to pay for the coat now?' Joan asked, distraught. She felt tears prick her eyes. 'I was going to wear it to the Palais.'

'You mean the Lotus,' Doris corrected her. 'C'mon, I'll pay our bus fares home.'

By the time Joan got back to Otley Road there were tears streaming down her face.

Her mother met her at the door. 'What's the matter, love?' she asked, whisking her inside with a quick look up and down the street to check that none of the neighbours had witnessed her blubbing.

'I lost me bonus at the hairdressers,' sobbed Joan, 'and now I can't buy the green suede coat.'

The thought of her beloved daughter going without the latest must-have item speared Mrs Cook to the heart. 'There, there,' she said. 'Don't worry, we'll sort something out.'

Joan cried herself to sleep that night, and the next day when she got up for work the reflection in the mirror made her gasp. Her hair, which had been perfectly curled the day before, was a stringy mess, her eyes were so red and puffy she looked as if she was suffering from a nasty tropical disease, and her skin was pale and blotchy.

'I can't go to work like this, Mum!' she pleaded. 'Don't make me.'

'Now, now Joan,' said her mother brightly, 'keep your chin up. It'll be right as rain, you'll see.'

Reluctantly, Joan pulled on her blue dungarees and scraped her ruined hair back from her face. Don't matter if it's a mess now, she thought, I've got no money to go out anyway.

As she rode the bus to work, Joan retraced in her mind the events of the previous afternoon, trying to think where she might have lost the purse. Could the man behind her in the bus queue have slipped his hand into her bag when she wasn't looking? Could someone have taken it while the bag was by her feet in the hairdresser's?

As soon as Joan walked onto the Hesser Floor, it was obvious that news of her catastrophe had spread fast. Girls shot her sympathetic looks and even people she barely knew seemed to be talking about her and pointing. They all lived for their bonuses, and her misfortune was quickly passing into legend, sending a chill down the spine of every sugar girl.

'God, you look like you've been socked in the eye,' remarked Doris helpfully, when she saw Joan's face.

Joan turned to Kathy instead. 'Don't suppose my purse has turned up here, has it?' she asked.

'No, 'fraid not,' said her friend. 'Sorry.'

That coat'll probably be gone by the time I get enough cash together again, thought Joan, turning miserably to her machine.

The day's work seemed to drag more than ever, and at the end of her shift Joan was desperate to run straight home and spend the evening under her bedcovers. But as she was about to leave, she heard Doris say, 'Now!', and saw her give Kathy a little push.

'Um, Joan,' said Kathy, with a shy smile, 'we've got something for you.'

Joan noticed that Rosie and a crowd of the other girls were also gathering round. What on earth were they up to?

From behind her back, Kathy produced a Tate & Lyle sugar bag, which was bulging with something that didn't look like sugar. She presented it to Joan. 'From all us girls,' she said, 'to make up for your purse getting nicked.'

Joan took the bag from her with both hands, realising as she did so that it was full of coins. Between them, her colleagues had managed to raise the entire sum of her lost bonus.

'You lot are brilliant!' said Joan, her puffy eyes crinkled with joy. 'Bleedin' brilliant!'

She raced off to catch the bus to Canning Town and arrived at Blooms out of breath and sweaty.

In the shop, she pulled out the sugar bag and poured all the coins onto the counter. The sales assistant, a middle-aged woman, looked at Joan with a twinkle in her eye. 'You've been saving up to get married, haven't you?' she said with a nostalgic smile.

'Nah, I'm here for me coat,' Joan replied.

'Oh, are you Joan?' the woman said, disappointed. 'Your mother's been in for it already.'

'What do you mean?' said Joan, scarcely believing what she had heard.

'Mrs Cook, she picked it up this morning.'

Joan was taken aback how quickly fortune had swung back in her favour. Not only did she now have her bonus back, but as a result of losing it she had got the coat for free!

She collected up the coins again and rushed back to Ideal Hairdressers. 'Same as yesterday, please,' she said, making herself comfortable in the seat.

'Bloody Nora,' said the hairdresser, looking at Joan's crumpled hair, which only yesterday she had sculpted to perfection. 'You must have had a heavy night.'

On Saturday evening, Joan slipped her new coat on and gave her mum an extra big kiss at the door. Mrs Cook beamed in delight. She loved nothing more than seeing her daughter going out looking the business.

After her friends' kindness in helping raise the money, Joan had backed down and agreed to go to the Lotus Ballroom, and she, Doris, Kathy and Rosie travelled to Forest Gate together on the bus.

The Lotus was above a shop on the corner of Woodgrange Road, opposite the roller-skating rink that the girls often frequented, and was always packed out on a Saturday night. As they approached, Joan could see the club's flashing light and felt a thrill of anticipation. She was wearing a skirt borrowed from her glamorous Auntie Iris, who had also plucked her eyebrows for her and lent her some killer red lipstick. She knew she was looking good, and she couldn't wait to see what the night would bring.

Inside, the ballroom was dark, lit only by little twinkling lights around the walls. It looked magical, thought Joan. There were a few tables and chairs scattered here and there but most people were up dancing. As they walked in, the band was playing 'Such a Night' and the singer was doing his best impression of Johnnie Ray, pretending to be knocked off his feet as he sang.

Joan was itching to dance. She knew she was a fantastic jiver – whenever she was thrown around the room by a half-decent partner people invariably asked if she was a professional, and she wasn't one to hide her light under a bushel. Before long she and her skinny friend Kathy were dancing their socks off with a couple of lads called Alan and Alfie, young soldiers on leave from their national service.

Alfie was tall, dark and a pretty good mover, but Alan had a baby face and blue eyes that Joan found irresistible. Every time she danced with Alfie her eyes were on Alan, but the walls of the room were lined with mirrors and she could see that whenever she danced with Alan, Alfie was watching her.

Evidently Kathy wasn't having such a great time. 'They both fancy you,' she complained, '– as usual!' She was used to her charismatic friend hogging the limelight.

'Don't be silly!' lied Joan, who was breathless with the exhilaration of dancing non-stop for the last hour, and wasn't ready to quit yet.

'I want to go home,' said Kathy. 'Will you get the bus with me?'

Joan was normally the last to leave a party, but remembering Kathy shyly holding out the sugar bag full of money at the factory she relented, and the two of them said their goodbyes to Doris and Rosie.

The boys they had been dancing with weren't so easily brushed off. 'Wait! Where are you going?' called Alfie, rushing after Joan, with Alan in hot pursuit.

'We're off!' said Joan, with a flick of her Grace Kelly blonde hair.

'Let me walk you home,' said the two men in unison. They turned to look at each other in annoyance.

'Suit yourself!' said Joan, feigning indifference. 'We're only going to the bus stop.' Secretly, she was delighted that Alan seemed as keen as Alfie. Kathy rolled her eyes.

Out on the street, the two men stumbled slightly and Joan realised for the first time that they were tipsy. It was a warm night, but she felt Alan's arm slip round her shoulders. 'Bit nippy tonight, ain't it?' he said, dimples forming on his baby face as he smiled.

But Alfie spotted his friend's sly move, and evidently wasn't impressed. 'Oi,' he said, 'I'm walking Joan to the bus stop.'

'Doesn't look like it, mate!' countered Alan, over his shoulder.

'That's not what we agreed!' said Alfie, yanking him away from her.

Alan bristled with anger. To Joan and Kathy's surprise the two began shoving each other as they continued to dispute their right to walk with her.

At first the girls giggled at the ridiculousness of the boys' behaviour, but soon the shoves had turned into punches. Kathy clapped her hand over her mouth. 'Oh Joan, they're going to do themselves damage!' she said.

Joan was still laughing. She was rather enjoying being fought over by two handsome soldiers – she felt like a glamorous screen siren with the power to drive men crazy, and it wasn't an unpleasant feeling.

As the taller of the two, Alfie had the advantage over his friend, and it soon became clear that he was winning the fight. Poor old Alan sloped moodily off and Alfie proudly offered Joan his arm.

She was sorry to see baby-faced Alan go, but the incident made Alfie come across as the bigger man, and now that she looked at him again he suddenly seemed more attractive.

Joan took his arm and they walked to the bus stop together, with Kathy trailing along behind them.

Before long, Joan and Alfie had become a firm couple. At the age of 16, possessing a handsome soldier two years older than herself felt even better to Joan than owning a whole wardrobe of green suede coats. She began to live for the few weekends when Alfie could come back to London from Catterick, and she always splashed her week's wages on new outfits to meet him in, just to see the awestruck look on his face.

On Fridays they both dressed up to the nines to kiss in the dark at the Imperial cinema in Canning Town, while on Saturdays they went out dancing. As they whirled around the floor together, Joan and Alfie drew admiring glances from the other couples and she felt giddy with elation.

On Mondays at work she provoked sighs and gasps from the other sugar girls with her tales of the romantic gestures Alfie had made over the weekend, and brought tears to their eyes describing the exquisite pain of saying goodbye to him at the station when he left.

To Joan's frustration, her parents persisted in their frequent trips down to the wretched caravan in Burnham-on-Crouch, demanding that she accompany them when they went there. Spending the days drinking endless cups of tea with her mum and dad, watching the boats bobbing tediously along the river and suffering her 11-year-old brother's aeroplane impressions, Joan felt almost crazy with frustration. She couldn't wait for the next time Alfie was in London for the weekend, and thought about all the dances they could be going to instead.

Joan was an instant hit with Alfie's parents, who had a butcher's shop, as well as with his older brother and sister. Like most people, they warmed to her chatty, lively personality, and they also cottoned on to the fact that, with her nice clothes and caravan near the sea, their son's new sweetheart was a cut above most factory girls. She was a good catch for a butcher's boy, and they made enthusiastic efforts to make her feel part of the family. Joan enjoyed the sense of belonging, having grown up in a less than happy household with a father who never showed her any affection.

Alfie showered Joan with hugs and kisses, and it felt wonderful, but the two of them had gone no further than that – any attempt to snatch more than a few minutes in private together was generally thwarted by their families.

One weekend, Alfie was coming to the end of a spell of leave, after which he and Joan wouldn't be able to see each other for a long time. Joan's parents were heading off to the miserable caravan, but she was determined not to miss out on her last two days with Alfie, so she begged them to let her stay behind.

Mr and Mrs Cook eventually relented, and Joan merrily waved them off. Then she rushed back indoors to plan her outfit for the evening. With Alfie going away for a while, she wanted to look her best.

She tried on five different possible combinations of dresses, skirts, tops and shoes before finally deciding on a red dress with a white trim, and white peep-toe sandals. Then she applied black eyeliner with little flicks out at the sides, like her Aunt Iris had recently shown her, standing back to admire the effect in the mirror. She couldn't wait for Alfie to see it.

When he knocked at the door, Joan jumped up from her dressing table and ran down the stairs as fast as her high heels would carry her. She threw the door open and Alfie whistled as soon as he saw her.

She beamed at his reaction. 'Where we going, then, soldier?' she asked.

'How about we spend the evening here?' he replied. 'Seems a shame to waste the house when your parents are away.'

Joan had to admit he had a point, though she felt slightly disappointed at not being able to show off her red dress and white shoes on the town. 'All right then,' she agreed uncertainly.

It felt odd to be alone in the house with Alfie. Joan wasn't sure what to do, so she made him a cup of tea.

He drank it, but seemed more quiet than usual, and kept looking at her strangely, with a kind of longing.

'What you staring at me like that for?' Joan said in the end, giving him a playful push. 'You're giving me the heebie jeebies!'

Alfie caught her arm before she had a chance to drop it, and pulled her in close for a kiss. It was deeper and more sensual than any of their previous embraces. Those had been snatched in the dark at the cinema, or on the doorstep at the end of the night before her father called her in – little more than pecks on the lips. This time, Alfie's tongue pressed its way into her mouth. She felt a thrill shoot through her, and giggled nervously.

Then Joan felt his hand move up her side, over the red dress, coming to rest on her breast. Instinctively, she pushed it down to her waist.

'Hey, there's no one here but us,' Alfie whispered. 'We're grown-ups, ain't we?'

'Course,' Joan said, indignantly. The last thing she wanted was for Alfie to think she was just a little girl.

The hand started to move up her side again, testingly. 'I'll be back with the Army tomorrow,' he said. 'I'll miss you so much.'

His words made Joan's heart ache. The prospect of being parted again was even worse than usual, knowing that they wouldn't be seeing each other for so long.

'Joanie,' he persisted, not getting a response, 'don't you want to show me how much I mean to you before I go away?'

Joan's mind raced. His desire for her made her feel beautiful and wanted. Yet despite her usual bravado and self-confidence, she only had the vaguest idea of what a man and a woman actually did when they 'spent the night' together.

But if she was going to find out, she reasoned, it was obviously going to be with Alfie – the only question was when. They weren't engaged yet, but they were hardly a flash in the pan. She knew his family, and he knew hers. It wasn't like he was about to disappear for ever.

She said nothing, and let the hand carry on sliding up the side of her dress.

Afterwards, Joan lay in Alfie's arms, rather shocked at what had just taken place. It had been painful and abrupt, not at all what she had expected. If she'd known what it was going to be like beforehand, she thought, she certainly wouldn't have rushed into it. Yet somehow the feeling of really being wanted had left her powerless to say no.

When Alfie left for Catterick, Joan felt a little surprised that life just carried on as before. There were her parents, arguing as usual. There were her friends, laughing and joking around at the factory. Wasn't the world supposed to look different after such a momentous event?

The only real difference was that Alfie's absence was no longer just the stuff of tear-jerking stories for the other sugar girls, but an uncomfortable fact that bothered her now more than ever. Their weeks apart seemed to drag on endlessly, and Joan's evenings spent alone at home were intolerable. At one point, she even suggested to her parents that they go to the caravan just to get away from it all.

There, she and her mother were sitting around the fire one evening, while her father and brother played football. Both women were staring into the flames when Mrs Cook suddenly said, 'Have you thrown anything away in there lately, Joan?'

'No,' Joan said, surprised. 'Why?'

Mrs Cook didn't reply, but when they returned home she marched her daughter straight to the doctor's.

Dr Imber delivered his verdict in a low voice, as if he were confiding a secret. 'Mrs Cook,' he said, 'I'm sorry to say your daughter is in the family way.'

'Thank you, Doctor,' Mrs Cook replied, perfectly polite as usual. She picked up her handbag and walked out of the room, Joan following behind her in a daze.

On the way home, Mrs Cook did not chastise her daughter, but she seemed more distant than usual, and it frightened Joan. All she could think about was that she needed to get hold of Alfie, fast. As soon as she could tell him what had happened, Joan was sure that everything would be all right. Alfie would propose to her and they could get married next time he was on leave, before she had even started to show. She imagined turning up to work with a ring on her finger – and the looks on the other sugar girls' faces.

Joan ran into the corner shop at the end of Otley Road, where Mrs Jones had the only telephone in the street. She asked the operator to put her through to Catterick and demanded to speak to Alfie urgently.

'You *what?*' Alfie exclaimed, when she told him the news. He sounded incredulous and angry at the same time. 'How's that possible? We only did it once, for God's sake.'

'I know,' said Joan, her hopes suddenly beginning to waver, 'but it's true.'

'Well, I don't know what to say,' Alfie replied.

This was not the answer she had been expecting. Where were the declarations of love? Where was the marriage proposal?

'You won't tell my parents, will you?' he asked, nervously.

Joan felt anger rising in her own heart. This was her brave, handsome soldier – the man who had fought for her outside the Lotus – and he was too scared to face his own parents?

'No,' she replied, 'I won't tell them. That's for you to do.'

'Thanks, Joan,' he said, weakly. 'I've got to go now.'

'When are you coming home?' Joan asked. She could tell that he was slipping through her fingers, but she wanted to hear it from his own lips.

'I don't know,' he said. 'I probably won't be home for a while.'

That evening Joan sat in the tin bath at home, the warm water enveloping her body. For the first time in her 16 years she wished she was no longer alive.

18

Ethel

Being in charge of a department full of teenagers, Ethel had learned to expect trouble, even if she tried not to look for it. Dealing with pranks was par for the course, whether it was girls setting off fire extinguishers or covering each other in sugar. But sometimes more serious cases of misbehaviour would occur, on which she had to take a harder line.

Although she disliked sacking anyone, and would try her best to avoid doing so, where dangerous behaviour was concerned Ethel had to operate a strict three-strikes-and-you're-out policy. One day she was on her regular rounds when she heard an unusual noise coming from behind the door to an electrical relay room. The room was off limits to regular staff and labelled, in large red letters: 'DANGER – NO ENTRY'.

Cautiously, Ethel pushed the door open. Inside, the source of the noise soon became apparent. In among the cables and wires which snaked around the little room, carrying the current which powered the entire department, was a sweeper, leaning upright on her broom and snoring away.

Ethel had always been supportive of the sweepers, who were generally looked down on in the factory, and had long championed their cause to anyone who would listen. 'Think of the mess we'd be in without them,' she would point out. 'How would we ever get anything done wading up to our ankles in sugar?' In any case, Miss Smith herself had begun her time at Tate & Lyle as a sweeper in the Blue Room.

Ethel knew that sweeping up was an exhausting job, and the desire to catch forty winks must be overwhelming. But there were limits, and sleeping in a room that was out of bounds on safety grounds went well beyond them.

'Wake up!' she shouted at the woman, 'You're not meant to be in here. Didn't you see the sign on the door?'

The snoozing sweeper jerked awake immediately, almost falling over her broom as she did so. Evidently embarrassed, she muttered a string of apologies before rushing past Ethel and out of the door.

A few days later, Ethel found herself in the same area of the department, and once again the tell-tale nasal clamour was audible above the soft hum of the electrics. She threw the door open with such a crash that the woman leapt into the air.

'Haven't I warned you?' Ethel said, exasperated. 'It's dangerous to be in here. You know if I catch you here again I'll have no choice but to let you go – no more warnings.'

The other woman nodded, before scurrying away.

The next day Ethel began her rounds with a sickening feeling. She felt sure of what she would find if she opened the door a third time, but to walk on by without checking would be a grave dereliction of duty. Reluctantly, she turned the handle and pushed.

There was the woman again, standing with her broom in one hand, not even asleep this time but looking completely shattered.

'Come on,' Ethel said softly, 'you know what has to happen now.' She took the sweeper up to the manager's office, where she handed back her broom and was formally dismissed from Tate & Lyle.

There were a number of crimes that would automatically lead to a sacking, and top of the list was theft. But the temptation to pinch a bit of sugar – particularly since it was still rationed until 1953 – must have been considerable to anyone surrounded by the stuff all day long.

One man was summarily dismissed when he got caught with sugar in the turn-ups of his trousers. On another occasion, a commissionaire and two foremen on the gate were fired when it was found they were deliberately misrecording the amount of sugar going out. Security was tightened immediately but not everyone was happy with the ensuing crackdown, and free-lance delivery drivers were often driven to distraction. One driver by the name of Terry was so frustrated when the commissionaires demanded he unload a consignment of sugar to be counted a second time that he simply tipped the lorry's contents out on the ground and drove off. 'You can stuff your contract!' he shouted at them as he departed.

Some thieves came in unexpected guises. One day, a rabbi arrived at the factory to bless a consignment of sugar that Tate & Lyle had agreed to donate in honour of a Jewish religious festival. The sugar girls found it hilarious to watch him blessing each packet of sugar as it went past on the conveyor belt – all the more so because one of their colleagues further down the line had begun her own ritual too, solemnly intoning, 'Fuck this sugar! Fuck this sugar!' as each bag went past.

So bizarre was the spectacle that it was a while before anyone noticed something else that was unusual about the rabbi's behaviour: every so often he would ruffle up his long dark coat, as if fiddling with something in his pockets. One of the girls had her suspicions. 'He's nicking the sugar, ain't he!' she told the charge-hand on duty.

'What am I supposed to do?' her superior responded. 'We can't ask a rabbi to turn out his pockets.'

'Course we can,' the young girl insisted, and proceeded to do just that. The guilty rabbi was promptly escorted from the premises and the blessed sugar repackaged for regular sale.

Of course, making off with a secret stash of sugar wasn't the only way of ripping off the company, and some workers tried their hand at more elaborate scams. One woman in the offices discovered that she could put in for all sorts of fraudulent claims through the company's health insurance scheme, going through the roster of girls in perfect health and putting them down for new glasses or sets of false teeth. When the money arrived to pay for them she would pocket it discreetly, signing a raft of false signatures in her register to confirm that every penny had been accounted for.

When the truth came out, the commissionaires frog-marched her out of the building, past her distraught manager, who wept to think that he had failed to spot what she was doing. Tate & Lyle were lenient, however, declining to prosecute and merely barring her from working in their factories ever again.

Not all rackets were quite so sophisticated. One Christmas an old hand at the Thames Refinery was seen flapping about in tears because she had lost her pay packet, including the usual festive bonus. 'It must be one of them new girls,' the woman wept. 'I knew they couldn't be trusted.'

The whole department submitted to searches and every locker was opened up, but nothing was found. With typical generosity, the company agreed to pay her the money again. But just as she was leaving with the second pay packet in hand, someone shouted, 'Hey! What's that thing sticking out of her shoe?'

The woman was ordered to take off her footwear, and out fell the first pay packet. It being Christmas, she was allowed to take home her bonus, but there was nothing she could do to save her job.

After thieving, fighting was the most common cause of sackings at the factory, although most girls knew how to get away with it. Joan Fittock, a young stacker on Ethel's shift, was waiting to clock off one day when she got into a dispute with a girl who had jumped ahead in the queue. 'Oi! Get to the back where you belong, you bleedin' chancer,' Joan shouted, at which the other girl promptly clocked her one in the mouth. Joan restrained herself until the two girls were in the cloakroom together, unseen by their superiors, and then walloped her for all she was worth.

If Ethel ever witnessed a fight, her natural instinct was to wade in and do her best to stop it. Early on in her days as a charge-hand she spotted two girls on her floor clawing at each other, and immediately rushed over to separate them. Her intervention had the desired effect, but afterwards one of the foremen took her aside.

'You shouldn't have got involved, Ethel,' he told her.

'Why not? I couldn't just stand by,' she replied.

'Because you could have got dragged in yourself and been hurt.'

He knew that some fights between sugar girls could be unexpectedly bloody. One day, when two girls on the Hesser Floor got into a row over a man, they arranged to sort it out later in the cloakroom. Before the allotted hour, one of the girls paid a visit to a boy on the lorry bank, who lent her a knuckleduster to use. The state of her opponent's face afterwards was too terrible for any supervisor to overlook, and procedures were initiated for her dismissal.

While many fights between sugar girls centred on men, sometimes disputes broke out over the most unlikely things. Most departments now had music playing on the factory floor, the result of a chance encounter during the war years when Oliver Lyle had walked in on a group of syrup-fillers giving an enthusiastic rendition of 'Knees Up, Mother Brown'. Far from punishing the young women as their forelady had expected, he promptly bought them their own radiogram – realising that a good singalong was one way to boost productivity. Other departments had since followed suit, and on the Hesser Floor a competitive edge had been added: every week, whichever team of girls bagged the most sugar was entitled to choose a seven-inch record, which the company would pay for. The new record would then be played repeatedly – some might say excessively – throughout the following week.

One team, under an older woman by the name of Aggie Nicholls, put out a tally count that was virtually unassailable. Aggie was something of a character, and so obsessed with her output, to the exclusion of almost everything else, that she didn't even bother putting in her false teeth at the start of the working day. She had been on the Hessers since they were first installed in the 1920s and, although picking the latest record was actually of minimal interest to her, she saw winning the competition every week as a matter of personal pride.

As far as Aggie was concerned, nothing was off-limits in the pursuit of this obsession. She would frequently misrecord her own tally, and when no supervisor was watching she would take her machine's waste output, which counted against the team in the final calculation, and secretly get rid of it. Worse, though, was the way she drove the other girls who worked with her. In Aggie's book, stopping the machine was the worst crime a sugar girl could commit, and any poor young woman who did so could expect to receive quite a dressing down, even if it was mumbled through a pair of toothless gums.

On occasion, such disputes would spill over into rows. One of the girls on Aggie's machine, Jean Mitchell, was having tea in the cloakroom with some friends before her shift, when Aggie marched in and began shouting at her for not starting work early. Jean did her best to listen patiently, but eventually became so exasperated with the barrage of complaints that she could take it no longer, and hurled her thermos flask at Aggie. The flask hit a beam in the ceiling, shattering the glass inside, and came down to hit Aggie in the face. All the girls scarpered, one of them shutting herself in a locker in terror, and Aggie stormed off to the toilets.

A few hours later, Aggie was sporting a black eye and a foreman came over to ask what had happened. Jean was convinced that she was about to lose her job, but to her astonishment Aggie replied without a moment's hesitation, 'Oh, I just fell and hit me head.' She might have been an obsessive, but Aggie was certainly no snitch.

Unconvinced by the explanation, the foreman asked around and eventually discovered the truth. But at Aggie's insistence Jean stayed in her job. Among the management Aggie held an almost legendary status, and when she asked a favour it was granted with no questions asked.

Company policy dictated that a union representative was required to attend all serious disciplinary meetings. On Ethel's shift the shop steward was now Betty Foster, the girl who had almost set herself on fire trying to avoid being caught smoking in the cloakroom. Betty was a straight-talking and reasonable young woman, and Ethel found her easy to deal with, even when they were technically on opposite sides of a dispute. The fact was that in most cases there was little the union could do to prevent a dismissal, and nine times out of ten they were simply there to witness that proceedings were all above board.

On one such occasion Betty was called up when a man had poured sugar into the glue trough of a Hesser machine, so desperate for a break from hauling away the stacked-up parcels that he had resorted to sabotage. It was an open-and-shut case – with numerous witnesses to the act, including Betty's friend Jeanie, there was nothing she could say or do to help him.

Nonetheless, it was a risky business playing witness to such dismissals, since resentment could end up being directed at the union rep for not being able to do more, rather than at the manager who was doing the firing. On one occasion a pair of stackers had been fighting on the Hesser Floor. One was transferred to syrup-filling – not much of a punishment, since the work there was easier than on the Hessers – while the other girl was given the sack. Betty had sat in on the dismissal but, as was often the case, didn't think that there was scope to intervene.

The fired girl obviously felt otherwise, because once Betty was outside the gates of the factory and on her way home she attacked her with a plank of wood, splitting her head open.

Betty ran back into the factory and sought refuge in the office block, where a foreman helped hold her scalp together and got her to the surgery. Once the nurse had applied ten stitches to the wound and Betty had recovered from the shock, she demanded that the police be called.

The foreman hesitated. 'I think that's a decision for management,' he told her. 'After all, you're not the one who fired her.'

Betty was furious. 'Give me the bleedin' phone,' she demanded, and dialled 999 herself.

As the foreman had predicted, Tate & Lyle were not happy that Betty had taken matters into her own hands, perhaps worried about adverse publicity if the fracas got into the local press. But even if the company wasn't willing to pursue the case, Betty wasn't going to let it drop. She testified against her assailant in court, and the girl was successfully prosecuted. Despite their displeasure, there was nothing that her superiors could do. Like all union girls, Betty knew her rights.

Sometimes, sugar girls would have to find more inventive ways of ensuring that justice was done, particularly when the offending party was one of their 'betters'. At the Thames Refinery, one of the office workers, a Mr W—, was notorious for wearing particularly soft-soled shoes which enabled him to sneak up on unsuspecting girls in the corridor and find some excuse to touch them up. In the staff restaurant, waitress Joan Adams had felt an unwelcome hand creeping along her stockinged leg under the table while leaning over to serve him his lunch. Joan was shocked, but the received wisdom among her colleagues was that you didn't go telling on people, and although many of them had experienced the same thing, none of them had felt able to speak out.

Joan discussed the situation with her boyfriend Stan, who worked for Tate & Lyle's shipping firm Silvertown Services Ltd. On hearing her story he was appalled. 'Well,' he announced, 'if the girls won't say anything, I will.'

The next day Stan went to a phone box just outside the factory, dialled the switchboard number and asked, in his most authoritative voice, to be put through to Wally King, who was in charge of the offices.

'Who's calling, please?' asked the receptionist.

'Um, it's Mr Peabody,' Stan replied, improvising.

Moments later, Wally King came on the phone.

'Mr King?' said Stan. 'You've got a Mr W— working for you, is that right?'

'Yes. Who is this calling?' the manager replied.

'It don't matter,' said Stan, 'but if I were you I'd tell him to keep his hands off the girls. He's getting too touchy-feely with them, and my girlfriend don't like it. I just thought you should know. Goodbye!'

A few weeks later, Joan was in the kitchen washing up the coffee cups, when her sister Margaret came in to see her. A visit from Mags was a rare thing, since she worked in the costing office and therefore normally associated with her 'posh friends' there, rather than her sister in the restaurant, a habit that had lent her the nickname 'Lady Margaret' among the other girls in their family. It was clear from the look on her face that something was seriously wrong.

Joan took her sister into the pantry and closed the door. As soon as it clicked shut, poor Margaret burst into tears. 'It's Mr W—,' she sobbed. 'I was walking up the corridor and there was no one about, and he come up to me and said, "Oh my dear, I see you're wearing different colours today." And he touched my boob.'

'He *what?*' A hand on a stocking was one thing, but molesting Lady Margaret was the final straw. 'I'll sort that bugger out once and for all,' Joan promised.

That afternoon she was setting off on her tea round, wheeling her trolley along to the offices, when she saw Mr W— creeping towards her from the other end of the corridor. His face lit up as he approached her.

'Oh *hello*, my dear …' he began to simper.

Joan mustered all her strength and gave the heavily laden trolley a great shove, shouting 'Out the way, Mr W—!' just too late for him to hop aside. The trolley careered into him, crushing his toes in their soft shoes and leaving him screeching and swearing in agony, and Joan made off triumphantly down the corridor.

From then on, Mr W— never bothered Joan or her sister again.

Although Joan had felt there was no option but to take matters into her own hands, in fact many charge-hands and foreladies at Tate & Lyle took their pastoral duties very seriously, and in addition to meting out discipline would spend a good deal of time worrying about the wellbeing of their young charges.

They would visit sugar girls who were off sick to see if there was anything they could get for them, make sure that those leaving to get married had their finances in order, and offer support to those going through difficult times with partners or parents. When a young worker called Maureen Richfield was having problems at home, her forelady Eva West invited her round to her house after work, offering a shoulder to cry on and plenty of tea and biscuits.

Sometimes, however, a girl made it clear that she didn't want help, and there was nothing that her superiors could do to intervene. Bella, one of Ethel's Hesser girls, was sporting a bump that seemed to be growing by the day. She was unmarried, with a boyfriend away at sea in the Navy, so her situation was socially perilous. Unwilling to face the reality of what had happened, Bella had done her best to hide her condition, both at work and from her parents, by wrapping herself up as tightly as possible with a length of bandage hidden underneath her uniform. But the truth of the matter was obvious to anyone who saw her, and after a while a concerned Miss Smith summoned Bella to her office.

'I just want you to know that we are here to support you if you need help,' she told the young girl. 'You can talk to me about anything you like.'

Bella did her best to look blank. 'I don't know what you're on about, Miss,' she replied.

'Are you pregnant, Bella?' Miss Smith demanded calmly, not letting her gaze falter from the young woman in front of her.

For a few moments Bella fell silent, and Miss Smith thought that she might be about to confide in her, but then the defensive young woman reasserted herself. 'Nah,' she said. 'Where'd you get an idea like that from?'

'All right then,' Miss Smith replied sadly, well aware that there was no more she could do. 'You can go back to work. Look after yourself.'

Bella worked on a four-pound packet machine on the Hesser Floor. One day, Ethel walked past her station to find that she was nowhere to be seen. She looked around the room, but there was no sign of her. 'Has anyone seen Bella?' she asked the girls on the neighbouring machines. One of them nodded slightly, and gestured with her eyes towards the floor.

Ethel followed her gaze. There was Bella, crawling underneath the machine, apparently trying to get at some spilled sugar.

'Bella, what do you think you're doing?' Ethel cried. 'Get out of there at once!'

'Sorry, Ethel,' came the reply. 'I was just trying to sort out a spill down here.'

Bella emerged on her hands and knees, with her bump scraping the floor beneath her. 'You mustn't do that again, it's very dangerous,' Ethel said anxiously.

It was clear enough to Ethel what Bella had been up to – she was desperate to lose the baby and had hoped that she might trigger a miscarriage.

If anyone tried to bring up the pregnancy again, however, Bella would only deny it. Sometimes, if a girl didn't want to be helped, there was nothing that her superiors could do.

19

Gladys

In the Blue Room, the fear of unmarried pregnancy was intense. While Gladys and her friends had all been coupled up for a year or more now, their men were kept firmly on the right side of the door at the end of a night. 'My parents say if we ever get pregnant, we'll be thrown out,' said Eva, wide-eyed. Her mother's greatest pride was that none of her seven daughters had so far 'had' to get married.

One afternoon at the end of the early shift, Miss Smith asked the Blue Room girls to come to the front of the factory. 'There's something I think you should see,' she told them, sternly.

The girls had no idea what she had in mind, and were not best pleased at having to stay on after their day's work was done. But you didn't say no to The Dragon, so they dutifully followed her.

A few minutes after they were all assembled, they caught sight of a small group of people dressed in black walking along the North Woolwich Road. As the group drew nearer to the factory, it became clear that they were part of a funeral procession, the coffin travelling in a horse-drawn carriage covered with flowers and surrounded by weeping relatives.

'Bella was a sugar girl,' said Miss Smith, her voice uncharacteristically wobbly. 'She wasn't married, and she got pregnant.'

A shocked silence fell over the girls as they took in her words. The procession came closer and they all bowed their heads.

Gladys couldn't help sneaking a peek at Miss Smith. It was clear she was struggling to maintain her composure, and tears had formed in her eyes. 'If any of you girls are ever in trouble,' she said, more softly, 'I want you to know you can come to me.'

The procession passed and went on its way, but the girls kept standing there, watching, until it was completely out of view.

* * *

Eric's engagement ring had started off as a source of pride for Gladys, even if he himself wasn't. But now every time she looked at it she felt uncomfortable. The girls were supposed to take their jewellery off whenever they were on the machines, and Gladys found herself more often than not failing to put the ring back on again afterwards.

'You're not wearing your ring,' Betty commented one night, over a cup of tea at Bianchi's. 'Is everything all right?'

'Oh, I don't know,' Gladys said. 'I suppose I just didn't feel like it today.'

The truth was that what had seemed like a game a few months back now felt more serious. Eric had just gone away again, and each time he went his reluctance to leave Gladys was even stronger, while all she felt was overwhelming relief at seeing the back of him.

She took the ring out of her pocket and put it in the palm of her hand. When she'd first been given it, it had seemed like a sparkling toy. Now she saw it for what it was: a promise, literally cast in stone. She felt sick to her stomach.

'You know you don't have to go through with it if you don't want to,' said Betty, watching her friend carefully.

'Oh, Bets, how can I chuck him now?' Gladys said. 'It'll break his little heart.'

It was late by the time Gladys got back to Eclipse Road, and her family were already asleep. But she knew she couldn't go to bed yet. She set the ring down on the table, vowing never to put it on again.

Gladys took a sheet of notepaper and a pen out of her mother's drawer. It was cowardly, she knew, but if she spoke to him face to face who knew what Eric might say to change her mind.

'Dear Eric,' she wrote. 'I'm sorry but …' What could she say? That she had never really loved him? Liked him, even?

'I just don't love you any more,' she scribbled, quickly. 'I'm sending you back the ring and I can't see you again. I'm so sorry. Gladys.'

She folded the letter, put it in an envelope, and dropped the ring inside.

The next day, having posted the letter, Gladys arrived home from work feeling lighter than she had in weeks, and virtually skipped through the front door.

'What are you so happy about, girl?' asked her mother suspiciously.

'I've chucked Eric!' Gladys beamed. 'I sent him back his ring and told him we was through.'

'Thank the Lord,' cried her father, raising his cup of tea in congratulation.

'You silly cow!' shouted her mother. 'What did you go and do that for?'

'Well, I had to, didn't I? I never really liked him,' said Gladys.

'Yes, we all knew that,' said Rose, exasperated, 'but why on earth didn't you just keep the ring?'

With Eric finally out of the picture, Gladys threw herself back into her two favourite pastimes – playing sport and messing about at work. Over the years, the other girls in the Blue Room had got used to her tomboyish ways, and she in turn now felt a genuine affection for everyone on the floor, not just her friends Betty and Eva. Being a relatively small department they were a tight-knit group, and it was rare for there to be any disharmony in the room. Even Maisie and Eva's ongoing rivalry had never boiled over into anything unpleasant.

It was therefore quite a shock when war broke out in the Blue Room. Ironically, it began with a windfall. A new girl called Lizzie came in one day in a flurry of excitement. Her boyfriend had just won a large sum of money and she was beside herself with joy. But her boyfriend's sudden increase in wealth coincided with an increasing sense of insecurity on Lizzie's part – made even worse when a pretty girl was in the vicinity.

Lizzie and Eva had always been very friendly with one another. Yet now, whenever Lizzie saw Eva chatting to her boyfriend – her glossy blonde hair tumbling down her back and her pretty, girlish face smiling up at him – it was as if a pitchfork had been stabbed into her heart. He was rich, she told herself, and that meant he could have anyone he wanted. And if he could have anyone he wanted, then he would probably want a pretty girl like Eva. No doubt Eva had realised it too, and was making the most of the opportunity, plotting to steal both him and his money!

The poisonous thoughts went round and round in Lizzie's head, growing stronger and stronger. The next time she saw Eva in the Blue Room, she stormed up to her.

'I know what you're up to – don't think I don't,' she said. 'You keep your hands off my man!'

Eva was shocked. 'Don't be silly, Lizzie, I'm your friend!' she protested. 'Why would I be after your boyfriend?'

'Some friend!' cried Lizzie, fighting back tears. Suddenly she shoved Eva, hard, pushing her over a sack of discarded metal print sheets. Twisted up inside the bag, some of the pieces were dangerously sharp, and it was only by good luck that Eva avoided a lacerated back.

The reel boys rushed over to help her to her feet, but not before Julie McTaggart had been alerted to the scuffle. Minutes later, Eva and Lizzie had both been sent to Miss Smith's office.

Betty Harrington told them to wait outside the door, and they stood there, one on either side, their faces turned away from each other. Eva was mortified at the thought of anyone seeing her outside the Personnel Office, knowing that word would soon get back to her father. He had probably already learned that she had been mixed up in a fight, and would be furious when she got home.

Finally the door to the office opened, and Eva and Lizzie walked in. Eva's palms were sweating with fear.

'Right,' said Miss Smith. 'One at a time, please. Eva, you can go first. Tell me what happened.'

Shakily, Eva gave her side of the story, trying to sound as grown-up as possible. She had nothing to be ashamed of, she kept telling herself. She hadn't started it.

Miss Smith sat back in her chair and considered what Eva had told her. 'Lizzie? What have you got to say?' she demanded.

Eva's heart was beating fast. What if Lizzie disputed her account of what had happened? If Miss Smith decided that she didn't believe her version of events, she might get the sack. No Browning had ever been fired from Tate & Lyle, and her family would see it as a disgrace.

Lizzie looked at the floor. 'It's true, Miss Smith. Like Eva said,' she muttered.

Eva turned to her in surprise.

'You do realise that scrap metal is very dangerous?' Miss Smith told Lizzie. 'You're lucky Eva wasn't seriously injured.'

'Yes, Miss,' Lizzie mumbled.

'I can't possibly send you back to the floor after this,' Miss Smith continued. 'You'll have to leave. But if after three months you can get a good report from your new employer, bring it to me and I'll consider taking you on again.'

Devastated though she was about the way things had turned out with Lizzie, Eva was relieved not to have to face her again in the Blue Room. She'd seen another side of her former friend, and it had scared her.

Lizzie, however, was furious at having lost her job despite having owned up to what she'd done. She was too angry even to make the best of the situation and take up Miss Smith's generous offer. Rumours that she was going to get her own back on Eva began to fly around the factory, and, like everything else, they reached Eva's father before long.

'Now listen to me,' he told his daughter over dinner that evening. 'The word is, she's going to deck you when you come out from the late shift on Friday.'

'Dad!' exclaimed Eva, horrified.

'Don't worry, darlin', I've already gone up Flo's office and told her about it.'

'Dad!' Eva said again, even more horrified that her father had been talking to Miss Smith about her.

'She said she can't give you the day off work, but she'll warn the commissionaires. You're to go into the gatehouse after your shift and wait there until the coast is clear.'

Eva nodded, dumbstruck.

Back at the factory, the upcoming battle was all anyone could talk about, even in departments where no one knew who Eva and Lizzie were. Some people, it seemed, were looking forward to seeing a cat fight.

The day before the showdown was due to take place, Eva's boyfriend John decided she could do with a backup plan. 'You need to be prepared,' he insisted, 'just in case something goes wrong and Lizzie gets her hands on you. Let me show you how to throw a proper punch.'

'John, you can't be serious!' she protested. The idea of pretty, girly Eva socking someone was ridiculous, even to herself.

'I'm deadly serious,' he said, furrowing his brow. 'Now, imagine I'm Lizzie. Go for me!'

'I can't!' Eva said, giggling. 'You don't look anything like her!'

'Eva,' he said, sternly, 'do you want to get beaten to a pulp? Now go for me. Hard as you like. Don't hold back.'

Eva sighed, then pulled herself up to her full height, which was not much, and hurled herself at her boyfriend, grabbing his golden hair in her fists.

'No, no, no,' he said, pulling her away by her wrists. 'That's what she'll expect you to do. Girls always go for hair-pulling and scratching. You've got to learn to punch like a man.'

John showed her how to make a fist, leaving her thumb out so it wouldn't get broken, and held up his palms to let her pummel them. Then he showed her how to protect herself with her left hand and attack with her right.

After a good 20 minutes Eva collapsed, exhausted, into a chair. 'I can't do any more,' she said. 'I'm not a fighter!'

'Well,' John said, 'in that case I'm coming to meet you at ten o'clock tomorrow night outside the Blue Room, and we're walking to the gatehouse together.'

At ten p.m. on Friday, as the machines ground to a halt, Gladys put her arm around Eva's shoulders. 'Come on, time to get you into the gatehouse,' she said. She, Betty and Eva left together, and John was waiting at the door as promised.

'Eva,' he said, 'I think you ought to know there's a lot of girls out the front of the factory.'

'What do you mean?' said Eva.

As they drew near to the entrance, she could hear jeering. Outside in the street, a large crowd had gathered to witness the forthcoming bust-up, and at the head of the rabble was Lizzie.

'Come on, quick – let's get inside,' said John.

Eva nodded, terrified, and they began to hurry over to the gatehouse. Outside, chants of 'She's gonna get you, she's gonna get you,' rang in the air.

Suddenly a thought dropped like a hard little pebble into Eva's mind. Why should she, who had done nothing wrong, hide away from a silly girl like Lizzie?

Eva stopped dead in her tracks. 'What are you doing?' asked John.

'I can't hide in the gatehouse,' she said. 'If I did that, I'd only be a coward. I'm going to face that girl. Alone.'

'What are you talking about? Can't you hear what they're saying?' asked John, frustrated.

'No, she's right,' said Gladys. 'C'mon, Eva.'

As John looked on in despair, Gladys, Betty and Eva walked out of the factory gate and onto the street. A buzz of excitement went through the crowd and it parted to let Eva through. She and Lizzie now stood face to face.

'You lost me my job,' said Lizzie.

'You deserved it,' replied Eva.

Fury flashed in Lizzie's eyes and she made a grab at Eva's beautiful blonde hair. She gave it a good yank and a few strands came out in her hand. Eva looked at them in horror. A shove was one thing, but Eva's hair was her pride and joy. Anger welled up in her and she was about to reciprocate in kind when she remembered the lesson John had given her. She clenched her hand into a small, tight fist and swung at Lizzie.

But Lizzie was fast – she ducked the blow and landed one of her own, the force of which knocked Eva to the ground. The crowd gasped.

Eva had blood in her eye where the other girl's nail had caught it. Looming over her, Lizzie looked impressed at her own handiwork. But she didn't have much time to gloat. Eva was back on her feet and all the more determined. She narrowed her eyes, focused on the area above Lizzie's right eye, and landed a good, hard punch.

Lizzie staggered backwards and the mob of girls grabbed her arms to steady her. Just then a commissionaire came pushing through the crowd.

'Eva!' he shouted. 'Your dad told you to come to the gate-house. Get in here now!'

Lizzie was still swaying from the punch, and Eva wasn't sure she had it in her to retaliate again. In any case, she didn't want to hang around and find out. She let the man lead her past the jeering girls and back into the factory grounds, with Gladys, Betty and a horrified John following close behind.

'Blimey,' said Gladys, once they were safely inside, 'where'd you learn to throw a punch like that?'

Eva looked at John, who gave her a proud smile, despite himself.

When Eva got home, however, her father was far from pleased with her. 'I told you to go to the gatehouse!' he fumed. 'You knew exactly what was going to happen if you didn't.'

'Dad,' she said, 'I couldn't do that. I had to fight my own battle.'

The next day, Eva arrived at work with her head held high, only to be told by the commissionaire in the gatehouse that she wasn't to go up to the Blue Room.

'What do you mean?' she asked. 'They didn't sack *me*!'

'Miss Smith said to send you up to the offices. She's waiting for you in the conference room.'

A summons to the conference room was even more serious than being sent to Miss Smith's own office, and despite her new-found bravado Eva was quaking in her boots as she walked there.

She knocked on the door. 'Come in,' boomed Miss Smith.

Eva pushed the door open hesitantly, revealing a huge long room with a large, highly polished table. At one end sat Miss Smith, along with several male managers whose faces looked familiar but whose names she did not know. Also at the table sat Lizzie, and – to Eva's horror – her own father. Lizzie, Eva noted, was sporting quite a shiner.

'Sit down please, Eva,' Miss Smith said, her face very grave. 'It appears you didn't follow my instructions yesterday, did you?'

'No, Miss,' Eva said, quietly.

'It also appears,' she went on, 'that Lizzie here has a black eye. And you, I see, haven't got off lightly yourself.' She looked at Eva's own injury. 'So may I ask what happened?'

'She pulled my hair!' Eva burst out, still outraged at the memory of it.

Miss Smith raised an eyebrow, and Eva was sure she saw one of the male managers next to her roll his eyes. 'Well,' said Miss Smith, 'you have got quite a mop of hair, haven't you?'

Half an hour later, the door to the conference room opened and Lizzie walked out, never again to set foot inside the factory. Eva, meanwhile, had been exonerated.

'I'll walk you back to the Blue Room,' Miss Smith told her kindly.

They stopped outside the department and Miss Smith asked, 'Will you be all right now?'

'Yes, Miss,' said Eva. 'And – thank you.'

Miss Smith nodded, and then marched away.

As soon as Eva entered the Blue Room, Gladys rushed up to meet her. She grabbed her right arm and raised it in the air. 'Win-ner, win-ner, win-ner!' she began to chant, and soon all the other girls joined in.

Eva blushed. She still didn't quite know how, but she had become the boxing champ of the Blue Room.

20

Joan

'A quarter of Pear Drops, please, and a couple of Sherbet Fountains.'

Mechanically, Joan pulled down the glass jar from the shelf behind her and weighed out the little sweets. She scooped them into a paper bag and added two Fountains from a rack behind her.

It was over a month since she had swapped working with bags of sugar for bags of sweets, and the time had not gone quickly. Joan's mother had whisked her away from Tate & Lyle before word could get out about her pregnancy, and she had not even had a chance to say goodbye to her fellow sugar girls. She had met up a few times since with Kathy and Peggy, but they were sworn to secrecy, and she knew the rest of the girls must be wondering why she had suddenly disappeared off the face of the earth.

Mrs Cook had found Joan her job at the Miss Candy stall of the East Ham Granada on the Barking Road. It was a stunning old 1930s picture palace, with a white and gold Wurlitzer organ that rose up out of the stage before every performance. But to Joan, confined to her little kiosk, it felt more like a prison.

A young couple wandered over to the booth and purchased a bag of Black Jacks, before walking off arm in arm. Joan gazed after them, remembering the happy evenings she and Alfie had spent together at the Imperial, the films barely glimpsed between kisses in the back row.

She had heard nothing from him since their brief conversation on the telephone. At first she had waited every day for a call, and checked the doormat each morning in the hopes of finding a letter, but as the days turned into weeks, and the weeks into months, she had resigned herself to Alfie's stony silence.

Joan's father, flabbergasted by the news that his 16-year-old daughter was pregnant, had been less willing to give up without a fight. 'I'll go round his parents' and sort them out,' he threatened. 'They ought to make him do what's right.' But Joan begged him not to get involved. She liked Alfie's family and was too ashamed to tell them what had happened if their own son hadn't let them know. Besides, she had decided that if Alfie chose to get in touch then that was one thing, but she was not about to see him pressured into marrying her against his will. She had seen what an unhappy marriage looked like, and would do anything to avoid one for herself.

At the time, such a principled stand was almost unheard of, but true to form Joan stood her ground. Eventually her father agreed not to press the issue, secretly rather relieved that he didn't have to see his threats through. Alfie's parents would remain blissfully unaware of the impending arrival of a grandchild, until such time as he chose to inform them of its existence.

Joan's spell as Miss Candy didn't last long. As soon as her bump began to show, Mrs Cook decreed that it was no longer safe having her in the family home, where a neighbour could chance to catch a glimpse of her. Joan was packed off to her Great-Aunt Gert's in Wanstead.

Like Joan's mother, Gertrude was a woman who enjoyed her airs and graces, insisting that Joan call her 'Truda' rather than Gert. The last thing the old lady wanted was for her neighbours to find out that she was sheltering an unmarried pregnant girl, so Joan had to hide out like a criminal, never daring to show her face beyond the front door. On the rare occasions when a visitor called, or when the postman knocked to deliver a parcel, she would have to retreat upstairs. Although her great-aunt's house was huge, for Joan it still felt as suffocating as the pokey little candy stall.

While she was there, Joan wore no new outfits – there would be little point since she never left the house. Her hair was no longer styled in the latest fashion, but hung lank down her back. She wore no make-up, since no one but her great-aunt ever got so much as a glimpse of her. She felt she would rather have spent a thousand weekends cooped up with her parents in their caravan than endure any more of this lonely existence.

One afternoon, while her great-aunt had gone shopping, Joan slipped out of the back door. There was a spacious garden, with grass and flowers and even an old tree at the far end, and for Joan – who had been trapped within four walls for so long – it felt like paradise. She lay down on the grass, taking care not to trouble the baby, which by now was large enough to kick if a sudden movement or noise disturbed it, and watched the fluffy white clouds pass overhead.

After a few blissful minutes, she saw something flicker out of the corner of her eye. Looking to the side, she could see the back windows of the next house along, and an unmistakable twitch from one of the curtains. Oh God, she thought, quickly getting up and hurrying back inside, doing her best to walk hunched over so that her bump was less pronounced.

That evening at dinner, Joan didn't dare mention her unauthorised excursion, but the next morning her great-aunt rushed up to her room in a state of agitation. 'Joan!' she whispered, 'the lady next door's seen something. You're going to have to leave.'

Joan merely nodded, resigned to whatever would happen next. 'I've sent a message to your mum at the caravan,' Gert continued, 'and in the meantime Polly says she can take you in. You'd best pack your bags, there'll be a cab arriving in a minute.'

Joan was excited at the thought of seeing Nanny Polly again, although since her Auntie Iris had moved out the house in Canning Town had lost some of its appeal.

True to form, her nan treated her with kindness and warmth, and that night Joan began to perk up again. At last she was back in her old neighbourhood.

But first thing the next morning there was a knock on the door: her mother had arrived to move her on again. So great was her shame, it seemed, that no one would dare to be seen with her for more than five minutes.

'I've found somewhere you can go to have the baby,' Mrs Cook told her. 'They'll take you this afternoon, just so long as you've been checked out first by the Royal Northern Hospital. It's in Holloway, so we'd better get going.'

Holloway? Joan couldn't believe it. That was miles away in North London – another world. She hadn't heard much about it, beyond the fact that there was a women's prison there.

As they sat on the train together, Joan was struck by the thought that the next time she made this journey it would be on her way back home, after she had given birth. By then, she realised, the baby inside her now would no longer be hers. The subject of adoption had never actually been discussed, but it didn't need to be. The idea of keeping the baby as an unmarried mother was unthinkable.

When they got to the hospital, Mrs Cook whispered, 'Here, put this on your finger,' and slipped her own wedding ring into Joan's hand. In the waiting room they took their seats opposite a pretty young girl sitting with her mother. The girl had short-cropped blonde hair and was sporting a gold band around her ring finger. Joan noticed that it looked as loose as the one on her own hand. I bet she's just like me, she thought, grimly.

Once Joan had been given the all-clear by the doctor, she and her mother made their way to the St Nicholas Home for Unmarried Mothers, just over a mile away. Number 31 Highbury Hill was a tall, semi-detached Victorian house, with dark ivy climbing up its walls.

Joan gave the wedding ring back to her mother, and they said their goodbyes. Mrs Cook did not seem angry or unkind, but Joan didn't sense any sympathy from her either as the nuns of the Crusade of Rescue came out and ushered her into the house.

A kindly young Sister with an Irish accent took Joan's bags and told her to follow her up the stairs. They climbed several flights to the top floor.

There, they entered a room that had been converted into a little dormitory, with four beds, each with a small built-in cupboard next to it on the wall. Across the room, French windows led onto a wrought-iron balcony.

'I'll let you make yourself at home,' said the Sister, putting Joan's things on the bed furthest from the door. 'Tea's in the basement in an hour.'

'Thank you,' Joan said, returning her smile. When the woman had gone, she opened the French windows and stepped out onto the balcony.

Joan breathed in the view. In the distance she could see Alexandra Palace, and below her a large garden that seemed to stretch a very long way. It really was a beautiful house, and bigger even than Great-Aunt Gert's. Despite the circumstances, Joan decided she would force herself to make the most of her time here.

An hour later, she ventured downstairs. As she crossed the ground-floor landing, she saw that the door to the front room was ajar, and inside she glimpsed a cosy sitting room with armchairs dotted around it. The door to the room behind it was closed, and a sign read: 'Nursery'.

I wonder why they need one of them, Joan thought, if we have to give up the babies.

She carried on down to the basement and found herself in a large kitchen with several big tables, around which sat a dozen young girls, most of them visibly pregnant, and half a dozen nuns of varying ages.

Joan slipped into a free chair. Opposite her was the pretty young blonde girl who had been waiting with her mother in the hospital.

I knew it, Joan thought to herself, as they gave each other a shy smile of recognition.

The blonde girl's name was Lynne, and to Joan's delight she turned out to be one of her room-mates. The other two in their dorm were named Mary and Pat, and as ever it wasn't long before Joan was chatting away with the other girls and making them laugh. Pat, a chubby Irish girl who had been a nurse before she got pregnant, was particularly friendly, and Joan relished the company after her lonely spell at Great-Aunt Gert's.

When they went up to the sitting room after breakfast the next day, Joan was surprised to see some other girls from the home carrying babies into the room from the nursery next door, which they cradled and cooed over as Joan and her friends sat chatting. Back up in the dorm, she asked Lynne why the infants were there.

'Oh, didn't they tell you?' she replied. 'They like the girls to breastfeed for at least six weeks before the adoption. It's good for the babies.'

Joan was thrilled. She had imagined that her child would be taken away as soon as it was born, but now it seemed she would get a brief chance to be a mother.

'Anyway,' continued Lynne, 'not all the girls are giving them up. Half of 'em change their minds after the birth, or their families do.'

Joan was shocked. She had been under the impression that keeping the baby was not an option, but Lynne was right. Of the 33,000 illegitimate babies born every year at the time, well over half remained within the family. Girls' parents would often claim that a new child was their own, hoping that their neighbours would accept what they told them. But Joan knew that there was no way her parents would take such a gamble, and risk the knowing stares and nosy questions of every busy-body in the neighbourhood.

'What about you?' asked Joan, looking at Lynne's ring finger, which was now distinctly bare. 'Don't you have to give yours up?'

'My mum says we'll keep it no matter what,' she replied breezily, 'even if my boyfriend doesn't ask me to marry him.'

Despite the positive outlook Joan had managed to maintain, the words couldn't help but sting. Might another solution have been available to her after all, if her own mother had been willing to help?

When they weren't chatting and giggling in the sitting room or around one of the tables in the kitchen, Joan and her new friends would often go out together for a stroll around Holloway. There was no need to stay hidden when they were so far away from anyone they knew, so they could wander the streets with impunity, and she soon found that it wasn't the forbidding place she had expected.

Joan's favourite hangout was a pie-and-mash shop on the Holloway Road which reminded her of Mrs Olley's on Rathbone Street, and she soon became a regular customer. 'That baby'll be born with a pimple on its nose, the amount of time you spend here!' the proprietor would rib her.

Her other favourite pastime was going to the pictures. The stylish Gaumont cinema at the corner of Tufnell Park Road was only a few minutes' walk from the Royal Northern Hospital, and a short bus journey away from the home. Joan was in there almost every week with one or other of the girls, catching the latest releases. With female friends to go out with once again, she no longer felt so lonely seeing the queues of couples traipsing in together, and with no boy around she realised she actually got to see more of the film.

But as their due dates drew near, the girls' minds inevitably turned to the difficult decisions that lay ahead. One day, Joan and Pat were alone together in the dorm, when Pat suddenly asked, 'Joan, can I tell you a secret?'

Joan was sitting on her bed, staring out of the window, and quickly turned round. 'Course you can. What is it?'

Pat's chubby face was contorted into an expression of deep concern. 'It's about my baby,' she said, biting her lip. 'Well, about its dad really.'

'Is he a coloured chap?' Joan asked instinctively.

'Yeah,' Pat exclaimed, surprised. 'So do you think I should keep it?'

'Well, so what if the baby's black?' said Joan. 'I reckon you'll love it just the same. If you could keep it as a white one, you should keep it as a black.'

'Thanks, Joan,' Pat said, looking more relaxed.

'Joan?' she asked, a few moments later. 'Will you be its godmother?'

Joan smiled. 'Course I will,' she replied.

One night, Joan and her mates had just settled into their seats for the latest film at the Gaumont. 'Here, is your chair wet?' she asked one of the other girls.

'No,' the girl next to her replied, tucking into her popcorn.

'I bet some filthy bugger's gone and wee'd in it. Budge up, I'm not sitting here.'

The girls all manoeuvred their hefty bellies out of their seats and moved up one.

By now the curtains were open and the credits were beginning to roll. A man at the end of their row stared pointedly in their direction, urging them to keep quiet.

'Better?' Joan's friend asked her, as she sat down again.

'I don't know. This one feels damp an' all.' Cautiously, Joan put her hand down to investigate.

On screen the film was starting, and the man at the end of the row shushed them loudly.

'Oh no,' said Joan, 'I think I know what it is.'

'You haven't?' The other girls all turned to her.

'*Will* you keep quiet?' the man demanded furiously.

Joan ignored him. 'Get me out of here,' she yelled. 'My waters have broken!'

The delivery went remarkably well, and just a few hours later Joan was happily holding a baby boy in her arms. 'I'm calling him Terrence,' she told the midwife proudly, as he suckled at her breast. 'Ain't he gorgeous?'

Over the course of the next few weeks, Joan and Terry spent almost every waking minute together, and every night he slept with her in her dorm. She had never thought of herself as the mumsy type, but caring for the baby turned out to be the most fun she had ever experienced. Sitting in the spacious front room with the other young mums, Joan felt more content than she could remember, and for once she had absolutely no desire to go outside and see the world.

'You two look so happy together,' one of the other girls told her, offering to take the baby's picture with her camera. Later, when she saw the photo, Joan couldn't believe that her doomed relationship with Alfie had created something quite so beautiful.

Before long, Lynne had given birth too and was nursing her own baby. One day, a young man knocked on the door of 31 Highbury Hill asking for her. The girls were allowed to have visitors but they couldn't bring them into the house, so she and the baby went out with him for a walk.

When they returned a few hours later, she excitedly told the other girls the news. The man was her boyfriend, and after meeting the baby he had proposed. Lynne, whose mother had promised to stand by her even if she was abandoned, was going to be married after all.

Joan gave her friend a big hug and told her how happy she was for her. But she couldn't help wondering whether meeting his own baby might have a similar effect on Alfie.

Although Joan and Alfie hadn't spoken since she had discovered she was pregnant, he was, after all, the father, and she knew that her only chance of keeping Terry was if she was married. She still refused to put him under any pressure or make any demands on him herself, but what harm could it do to meet up?

Joan wrote to her old friend Kathy and asked if she would come and visit her. When Kathy arrived, she took her for a walk up the Holloway Road.

'I've got a favour to ask,' she told her.

'Oh yeah? What is it?'

'Do you reckon you could get in touch with Alfie? I want him to come and visit me and Terry. See if that don't change his mind.'

'Course,' Kathy told Joan, with a squeeze on the arm. 'I can get a message to one of his mates. We can't wait till you're back home where you belong,' she added. 'This place is one hell of a trek.'

'Yeah, I know,' said Joan, 'but it ain't so bad as it looks.'

Word arrived that Alfie had agreed to pay Joan a visit, and she excitedly began preparing for the big day. First she went out to a local tailor's and ordered a smart new skirt suit. Then she headed over to the Jones Brothers department store on the Holloway Road and splashed out on a bit of new make-up. She was determined to look as good as she possibly could, so that Alfie couldn't help but pop the question.

When the appointed day finally arrived, Joan waited nervously in the front sitting room with her baby in her arms, peering out of the window until she saw Alfie approaching along the pavement. 'Come on, Terry,' she whispered, 'it's time for you to meet your daddy.'

She strode out of the grand front door of the Crusade of Rescue, feeling like a million dollars in her new outfit. 'Alfie!' she called, hurrying down the steps to meet him with Terry in her arms.

'Hello, Joan,' he said, giving her a peck on the cheek.

Joan held the baby up to him. 'This is Terry,' she said.

Alfie peered into his little face and stroked his cheek before standing up straight again. 'Shall we go for a walk, then?' he asked.

One of the nuns brought a pram out for them and they wandered up to Highbury Fields. There, they saw men in white jumpers playing tennis, well-to-do ladies taking a stroll between the rows of trees and men walking their dogs around the green. Every so often they would pass a family spending the morning out together: mum and dad and a little baby or two. Joan smiled at them and they smiled back. *I wonder if they can tell,* she thought to herself. *Or do they think the three of us are the same as them?*

They walked down as far as the Boer War memorial, and then turned and headed back up the hill. Alfie asked how Joan and her parents had been in the time since he had seen them last, and how her brother was getting on at school. He told her how things were in the Army, and how much he was looking forward to the end of his national service.

But the question Joan was waiting for never passed his lips. There was no stopping suddenly and getting down on one knee, no urgent squeezing of her hand with a promise whispered into her ear. They chatted idly, wandered back to the home, and he departed, leaving everything just the same as it had been before.

Joan was inconsolable. That night she cried herself to sleep, hugging her baby to her breast. The great plan had come to nothing – in spite of her efforts Alfie had remained obstinately silent, just as he had on the phone all those months before. Once again, that silence had killed all her hopes for the future. It had condemned her and Terry to part.

A few days later, Kathy called the home to see how Joan was doing. 'I'm sorry things didn't work out with Alfie,' she told her.

'I was so sure he'd change his mind,' Joan replied, still devastated by the failure of her plan.

'Well, he's a fool if you ask me,' Kathy said. 'He don't know what he's talking about.'

'Have you spoken to him, then?' Joan asked, suddenly.

Kathy hesitated. 'Yeah,' she admitted.

'What did he say?' Joan asked.

'I don't know if I should tell you, Joan. I don't see as how it would do any good.'

'Come on, Kath,' Joan pleaded. 'I've got to know.'

'All right then,' Kathy replied uncertainly. 'He said he didn't like the cut of your skirt, he thought it was too short. He told me he wasn't sure the baby was his after all.'

'Well, who the hell else's could it be?' Joan felt as if her veins were pumping pure rage. How dare Alfie say that about her? And all because she had bought a new outfit to look nice for him.

'If you ask me,' said Kathy, 'I reckon that was just an excuse. He was looking for a way out and that was the best he could come up with.'

Joan went silent. There was nothing more to say. She had failed, and now her baby was going to be taken away from her.

In her final weeks at the home, Joan was filled with desperation as she waited for the day when she and Terry were to be parted. The two of them had grown closer than ever, and she could scarcely bear to think about losing him.

Sure enough, though, the fateful day arrived, and his departure from her life was signalled by the reappearance of her mother. 'I've come to help,' Mrs Cook informed her neutrally, 'and once we're done here, you can come with me to stay at the caravan.'

The nuns gave Joan a piece of paper with the address of Terry's adoptive parents, together with directions, as she and her mother were to take him there themselves. Joan dressed him in a little outfit she had bought on the Holloway Road, said a tearful goodbye to her friends at the home and followed her mother out of the door.

On the bus, it was all she could do to stop herself from bursting into tears in front of all the other passengers, and her mum's constant attempts to make polite conversation didn't help. Still, for Terry's sake, she didn't want to show her distress. He was happily snoozing in her lap, and the fear of upsetting him and spoiling their last moments together was enough to help Joan keep a lid on her own emotions.

Eventually, they got off the bus and took a short walk to a long, tree-lined street flanked with tall Victorian houses. Joan's mother took her by the arm and gently guided her up to one of the doors. Through the large bay window to one side she could see into a spacious living room, where several little sheets were drying on a clothes-horse and a stash of clean cloth nappies were piled up on a sideboard, ready for the new arrival.

Joan's mother knocked boldly on the door, and it was opened by a kind-looking woman. A smile spread rapidly across her face as she saw Joan and the baby. Mrs Cook stepped discreetly to one side to allow her daughter to approach the threshold.

'He's beautiful,' the woman cooed, gazing into Terry's little face.

'Yeah,' was all Joan could say in reply. She felt as if the life had been drained out of her. The rage that she had felt before was gone, but nothing else seemed to have taken its place.

Slowly, she lifted Terry up towards his new mother.

'Don't worry, we'll take good care of him,' the woman told her, gratefully accepting the little bundle.

Joan was about to let her arms drop to her sides, but Terry reached out a tiny hand in her direction. She offered him her little finger, and he gripped it firmly, smiling. 'Goodbye, little one,' she whispered. 'Thanks for everything.' Then she pulled her finger away.

Joan turned to look at her mother for a moment, hoping for a mirror of the turmoil she was feeling inside, but all she saw was a face set in perfect serenity. She looked back towards the house, but the great front door had silently closed. She and her mother were shut out in the cold.

'Come on, Joan,' Mrs Cook said, gently taking her hand and leading her away.

Joan fumbled for the little photograph inside her pocket, making sure it was still there. It was all she had left of Terry now. She gripped it, as the tears streamed down her face.

That weekend at the caravan, Joan sat in front of the fire, still feeling like little more than a dead weight. Her arms felt empty with no baby cradled in them, and she let them hang down limply in her lap. Her breasts were leaking milk that was no longer needed.

The sight of her daughter so obviously distressed seemed finally to move Mrs Cook to pity. She came and sat down next to Joan, reaching out and pulling her into a hug.

For what seemed like hours, the two of them sat like that together, bathed in the warmth of the fire. 'You poor soul,' Mrs Cook whispered. 'Oh, whatever have you been through, my poor girl?'

21

Ethel

The winds of change were beginning to blow through the factory. News had filtered down to the girls that the old Hesser Floor was going to be wound down and the sugar-packing operation moved to a brand-new building being put up in the yard. The two new floors would be known as the Rainbow and Harlequin rooms, and the girls would be transferred there gradually as the machines were installed one by one.

For one of Ethel's sugar girls, Eliza, the news was particularly exciting, since her boyfriend Ron was part of the team from Gleeson's, the builders who were constructing the new building. Eliza found that if she walked out onto the steps outside the department she could often spot him down below. 'Cor, I feel like Juliet on her balcony,' she told the other girls after spending her toilet break waving down to him and blowing kisses.

After many months, the Rainbow Room was finally complete. Ethel was delighted when she and her friend Beryl Craven were asked to get the new floor up and running. At first, the department would be offering just one day-work shift, but in time, as more machines were installed and extra staff were found to run them, a two-shift system would be introduced and the two young women would head up a shift each.

A team of men and girls were working hard to get the new packing machines ready as quickly as possible. Ethel stopped to admire the handiwork: the brightly coloured machines were based on a new design, with two heads instead of one, which meant they could process nearly double the quantity of sugar, churning out 150 bags every minute. The packing – long considered the most gruelling part of working as a sugar girl – would from now on be done automatically.

The Rainbow Room was appropriately named since the new machines installed there came in different colours – Orange, Apple, Lemon, Scarlet, Lavender, Ocean and so on – while the Harlequin Room was to have a similar mix. When Ethel first entered the new building, she found a workman gazing at the stairs between the two floors. 'We can't decide what colour to paint them,' he commented.

'Well, it is called the Rainbow Room, isn't it?' she replied. 'Why don't you paint each step a different colour?'

'Brilliant!' the workman said, before setting off up the road to Pinchin Johnson's paint factory.

Once the machines were up and running, refinery director Oliver Lyle came along to see them in action. One of Ethel's new girls, Frarnie Swallow, was fixing a problem with the belt when he arrived on the floor, while Betty Foster and Jeanie Pearse were standing around waiting to get the machine going.

'Good morning,' said Mr Lyle. 'I've come to see how you lot are getting on.' He went along the line of young women, shaking their hands enthusiastically until he came to Frarnie, who was horrified to realise that her hands were still dirty from the job she had just been doing. 'Sorry, sir,' she said awkwardly, wiping them on her dungarees.

'Nonsense!' the old man said, grasping her hand and shaking it for all he was worth. 'Nothing wrong with a bit of grease! Can't run the machines without it, can we?'

Frarnie blushed. 'No, sir. Of course not.'

As well as the colourful machines, some other new arrivals were also turning heads among the sugar girls. At lunch one day in the canteen, they were surprised to see Miss Smith walk into the room with a black woman – the first she had ever hired to work at the factory. 'Look! Look!' everyone whispered, trying to get a glimpse of the new recruit. But Miss Smith's presence, as she had no doubt intended, ensured that their stares were not too obvious and that they kept their thoughts to themselves.

Before long, the Rainbow Room had begun to live up to its name, and not one but two black women were working on the machines there.

Monica Liverpool had recently come over from the Dominican Republic. She was a hard worker, but Ethel found that she was frequently being brought before her accused of some minor crime or other. It was hard to know whether the accusations were genuine complaints, or if there was an element of prejudice lying behind them. Ethel would try her best to listen to both sides, but generally Monica seemed to be blameless.

Edna Henry had grown up a few miles away from the factory, in Forest Gate. As a little girl she had heard tales of her grandfather working at Tate & Lyle as a pansman. Edna had never known her mum's parents – an Orthodox Jewish family, they had disowned their daughter for marrying a sailor from Trinidad – and the stories that her mother told her about factory life were all that she knew of them.

When Edna left school she had been determined to follow in her grandfather's footsteps and get a job at the factory. At first her mother had done her best to frustrate Edna's plans, worried about the company's reputation for loose morals.

'You're not going there, it's a knocking shop,' she had declared, arranging a placement at a dreary little dressmaking firm instead. Several years later, and by now married with children, Edna finally secured her dream job.

Once in it, however, she found she had new battles to fight. The Rainbow and Harlequin rooms had both been running successfully for many months now, and such was the need for new girls as more and more machines were added that opportunities for promotion were coming up increasingly often. A vacancy came up for a key girl – the equivalent of a driver on the old machines – and contrary to the traditional practice of such appointments being made by the forelady or charge-hand, under new rules any girl could apply.

By now Ethel's sister-in-law Honour was working in the sugar-packing department, on a different shift from Ethel's, and had risen up through the various jobs on the machines. When the post of key girl came up, she decided to put her name down.

Edna, meanwhile, had also decided to throw her hat into the ring. She had started at the factory a little earlier than Honour and had never missed a day through sickness, so she was sure her application would be successful.

Evidently, the powers that be did not agree, and a week later Honour's name was posted on the departmental board. The other key girls were delighted – with her cheerful personality and easy-going nature Honour had quickly made friends on the floor.

Edna, however, wasn't about to take it lying down. The job was hers by rights, she felt, and she refused to see it go to someone else, even if she was a charge-hand's sister-in-law.

Edna gathered her courage, made her way up to Mary Doherty's office and knocked on the door. 'It's not fair,' she told the surprised forelady. 'I've been discriminated against. I've got longer service and better timekeeping than Honour. And if you don't believe me, you can check for yourself.'

'All right then, I will,' replied Mary, 'but I'm sure you'll find that's not the case.'

Edna waited resolutely as Mary dug out the relevant records. Having compared the two sets she was forced to concede that Edna was right.

'Am I the new key girl then?' demanded Edna.

'Yes, I suppose you are,' came the reply.

Satisfied, Edna returned to the factory floor and resumed her work.

The other key girls were not exactly welcoming, however. When Edna went to sit with them at break time, they promptly stood up and relocated to another part of the room. Not to be deterred, Edna moved with them. They stood up en masse and moved again.

Eventually, she resorted to blocking their way. 'Look,' she told them, 'wherever you go, I'm going. I'm a key girl, same as you are, and if you don't agree you can go up the office and ask them.'

The other girls were forced to admit defeat, and from then on treated 'Ed' as one of their number. Honour, meanwhile, had to wait a little longer for the promised promotion.

Edna was never afraid to ruffle a few feathers if she felt that something was not above board. The next time she clashed with Mary Doherty it was over a bonus payment which the forelady had refused to pay to her. Mary eyed her coolly as she gave her explanation. 'You didn't start on the first day of the month, so your service isn't complete.'

'That's ridiculous,' Edna remonstrated. 'The first day of the month was a Sunday.'

'Well, I'm afraid those are the rules,' the forelady replied, turning back to some paperwork on the desk in front of her.

'In that case, I'd like to make an appointment to see Miss Smith,' Edna retorted.

'You can't do that – Miss Smith is a very busy woman.'

'Yes I can,' Edna replied, marching out of Mary Doherty's office and straight down to Personnel. As she had predicted, The Dragon proved as fair as she was fierce, and agreed that Edna's interpretation was the right one. Reluctantly, Mary Doherty signed off the bonus.

Edna soon grew restless in the Rainbow Room. She began to work her way around the factory's various departments, applying for a new transfer every so often until she had tried most of the women's jobs on offer, from sugar-packing and syrup-filling to the canteen. Wherever she went, she brought her strong sense of justice to bear, and never more so than during a stint in the can-making department, where she clashed with a shop steward by the name of Carol.

Coming into work one morning, Edna noticed that a girl called Dawn Riley was missing. Dawn's mother had recently been diagnosed with cancer and the management had let her work part-time so that she could get home to make her mum's dinner.

'Has Dawn switched her shifts?' Edna asked Carol.

'Oh, no, she's been sacked,' came the reply.

It seemed that, having trialled their sympathetic arrangement for a few months, the bosses had decided it was more trouble than Dawn was worth, and she had been swiftly dismissed.

Edna was devastated. 'That poor girl! What are you going to do about it?' she asked Carol. 'You can't just let them get rid of her.'

'What can I do?' replied Carol, feebly. 'They've already made their decision.'

Edna was not to be put off. 'Give me permission to speak for Dawn,' she pleaded. 'If you won't fight for her, I will.'

With Carol's cautious blessing, Edna marched upstairs to speak to Bill Elliot, the manager responsible. This time she didn't hold back.

'It's a bloody disgrace what you're doing,' she told him. 'That poor girl is going through enough. You're lucky she's working part-time, and if you dare try to dismiss her I'm going to take it further.'

Bill was so shocked at the impassioned outburst that he promised to look into the matter. Later that afternoon he called Edna back to his office to tell her the good news: they had decided not to get rid of Dawn after all, and she was to be reinstated under the previous arrangement.

The next morning a very happy Dawn was back on the factory floor. Carol walked up to Edna. 'I want you to know I'm resigning as shop steward,' she announced.

'Best day's work you've ever done,' replied Edna.

Soon she was installed as Carol's replacement, making her the first black woman in the factory to become a union rep.

Edna's determination to stand up to injustice stemmed from her childhood. Her father had died when she was young and her mother had remarried, this time to a Jamaican man who worked at Pinchin Johnson's paint factory. Edna's stepfather was an aggressive, violent man with a serious gambling habit, and he enjoyed having a new daughter to boss around.

Each evening he would demand that the young girl read him the racing results from the paper. Having seen her mother's hard-earned money forcibly taken to fund her stepfather's flutters, Edna would take her own small revenge by pretending to get the names of the horses mixed up, eliciting silent fits of giggles from her mother.

But there was precious little laughter in the family home, and before long Edna's mum was being regularly beaten by her new husband. One evening he came home demanding that she hand over her housekeeping money so that he could go to the dog racing at West Ham Stadium. She refused, and before long a fierce row had started.

Edna's mother tried to get her to leave the room, but the little girl refused to go, standing squarely between her mum and her increasingly furious stepfather. He shoved Edna aside and soon had his hands around his wife's neck, forcing her down onto the floor of the kitchen and choking her. Without thinking, Edna grabbed the nearest heavy object to hand – a metal poker – and brought it crashing down on his head.

Her stepfather let out an agonised scream, letting go of Edna's mother and turning to face the child. 'You're dead!' he bellowed, lunging to grab his cut-throat razor. Edna ducked, scrambled between his legs and ran straight for the front door, hurtling down the road to hide in the grounds of the local timber yard.

She crouched there, terrified, all night long – too scared to come out, even when her mother came by, calling to her that her stepfather had calmed down. Eventually, when Edna thought he would have left for work the next morning, she timidly made her way back home.

Despite the incident, Edna's mother stayed with her new husband. Edna kept out of his way as much as possible, but she never forgave him for the way he treated her mother.

Once Edna became an official representative of the women at the factory, she made it her business to study as many employment law textbooks as she could get her hands on, determined not to let her superiors take advantage of the girls' lack of education to get the better of them.

One winter's day, she arrived for work at six a.m. to find that the factory floor seemed far colder than usual. She asked Des Nolan, a foreman, to come down to the floor, and to bring a thermometer.

'I reckon it's too cold for us to work today, Des,' she told him, aware that the minimum working temperature was 61 degrees Fahrenheit. Edna escorted him over to the coldest part of the room, as per the rules she had diligently memorised, and sure enough, the reading was well below the acceptable limit.

'You could keep your hats and coats on,' he suggested.

'No, sorry, Des,' she told him, 'we're not allowed to – it's dangerous. They might get caught in the machines.'

Des agreed that the girls could go and wait in the canteen while the room was heated up. Edna and the others sat huddled over steaming cups of tea, waiting for word from the floor. Before long another manager appeared. 'It's much warmer now,' he informed them. 'You'd better come back to work.'

'Wait here,' Edna told the girls, as she went back to the floor with the manager. Sure enough, it was still cold. 'It hasn't warmed up at all,' she told the man. 'Were you planning to light a fire in here or something?' She marched back to the canteen and rejoined the others.

By this point the girls were getting anxious. 'They'll dock our pay, Ed,' they told her. 'We're going to lose our wages.'

'Don't you worry,' she replied. 'As long as we're on site they can't dock us a penny. If they don't provide the facilities for us to work in, we ain't obliged to work.'

As the time ticked by, the girls became giddy with their own bravery, and not a little high on all the caffeine they had consumed. After a whole eight hours in the canteen, Edna told the managers the women's shift was over and they were leaving.

'Cheers Ed!' the girls called out, as they headed home. But Edna knew their bravado masked the fear that, by following her, they were risking their livelihoods.

The next morning, the girls turned up for work as normal and nervously clocked in. When they arrived on the floor they were ecstatic to find that they were still in their jobs, their foreman was suitably humbled, and – most importantly – their factory was lovely and warm.

As time went on, new waves of immigration from the West Indies meant that Edna and Monica were no longer the only black women in the factory. The Jamaicans and Trinidadians embraced Edna as one of their own, but when it came to the Dominicans and Saint Lucians, relations were rather frostier. To make matters worse, these women spoke a form of patois which to Edna was incomprehensible. One day as she was passing by a rowdy group of Saint Lucians, one of them turned to her and whispered, 'En chou manman-ou.'

Perturbed by this mysterious remark, Edna went over to the Rainbow Room and pressed Monica for a translation.

'They say, "In your mama's arse",' was the helpful response.

'Well, that's nice!' responded Edna. 'What am I supposed to say to that?'

Monica thought for a moment before whispering urgently, 'Lanng kaka manman-ou.'

'All right,' said Edna, 'what does that mean?' But Monica just smiled and went back to her work.

The next day as Edna walked past the group of Saint Lucians, she hollered at them slowly and deliberately, 'Lanng-ka-ka-man-man-ou!'

They gasped, glaring at her with rage in their eyes. But from then on they never bothered Edna again.

The next time she saw Monica, Edna asked what exactly she had said to them.

'Lick your mama's shit,' was the reply, and the two women burst out laughing.

Over the years, Edna found opportunities for promotion through the union, until eventually she was made the representative for the whole refinery, bringing her unique style of negotiation and her strong sense of right and wrong to pensions meetings, pay disputes and arbitration at the highest level.

Always a thorn in the side of the management, it came as a surprise to Edna when her manager Bill Elliot offered her a promotion to supervisor. At first she was suspicious of his motives. 'Is this about my ability or buying my silence?' she asked him.

He assured her that there was no question of her having to leave the union just because she accepted the promotion. But Edna told him that she felt there was no way she could represent her fellow workers if she was no longer one of them.

The manager had only one more card to play. 'It'd mean a lot more money,' he pointed out.

'I don't care,' was Edna's reply. 'Money don't mean a thing to me. Principles do. I don't want the job.'

Of all Edna's achievements during her time at Tate & Lyle, perhaps the most significant was her multi-skills programme, a scheme she devised and championed which ensured that every floor worker learned how to do the jobs of her colleagues, inspired by her own experience of transfer after transfer around the factory. This meant the possibility of variety in an otherwise tediously repetitive job, and combined with an equal opportunities policy it ensured that the workers were paid the same rate.

Bill Elliot, her one-time adversary, grew to respect and value her contributions. 'You've shown a lot of balls, Ed,' he told her at the party held in 1989 to celebrate her retirement.

As she explained to him, all she ever wanted was fair treatment between equals. 'Just 'cos you're a manager, there's no law that says we're different,' she told him. 'You wear white overalls and I wear green, but we both work for Tate & Lyle.'

22

Gladys

In the Blue Room, women's contracts were terminated when they got married, and with Betty's wedding day fast approaching, Gladys knew she would soon be facing life at Tate & Lyle without her best friend.

Gladys tried not to think about the future and instead threw herself into preparations for Betty's last day. Stealing some cardboard boxes from work, she went home and set about cutting shapes out of them with her father's pocket knife. The biggest box she flattened and cut into an L-shape, and the others she carved into several bell-shaped pieces. Then she covered the pieces in tinfoil, made holes in the tops and threaded string through them.

When Betty arrived at work the next morning, Gladys snuck up on her and threw the biggest piece over her neck so it hung down her back like an L-plate. Then, with Betty giggling away, she set about festooning her with silver bells. Meanwhile a bench on one side of the room was quickly filling up with cards and gifts from all the other Blue Room girls. By the time they were finished with her, Betty looked like a Christmas fairy who had flown off with all the presents from under the tree.

After their shift, the whole department went for a goodbye fry-up at their regular café opposite the factory. 'I'm going to miss you lot so much,' Betty said, throwing her arms round Gladys and Eva and giving them a squeeze. 'You're the best friends I've ever had.'

Gladys couldn't bring herself to reply, but tears dropped into her mushrooms on toast. This was the beginning of the end for the Blue Room as she knew it. Eva, Maisie and all the other girls who had recently got engaged would soon be following in Betty's footsteps.

'Why do we have to leave when we get married? It's so unfair,' she protested.

Betty looked at her. 'Aw, Gladys, we've just got to find you a bloke to get engaged to,' she said, kindly.

'Nah,' Gladys said, forcing a smile, 'I tried that once before, remember?'

Betty was married on a beautiful July day, and she and Sid moved into a brand-new flat. Gladys and Eva went round to visit and Betty proudly served them tea in her new living room. The old giggly, daredevil Betty might have been less in evidence, but a calmer, more contented one had taken her place.

Back at Tate & Lyle, Gladys's younger sister Rita had joined the company and was working in the can-making department. Rita had a shock of curly red hair just like Gladys, and the two were constantly being taken for twins – an annoyance to both girls. 'Surely I don't look as old as *her*,' Rita would say, sulkily, while Gladys despaired that she was still being mistaken for a school leaver. She also had the niggling feeling that, with her younger sibling coming up behind her at the factory, she should have moved on by now herself.

That summer, every weekend seemed to be taken up with a different couple tying the knot, and by the time autumn came round Gladys had become well and truly sick of wedding cake and fish-paste sandwiches. The latest Blue Room bride was a girl called Dolly Stone. Her wedding was in Canning Town and, after food at Dolly's parents' house, the party decamped to the Trossachs pub on the Barking Road.

It was tipping it down, and the guests arrived soaked but keen to warm themselves up again with as much drinking, dancing and singing as they could muster. A man was playing the piano in one corner, and the punters were taking turns to sing. Usually Gladys would be first up, clowning around and making an idiot of herself, but this time she found herself hanging back.

Gladys didn't normally drink – she'd always been high-spirited enough to have fun all evening on lemonade – but tonight she was on the gin and tonic. It was the favourite tipple, she realised glumly, of her mum, whose ritual after drinking it was to come home from the pub and disappear into the toilet in the back yard to cry for hours on end.

Oh God, she thought, was she turning into her mother? Quickly, she stepped up to the piano and whispered in the ear of the pianist.

There was only one song she could face doing tonight – only one song that would sum up her state of mind. It might be a wedding party, but they'd just have to lump it. She cleared her throat and began belting out 'Blue Moon'.

As she looked around the room full of half-drunk, happy couples, Gladys felt as if the song had been written just for her. This was her lot in life, she realised – always the joker, always the tomboy, and always destined to be sad and single.

The other guests ignored her and whooped in delight as Dolly kissed her new husband. Outside, the rain was pounding against the pub windows. Maybe it was just the gin, but she couldn't help feeling that the whole world was doing its best to make her miserable.

Out on the street, a bus trundled along in the rain. Among its shivering passengers were two young men on their way back from the pictures at the Boleyn cinema on the Barking Road. They were headed to the Abbey Arms pub for a nightcap.

'It's tipping it down,' said one of them. 'Let's get off at the next bus stop instead – there's a pub right next to it.'

When the bus drew to a halt, they jumped off and dashed through the rain, heaving open the door of the Trossachs and falling inside.

Gladys, still singing, looked up and saw the two men. One of them, she noted, was a rather good-looking, well-built young bloke wearing glasses. There was something strangely familiar about him, she thought. It couldn't be – could it? It was.

Bum Freezer!

Gladys almost forgot to keep singing. John, the scrawny kid she used to kick a football about with down at Beckton Road Park, whom she had taunted for the too-short leather sports jacket his mum made him wear, had grown into a strapping young man, muscular and tanned from his time in the Army.

She felt suddenly self-conscious. What would he think of her now – the former mouthy tomboy, wailing out a soppy song like this? She did her best to mumble the rest of the lyrics with her head down, before slipping gratefully away from the piano and shoving her way through the crowd towards the ladies' loos.

Just before she got there a hand tapped her on the shoulder. 'Hello, aren't you the girl with the lovely legs?' The voice was quiet, as John's had always been, but deeper now.

Gladys turned round to see him smiling at her. 'Bum Freezer, ain't it?' she grinned back. 'What are you doing here?'

John told her he was out of the Army and living in Forest Gate. His mother and sister had both died of tuberculosis, and John was the only child his father had left. He had returned home to the East End to be with him, and to fulfil his ambition of working as a lighterman in the docks.

As they talked, Gladys forgot about the rain outside, the happy couples around them and the glass of gin and tonic in her hand. Chatting to John was so easy, just the way talking to an old friend should be. Only this time she couldn't take her eyes off him.

John seemed equally engrossed, but as Gladys listened to him talk in his soft, serious voice, she felt a twinge of guilt for how she had treated him in the old days. Back then, he had seemed like a bit of a wimp to her, but now she saw that he was just gentler and more thoughtful than other men. She was louder, tougher and cheekier than any girl she knew. They were like chalk and cheese, really. What was the chance of him fancying her now?

When the landlord called time at the bar, it was as if a spell had been broken and they both looked around, surprised to find that they had been chatting for hours. John straightened up as if shaken awake. He looked at Gladys for a moment, then said, quietly but confidently, 'Can I take you out next week?'

The old John would never have had the guts to ask, thought Gladys. And the old, jokey Gladys would have shrugged him off.

'Sorry, mate,' she said, before she could stop herself, 'I'm on two-to-ten next week.'

She could have slapped herself.

'Well,' said the new John, gently persistent, 'how about the week after that? *Singin' in the Rain*'s on. I reckon it might suit you.'

On Monday the following week, Gladys rushed home after the early shift to get ready for her date. The Teddy Girl look was in, and Eva had convinced her to get a brand-new outfit made at Phil Freeman's, the tailors near Rathbone Street: a brown birds'-eye patterned jacket and tight, knee-length pencil skirt. She eyed the latter suspiciously; her last one had split up the back when she was dancing too energetically one evening at the Tate Institute, and had to be held together with safety pins for the rest of the night. At least tonight she was only going to the pictures.

More worrying were the pointed stilettos she had bought to go with the outfit – hand-made at the shoe shop near Trinity Church on the Barking Road. 'Stick toilet paper up the toe, otherwise your foot will slip and you'll go flying,' Betty had warned her. Gladys's family used newspaper for bog roll, so she rolled up a bit of that and shoved it as far down the elongated nose of the shoe as it would go.

As she hobbled down the stairs, the skirt stretching almost to breaking point with each step, Gladys heard her father give a rasping laugh. 'Yeah, yeah, get a good old look!' she snapped, wobbling slightly on her stilettos. But she knew that, if she were sitting in his seat, she'd be laughing her head off too. Why were women supposed to wear such impractical things for the sake of blokes?

It was a relief to finally collapse into her seat on the bus and rest her poor feet as it made its way along the Barking Road. But now that Gladys had the space to think about what she was doing she found herself gripped by an unfamiliar fear. For the first time she was going out for the night with someone she actually liked – and it terrified her. What if John ran out on her, or stood her up?

As the bus approached the stop before the cinema, Gladys felt as if her feet were welded to the floor. She just couldn't get off without knowing for certain that John was there waiting for her. There was nothing for it but to stay on the bus and go right past the cinema to check that he really was outside, even if it meant hobbling all the way back.

Other passengers disembarked, but Gladys stayed put. As the bus drew away from the kerb, she huddled down in her seat until just the top of her head was visible, and peered out of the window. The people around her might think she was mad, but she didn't care. She just needed to know.

They neared the Boleyn and Gladys held her breath. She could see a crowd of people outside the cinema, talking and laughing. But where was John? She sat up straighter to get a better look. At that moment, John stepped out from behind a tall man in a hat, with what looked like cinema tickets in his hand. Gladys breathed an enormous sigh of relief, and then, remembering herself, quickly huddled down again in her seat until the bus was safely out of sight.

By the time Gladys had walked back to the cinema she was late and her feet were aching. But when she reached John she realised he had a look of relief on his face, too. He'd probably been wondering where on earth she was, and also worrying that she'd changed her mind.

'You look lovely,' he said softly, offering her his arm, and she followed him, tottering slightly, into the cinema.

For the first time in her life, Gladys didn't mind one bit sitting in the back row, and she was so busy canoodling with John that they didn't get to see very much of Gene Kelly and Debbie Reynolds. By the time they emerged from the dark, all the worries and insecurities that had gripped her had fallen away, and she felt as free and chatty as she had when they were 13 and hanging out together in the park.

As they walked hand-in-hand along the Barking Road, the skies broke, and it began to pour. Gladys's make-up was melting and her new outfit was getting soaked, but she didn't care. Soon she was twirling around the lampposts like Gene Kelly, singing her heart out.

John ran after her, laughing and splashing in the puddles.

When Gladys and John decided to get married, her mother Rose was all in favour of the engagement, and it was as though poor Eric Piggott had never existed. 'Little Johnny talks so posh now, don't he?' she said, approvingly. 'Who would've thought he'd grow up like that.'

Although John's accent hadn't changed since he went away, Gladys knew what her mother meant. His soft, serious tone of voice lent him a kind of gravitas, and he was a thoughtful, intelligent man. John was now working down at the docks, which her father also approved of, where he was known as The Albert Dock Lawyer for his ability to pen convincing-sounding formal letters for any of his colleagues who needed them. But like his fiancée he also enjoyed a good prank, and he and his friends could often be found firing large dollops of mud with a catapult at the portholes of the big liners, blocking the views of the richest passengers on board.

Gladys's parents might have been won over, but at John's house it was a different story. His father had remarried and his new wife, Maude, made it very clear that she didn't want a half-gypsy girl as a daughter-in-law. 'Don't expect me to come to your wedding,' she told John.

'She'll come round, just be patient with her,' he assured Gladys, whose first instinct was to give Maude a piece of her mind. Instead, she and John began saving diligently for their big day, hoping that Maude would change her tune when she realised that the event was going ahead with or without her blessing.

A month before the wedding, John's father took him to one side. 'I'm sorry, son,' he said, 'but Maude don't want to go, and if she ain't going I can't go without her.'

Given the non-attendance on John's family's side, Gladys was determined to throw a party that everyone would be talking about, with as many of her Tate & Lyle friends there as possible. She therefore took the relatively unusual step of hiring a hall – a little tin hut at the bottom of Cumberland Road, a few minutes' walk from her parents' house. Soon, sorting out the wedding was turning into a second job for Gladys, taking up every free afternoon when she was on the early shift, and every free morning on the late one.

With most of the money going on the party, there wasn't much left over for the wedding dress, but Gladys wasn't bothered. She bought an off-the-peg white cocktail dress from C&A for five pounds, and a matching one in turquoise for her sister Rita, her bridesmaid.

With all the running around, Gladys hadn't had much time to think about the fact that she, too, would now have to leave Tate & Lyle. There would be no more trips to the café at break time, no more driving Miss Smith and Julie McTaggart up the wall, no more netball and athletics – and most of all, no more Blue Room girls. The department where she had once turned up as an outsider in her baggy dungarees had come to feel like a family, and now that family was breaking up. As her old friends left, new girls were starting in the Blue Room, and to Gladys they looked like children.

'Gawd, that's what we must've been like,' she said to Eva, watching them laughing and mucking about. 'Poor old Julie!'

On her last day at the factory, Gladys was 15 minutes late as usual. She didn't have to shake Betty awake any more, but being tardy had become a sort of tradition, and she wasn't about to break it now. At the gate, Mr Tyzack gave her a nod. 'Late again,' he tutted. 'Yep,' said Gladys, 'you know me.'

When she got in, the girls had filled her bench with presents, as she knew they would, and Eva slapped a great big L-plate on her back. 'Who would've thought I'd last this long, eh?' Gladys said, with a giggle. 'I must've nearly got the sack a hundred times.'

'Well, thank God you were good at the relay, that's all I can say,' Maisie laughed.

There was still one last trip to be made to Miss Smith's office, however, before Gladys could leave the factory once and for all. She had to go and see her to receive her severance pay – a week's wages for each year she had worked there.

As she made her way across the yard, Gladys cast her mind back over every misdemeanour, every run-in she and Miss Smith had ever had. The Dragon had certainly done her best to intimidate the young Blue Room girl, but Gladys had seen her victories too – scuppering the perfect line-up in the beauty contest, terrorising the bosses with mice and getting away with it, and riding in the telpher.

Over time, she realised, she had also seen another side of Miss Smith – the woman who had looked after Betty when she was down, who took orphans under her wing, who blamed herself for Bella's death, and who hadn't given up on a lippy little cow like Gladys.

'Hello again, Gladys,' said Betty Harrington, as she entered the office for the last time.

'Don't worry, Betty, for once I'm not in trouble,' she replied.

'We're going to miss your face around here,' said Betty Phillips. 'We've got used to seeing it so often.'

Miss Smith looked up from her desk as Gladys came in. 'So, you're really leaving,' she said, with a thoughtful look on her face.

'Looks like it,' said Gladys, gesturing towards the L-plate around her neck.

Miss Smith handed her an envelope with her pay in it. 'Well, I'd like you to give your husband-to-be a message from me,' she said.

'Oh yes, Flo?' said Gladys, daring to use her Christian name for the first time. 'And what's that, then?'

'Tell him,' she replied, with a mischievous twinkle in her eye, 'that I wish him all the luck in the world!'

23

Joan

The Cook family had done their best to put the shameful business of Joan's illegitimate baby behind them, moving to a flat in Melford Road in the hope of making a fresh start. For Joan, however, the building harboured a constant reminder of the life she had lost, since their downstairs neighbour worked for Tate & Lyle.

Her own former Tate & Lyle friends, meanwhile, were moving on with their lives. Kathy had left the factory and was working at a holiday camp, where she had met a lovely Irish man called Peter. Soon they had married and moved away. Peggy had left Tate & Lyle when she got married and was now working in the offices of a sack factory. Joan went round to see her and her new son Clive. Although she was happy for her friend, it was difficult witnessing the simple family life that she herself had been denied.

All she had to remember Terry by was the one little photograph she treasured. How much would he have already changed from the baby in the picture, she wondered, as she stared into his little eyes. Would he still remember her by now, or would he think that other woman was his mother?

Meanwhile, life marched on, dragging Joan, helpless and listless, along with it. When her mother again brought up the idea of her working in an office, Joan didn't have the energy to fight it. Mrs Cook made arrangements for her to attend an interview with a lady called Mrs Cameron Burrows at BM Philips, a coconut importer in Monument, and Joan mutely agreed.

The interview was conducted over lunch at a smart restaurant near Billingsgate Market, and Mrs Cook was delighted when Joan reported back that she had been served a cream cheese and banana salad. Joan had to admit it was the most delicious thing she had ever tasted.

'This is the start for you, my girl,' said her mother, beaming. 'You'll see.'

Joan realised it was true – with a new address and a new job where nobody knew anything of what had happened, it would be quite possible to simply reinvent herself. But somehow the old spark, the old vitality that had been the very cornerstone of her personality, was gone. Answering the phones at BM Philips, she simply couldn't disguise the loss and unhappiness in her voice.

Before long, Mrs Burrows decided she couldn't allow Joan to stay in the role. 'I don't think phone work suits you just now,' she said, kindly, 'but how about a little job in bookkeeping instead?'

Joan nodded, her cheeks burning. She felt she had fallen at the first hurdle.

She was duly sent downstairs to learn the ropes from a friendly girl named Eileen, who was around her own age and who lived in a prefab house in Beckton. Alongside her were two other office girls, Jackie from Dagenham and Pat from Blackfen.

Joan recognised in them the same lust for life that she remembered having herself when she had started at Tate &

Lyle, eager to join in the social life there. The three girls were always going out in the West End, and they made an effort to invite Joan along, but she felt too jaded to accept their offers.

One day, however, Eileen burst into the office with the news that Frankie Vaughan was doing a concert and that she had managed to get hold of four tickets. 'You've got to come, Joan,' she insisted. 'We can't let that ticket go to waste!'

Joan knew Eileen could probably flog the ticket for twice what she'd paid for it, and was just trying to find a way to include her. She was won over. 'Well, in that case I'd better take it,' she said, smiling.

That Saturday, Eileen, Pat, Jackie and Joan put on their glad rags and headed into town together. Joan hadn't dressed up for anything in ages, and she realised it felt good.

Going out with Eileen, Pat and Jackie soon became a regular event, and Eileen in particular was becoming a close friend. But Joan still felt as if she were holding a part of herself back, in a way that she hadn't with Peggy or Kathy. She knew she couldn't risk telling Eileen or anyone in her new life about Alfie and the baby she had given up, and that meant there was always a certain distance between them.

One day Eileen told Joan that her uncle was getting married and she didn't have a guest to take with her to the wedding. 'Do you want to come with me?' she asked.

Joan was touched that Eileen would invite her to a family event, so she agreed. It was an afternoon wedding in East Ham, and when the service was over everyone went back to Eileen's grandmother's house in Aragon Road to party the rest of the night away.

After a few drinks most of the younger guests, and a few embarrassing older relatives, were dancing around energetically in the little front room. Joan was doing her best to ignore Eileen's pleas to join them, busying herself with the buffet.

'Oi,' said Eileen, nudging her spoilsport friend, 'that bloke over there keeps looking at you. Think maybe *he* can get you to dance?'

Joan looked up from her sandwich and her eyes met those of a very tall young man. He smiled shyly at her.

'Oh God, no,' said Joan. The man had nice broad shoulders but his face was marred by a white scar running over the top of his left eye.

'He's coming over!' giggled Eileen. 'I'll leave you to tell him yourself.'

'Wait!' Joan hissed, but it was too late. Emboldened by Eileen's exit, the man hastily shuffled over to take her place.

'Hello, I'm Lenny,' he said, in a voice that was surprisingly soft and quiet given his looming frame.

'Nice to meet you, Lenny,' she replied, staring straight ahead. 'Joan.'

'Would you like to dance, Joan?' he asked.

She chuckled. If anyone could dance till she dropped it was her. The poor bugger wouldn't have a chance of stealing a kiss.

'I bet you one pound that I can keep dancing longer than you can,' she told him.

'Deal,' he said, reaching out his hand. She shook it, and followed him into the middle of the room.

An hour and 20 minutes later, Joan and Lenny were the only couple still dancing. Most of the guests had either left or collapsed tipsily into chairs, while a few little boys were picking at what was left of the buffet. But Joan was determined not to give in. For a start, a pound wasn't nothing, and secondly, she couldn't stand to lose at a dancing contest, of all things.

Lenny's resolve was strong too, though. Despite the sweat on his brow and the increasingly languid movements of his long arms and legs, he hadn't given up. You had to hand it to him, thought Joan – the bloke had persistence.

Suddenly, the needle on the record player was yanked away and Eileen's grandmother announced that she'd had enough and was heading off to bed. The light was turned off and, quick as a flash, Lenny pulled Joan onto his lap and planted a kiss on her lips. It came as such a surprise, and she was so exhausted, that she didn't protest.

'I've got to go,' she said, as soon as he drew away. 'It's late.'

'I'll drive you home if you like,' Lenny replied, hopefully.

Joan was about to say no, but the word 'drive' stopped her in her tracks. She was still a Cook girl, after all, and here was a man with his own car.

Joan let Lenny help her into her coat and followed him out onto the street. They walked up the road and came to a stop in front of the scruffiest old banger she had ever seen in her life.

'You don't mean that's your car?' she asked him, horrified.

'Oh, no,' he said, 'it's not mine. It's my brother-in-law's. He's a lobster fisherman in Jersey. I'm just borrowing it for the weekend.'

Joan climbed in, speechless, wondering what her poor mother would say if she saw her draw up at Melford Road in such a monstrosity – and next to a man who was certainly no oil painting.

When they neared her neighbourhood, Joan spotted an opportunity. 'This is me,' she lied. 'Roman Road. You can stop just here.'

Lenny pulled over. 'Can I see you again?' he asked.

Joan considered him for a moment. He was shy, quiet, and not a looker by any means. In fact, he was about as far away from Alfie as you could get. For her that sealed it.

'All right,' she said. 'Where are we going to go?'

Over the next few weeks, Joan discovered that it was possible to go to the pictures with her new man without running the risk of being spotted by friends or family. When the film finished, she would wait in the cinema toilets until everyone else had gone home and he was standing alone outside. Just as he was on the point of giving up and walking off, she would run and catch him up, putting her arm through his. Whenever he dropped her home, she would say goodbye to him on Roman Road as before, and walk the rest of the way back on her own.

In temperament the two of them couldn't have been more different. While Joan was rediscovering her former outspoken, sociable personality, Lenny was an introvert, never happier than when he was on his own, tinkering with an engine. A fork-lift truck repairer at the Keiller's jam factory in Silvertown, his greatest ambition in life was to own a sky-blue Citroën DS. Before long he was giving Joan driving lessons in his brother-in-law's old banger, and she discovered that despite its appearance she rather liked being behind the wheel. A scooter was duly provided, courtesy of Mr and Mrs Cook, and from then on Joan could be seen zooming from the East End to Monument every morning.

To Joan's surprise, the features that had at first seemed off-putting in Lenny's face gradually became lovably familiar, and she grew to care less and less about them being spotted together. Soon she couldn't bear to be away from him, and even a few days apart felt painful. After all the losses Joan had suffered, being separated from those she loved had become hard for her.

Those losses still played on her mind, and as their relationship progressed the secret she was hiding from Lenny weighed heavily on her. Joan knew her mother would be horrified if she discovered that, after all the efforts made by the Cooks to erase Joan's scandalous past, she was now considering volunteering information about it to Lenny. But she believed it was the right thing to do. In any case, if Lenny was worth his salt he would stand by her. If he didn't, then he wasn't the man she wanted to be with.

Despite her conviction, she was annoyed to find that she was incredibly nervous about telling him, and somehow the right moment kept eluding her. Finally, she blurted it out one night over pie and mash.

Lenny chewed thoughtfully as he heard the full story. He was naturally a good listener, which made it very easy for Joan to go on talking indefinitely, but for once she forced herself to stop. All that really mattered now was his response.

'Joan,' he said, softly, 'I love you. The past is the past. It don't change anything now.'

Joan felt an enormous wave of relief wash over her. Finally someone in her new life understood who she really was. Even though she continued to keep the secret from the girls at work, she felt lighter and freer around them than she had before.

But if Joan thought that telling Lenny about the baby would bring her peace, she was wrong. A letter arrived not long afterwards, and enclosed was a form finalising Terry's adoption. Joan's pen hovered over the space where her signature was required – Lenny's words had opened up a tiny chink of hope in her mind.

Later that day she called the Crusade of Rescue and, bracing herself for the reply, asked how Terry was getting on with his adoptive family.

'Oh, hello, Joan,' said one of the nuns, cheerfully. 'Yes, your boy's doing very well. In fact his new parents are so happy with him that they've taken another one from us.'

Joan could see the happy family in her mind's eye: mum, dad, two kids. Could she really shatter that perfect picture?

Muttering her thanks, she hung up and tried again to sign the form. But again her pen wavered. She simply couldn't do it until she had opened the door to that niggling hope and confronted it properly. Lenny loved her. She knew he was serious about her. Would he be willing to try and help her get Terry back, and make that perfect family theirs, not someone else's?

The next time they met, Joan showed him the form. 'Lenny,' she said, shakily, 'can I – can we – try to do anything about this?'

Lenny held her hand and looked into her eyes. He loved her with all his heart, but he had already done far more than many men of his generation would have been able to.

'No, Joan,' he said, quietly but firmly. 'I'm sorry, but we can't.'

Joan nodded, her eyes filling with tears. By now she had learned the hard way that there were some battles in life even she couldn't win.

Joan kept the little picture of Terry with her always, but she closed the door on her hopes of ever getting him back. Over time, when she recalled the nun's words on the phone that day, they seemed reassuring rather than painful. She was glad his new family were so happy with him, and felt proud to have played a part in that happiness. Soon she found she could no longer remember Terry's birthday.

All the same, she always hoped that one day, many years down the line, a young man might knock on the door and ask if Joan Cook was his real mum.

After a year and a half of courting, Joan and Lenny were married. This being the Cook family, there was no living with the in-laws while painstakingly saving for a deposit, or even any need for a dreaded mortgage. Joan spotted a house on Roman Road, the very street she'd once fooled Lenny into believing she lived on, and told her dad she wanted to buy it. 'How much do you need?' John Cook asked her, and the next day she was walking up to the house with the entire amount in cash stuffed underneath her jumper.

Nor was their honeymoon a run-of-the-mill affair. Joan was determined that she and Lenny would be the first people they knew to have a foreign holiday, and when she spotted an advert in the *Daily Mirror* for Hotel Ricardi, just outside Rimini, she was seduced by the exotic-sounding name. She wrote at once and booked the biggest room they had.

As she and Lenny stood staring at the aeroplane they were about to board, however, the reality of it suddenly hit her. They were actually going up in the air! For once, Joan was a gibbering wreck.

Worse, the plane was full and she was forced to sit up one end while Lenny anxiously took a seat at the other.

Eventually a kind old man offered his seat to Lenny's fretful new wife.

Once they reached Italy, the luxury holiday Joan had envisioned was laid out before her: it was blissfully hot, the hotel was beautiful and the beach was perfect. But, to her surprise, she hated everything about it. Much as her family had done their best to rise above their origins, she was an East End girl through and through, and she couldn't wait to get back home.

When she stepped off the plane back in England, Joan had to resist the urge to throw herself down on the tarmac and kiss it. From that day forth, the furthest she and Lenny ever went was to visit his lobster-fishing relatives in Jersey.

But the holiday proved to have one rather more positive legacy. Joan spotted a competition in *The Sun* for 'the funniest 25-word story about your love life' and was determined to win it – especially since the prize was a double divan. Relishing the chance to put her cheeky way with words to use again, she sat down and wrote:

> *My husband opened a bottle of champagne in our honeymoon bedroom. As the bottle popped, it shot under the bed, leaving him holding the cork.*

A week later, Joan opened the paper to discover that she had won the bed. But more importantly, there were her words in print on the page, with her name underneath them. She might have been bottom of her class at school, but now she could hold her head high: she was a published writer.

Not long after they were married, Joan had left her job at the coconut importer and she was working as a wages clerk at Dickie Bird's ice cream when she discovered she was pregnant. Instantly, she thought back to her 16-year-old self, lying in the bath, wishing she was no longer alive. How different things were now: she was a married woman with her own house and a husband who she knew would be over the moon when he found out. Just a few years earlier, the same piece of information had destroyed her world.

Lenny rushed round to tell his parents, and began planning a nursery for the little boy or girl. Joan's own parents welcomed the news that she was pregnant as if they had never heard it before. No one mentioned the child that had never been acknowledged. Everyone played the part of the delighted family to perfection. Happy as she was, the contrast was painful for Joan. She did her best to hide her darker thoughts, but she suspected that Lenny could tell.

They were at home together one day about three months later, talking about paint colours for the new nursery, when Joan felt a sudden pain in her stomach. 'Back in a sec,' she told Lenny, running to the toilet. When she sat down, she realised she was bleeding.

Lenny was taking no chances and immediately called an ambulance. By the time it arrived Joan was haemorrhaging badly, and she was distraught. Could it be that after having to give up a perfectly healthy baby, now the one she was able to keep was dying?

As she was carried into the back of the ambulance on a stretcher, Joan sobbed uncontrollably, and passers-by stopped to stare. 'Don't cry, don't cry,' said the young nurse, patting her hand anxiously. Joan pushed her away. She didn't care what anyone thought. As they drove away with the siren blaring, she was crying now not just for the baby she was losing but for the one that she had already lost.

At Mile End Hospital, the doctor leaned in and whispered, 'Are you sure you haven't done something to yourself?'

Joan's eyes were streaming and she could hardly see him through the blur of tears. She wanted to scream but she was so choked with crying that she couldn't catch enough breath even to speak.

'No,' she managed to sob, 'of course not.' Then she passed out.

Joan was in Mile End Hospital for a week and had several blood transfusions. When she came round, she discovered she had been put on a ward next to a young girl who had just given birth to a perfectly healthy baby boy.

The girl was blind, and she didn't have a ring on her finger. Joan blinked at her, unable to comprehend the injustice of it. 'How are you going to look after him?' she demanded, before a nurse came and hastily drew the curtain between them.

Back in East Ham, Lenny was anxious to do everything he could to look after his wife, insisting she go part-time at work and take it easy. On her days off, Joan spent a lot of time staring at the wall, thinking through all the events of the last few years. She was still barely into her twenties, yet already she'd had her heart broken by the man she thought she would marry, been forced to give up her first baby, and lost her second before it was born. She realised that, for all the money they had, her family were as helpless in the face of fortune as their neighbours.

But that didn't mean she couldn't fight back. Joan thought of the days when she had stood up to her father as his blows rained down on her mum's head. She thought of the pain she had managed to turn into pride, knowing that the child she had given birth to was now making another family happy. Joan had never been a victim, and she was not about to start being one now.

'Lenny,' she said, when her husband came in from work, 'I want to try for another baby.'

'Are you sure?' he asked, concerned. 'It's only been three months.'

'I'm sure,' she said, kissing the scar above his left eye.

Nine months later, Joan returned to Mile End Hospital. There, she gave birth to a beautiful baby girl weighing 11 pounds 6 ounces, and took her home.

24

Ethel

Ethel's younger sister Winnie had recently got married, and she was leaving the little house she shared with Ethel and Archie for a flat in Poplar. Since the syrup-filling department was off-limits to women once they were wed, Winnie would no longer be working at Tate & Lyle with Ethel either. Nonetheless, she could not have been happier in her new life, and her joy was only multiplied when she learned not long after the wedding that she was pregnant.

'I'm so excited, Et,' she told her big sister when she came round to visit. 'I'm going to have a little family of me own now.'

Archie's sister Honour had also recently got married, to a colleague at the factory named Johnny Gibbons, and Ethel wondered how long it would be before they started a family as well.

After Winnie had given birth, Ethel went up to the hospital in Poplar to bring her a change of clothes and take her home. When she entered the ward, she spotted her little sister lying in bed, cradling a tiny baby. 'Come on!' Winnie beckoned her closer. 'Say hello to Tony. Tone, this is your Auntie Ethel.'

Ethel examined the little crumpled face. 'He looks very nice,' she told Winnie approvingly.

'I'm so happy, Et,' her sister replied, beaming.

Ethel put an arm around Winnie's shoulder, squeezing her tight. The baby made a gurgling noise, and began to drift off to sleep.

'Don't you want one of these?' Winnie whispered. 'I always thought of you as a brilliant mum.'

'We're all right, Win,' Ethel replied, laughing. 'If that's what happens then we'll let nature take its course, but I've got my job at the factory.'

Ethel had watched numerous sugar girls leave Tate & Lyle to start a family over the years, but she had no particular desire to have a child, and would quite happily have stayed there forever. She had a supportive husband and the freedom and independence of her own career, almost unheard of for a woman of her background in 1950s London. It seemed that her mother had been right to expect great things of her.

Not long after, Ethel was inspecting one of the machines at work when she was struck by a peculiar giddy feeling. Her legs felt weak beneath her, and her vision was beginning to blur. 'Excuse me a minute,' she said to the girl at the machine, as she wobbled off in the direction of the cloakroom.

Just before she got to the door she felt herself sway more profoundly before suddenly falling towards the ground. It was lucky for Ethel that Honour's husband Johnny happened to be passing through. He rushed over and managed to catch her before her head hit the shiny tiled floor. Scooping her up into his arms, he carried her into the cloakroom, and gently sat her down.

Ethel came round relatively quickly. 'Are you all right?' Johnny asked, anxiously. 'Do you want me to get someone?'

Ethel put her hand up to her head. 'I'm fine, I'm fine,' she insisted. 'No need to fuss. I'll be right as rain in a minute.'

Before long she was up on her feet and back on the floor, busily pacing around the department.

A month later, Ethel was eating her lunch in the canteen when again the dizzy feeling came over her. She calmly pushed her plate of food to one side, making a space big enough for her head on the table in front of her, and then allowed the faint to take its course. She woke up once again to find that a crowd had gathered around her, but she was on her feet within minutes, assuring them that nothing was wrong.

When the fainting attacks recurred the next month, Archie insisted that Ethel go to the doctor. 'This can't go on,' he said. 'We've got to find out what's wrong with you.'

Reluctantly, Ethel admitted he was right.

A few weeks later, Ethel sat in front of the doctor as he read through her test results. 'Everything appears to be normal,' he said, somewhat baffled. 'My advice to you, Mrs Colquhoun, is to have a baby. That ought to sort you out.'

Though she hadn't previously given the idea much thought, once Ethel had been set the challenge of conceiving a child, she was determined to succeed at it. However, despite her and Archie's best efforts over the following months, she was frustrated to discover that in this area of her life success was elusive.

'Well, you told me what would cure me,' she complained to the doctor, 'but nothing's happening.'

'Mrs Colquhoun,' he said carefully, 'you do know there are certain times of the cycle that are advantageous, don't you? The fourteenth day onwards is the best time to try.'

Ethel returned home with this new piece of information. 'Right you are, then,' said Archie, and they waited for the auspicious date to arrive.

When it did, they dutifully climbed the stairs to bed, but before they had even reached the top they were both cracking up at the ridiculousness of the situation. 'Oh Arch,' said Ethel, 'we mustn't laugh!'

They tried their best to suppress their giggles, but as they got under the covers, one look at Archie's face, trying hard to assume an expression of serious concentration, made Ethel burst out laughing again, and he was soon following.

It was no good – the knowledge that the doctor had prescribed their night together had made it impossible. Eventually they were so exhausted from laughing that they fell asleep.

In the middle of the night, the two of them woke up and, with the pressure off, the intended act finally took place. The next morning, as Ethel was leaving the house, her neighbour couldn't help remarking, 'I heard you and Archie last night – what were you two laughing your heads off about?'

'Oh nothing,' said Ethel quickly, scurrying off up the street.

The prescription worked, and soon Ethel was expecting. Like all those sugar girls before her, she was now faced with the necessity of having to tender her resignation, as the rules of the factory dictated.

As her bump grew larger and larger, Ethel tried not to think about what the baby's arrival would mean, but now and then she caught herself worrying about leaving Tate & Lyle. She had dedicated herself to the factory, and it had rewarded her richly.

But if she was no longer a sugar girl, then what was she? Her anxious ruminations were not helped by the constant stream of comments that seemed to follow her everywhere she went. 'Ooh, you must be looking forward to being at home with the baby ... Won't it be a relief not to come in here day after day? ... I bet you can't wait till you hang up that white coat for good.'

When her final day at the factory came around, Ethel faced it bravely. The girls on the floor had shown their usual generosity in the presents they bought for her and the baby.

'I bet you're all just pleased to see the back of me,' Ethel joked, wiping a tear from her eye. She hugged a few of the girls, before gathering up the gifts and heading home.

It was only once she was alone in her own house that Ethel really allowed her emotions to come out. She cried and cried all night long, distraught at the thought of never going into the factory again. Tate & Lyle had been her world, and the sense of loss was enormous.

Ethel was taken into hospital at six a.m. one Saturday with complications, and baby Colin was born a week later by caesarean section. She was seriously ill afterwards and lay in her hospital bed for two weeks while Archie waited anxiously at home, calling up every day to ask if his wife could be discharged yet.

Colin had been put on another part of the ward, and as soon as Ethel came round she asked after him. 'He's ginger, like his dad,' she was told. 'We've been showing him off round the ward 'cause he's got more hair than we've ever seen on a baby!'

After a while the nurses said they would bring Colin to her

to breastfeed. Although she was exhausted and groggy from the drugs she had been given, Ethel couldn't wait to meet her baby and did her best to sit up in bed. Two nurses arrived in the doorway, one of them clutching a small bundle from which a couple of tiny arms were protruding.

The other nurse helped Ethel adjust the hospital gown she was wearing, and put the child to her breast, but he didn't take.

'What's wrong?' Ethel asked anxiously.

'Just try again,' the nurse replied, trying to push the baby towards her.

Ethel knew she was feeling a bit out of it, but looking down she was sure the baby's hair looked more brown than red.

'I thought you said Colin had ginger hair,' she said, panicked.

Just then another nurse appeared in the doorway, laughing her head off. 'You do know you've got the wrong baby there!' she told her colleagues, who all burst out laughing as well.

Ethel felt so horrified she could have hurled the baby across the room, but the nurses quickly whisked him away and left, still laughing. She lay back down on her bed, feeling sick to her stomach. She knew if she'd had her normal strength she wouldn't have let them get away with what had just happened, but she felt too ill to fight.

After a while, Ethel's strength returned to normal, and by the time Archie was finally allowed to take her home, she and baby Colin had formed a close bond. But the experience in the hospital had put her off ever having another child.

As they were leaving, one of the nurses called out, 'See you next year, mother!'

'You won't see me no more,' retorted Ethel.

As a full-time housewife and mother, the diligence and perfectionism Ethel had once brought to bear at Tate & Lyle were now employed in making sure that her home was clean and tidy, and she spent hour after happy hour scrubbing, mopping and polishing until every surface sparkled. Now when guests came to visit, they invariably commented that Ethel's was the most spotless house they had ever been inside.

Archie assured her there was no need for her to go back out to work, and that they could survive perfectly well on just his wage. After 18 months, however, he had to admit that they were struggling a bit.

'I'll get another job, Arch,' Ethel offered.

'No,' he insisted. 'You ain't going back to work until Colin's at school.'

Ethel returned to the housework and childcare. But she didn't let the idea drop, and when she heard there were part-time jobs going at the Standard Telephone and Cables factory in North Woolwich, she was determined to convince Archie that she should apply.

'It'll only be in the evenings,' she told him, 'so it won't be like I'm working full time.'

'All right then,' he said, resignedly, 'if that's what you want.'

Ethel was delighted to be back at work, and the arrangement meant she could still spend all day cleaning the house to perfection and spending time with Colin. But soldering electrical parts as a factory floor worker was hardly the same as being a charge-hand, and she couldn't help missing her beloved Tate & Lyle.

A few months later, Ethel was at home one morning when she heard something drop through the letterbox. She went to the front door, collected a letter from the mat and wandered back towards the kitchen, opening the envelope absent-mindedly. As she unfolded the paper inside, she stopped dead in her tracks. There at the top right-hand corner was the Tate & Lyle logo, embossed on the page, and at the bottom she could make out the familiar scrawl of Miss Smith's signature.

Dear Ethel,

I hope that all is well with you since you left us, and your family are in good health. I am writing to let you know about a new part-time evening shift we are starting in Small Packets. Could you come down to see me about this? If so, please make an appointment with Betty and I should be pleased to discuss it further with you.

My regards to Arthur and the baby.

Yours sincerely,

Miss Florence Smith

Ethel could hardly believe her eyes. A part-time evening shift like the one she was working at Standard, but at Tate & Lyle! Archie had barely got through the door that evening before she had thrust the letter into his hands. 'Look, Arch,' she cried. 'Miss Smith wants me to go in about a job!'

Archie was less delighted than his wife, remembering the sleepless nights he had endured while Ethel tossed and turned thinking about the Hesser Floor. 'You're not going back there if you're going to start worrying like you did before,' he told her.

'I won't do that no more, Archie. I promise I won't!'

It was clear there was no keeping Ethel from Tate & Lyle, so he agreed she should call and make the appointment.

A few days later, Ethel arrived at the entrance to the refinery, wearing her very best dress. It was two years since she had last been inside, and it felt like a lifetime since she had stood at the old factory gate as an anxious 14-year-old. She looked up at the imposing stone frontage that now stood in its place, bearing the square-shouldered letters:

TATE & LYLE LTD. PLAISTOW WHARF

Despite all that had changed, a bit of her felt nervous this time round, too. She still didn't know what job Miss Smith had in mind for her. What if she wanted Ethel to start at the bottom again, as a mere machine worker in the same department where she had once been a charge-hand?

The door to the Personnel Office was open, and Ethel knocked quickly before letting herself in. Miss Smith had her head buried in a filing cabinet while the two Betties were busily typing away.

'Hello, Miss Smith,' Ethel said.

'Ethel!' she replied, looking up with a warm smile. She stepped forward and shook her hand, before ushering her to a seat on the other side of the desk.

'I was just looking out your file,' she told her, setting it down on the table between them and flicking through it.

Ethel stared at the file, which charted every twist and turn of her career at the factory: from her first day as a humble sugar packer in the final months of the war, through her promotion

to the office and demotion back to packing again, to her brief
unsuccessful spell on the tally shortly after her mother's death,
her return to packing for a third and final time, and her ascent
through the ranks from filler to driver and finally to the factory's youngest charge-hand.

She held her breath, waiting to hear what her fate would be.

'So, what do you think?' Miss Smith said at last. 'Would you
like to come back – as a charge-hand on the evening part-time
shift?'

Ethel was too stunned for words.

'Of course, we'd take your previous service into account, so
for the purposes of your pension and other benefits it would be
as if you'd never left,' she added quickly. 'And the rate has gone
up since you were here previously.'

Ethel was silent for a moment, struggling to take in what she
was being told.

Miss Smith leaned foreword, hopefully. 'Do you have any
questions?' she asked.

Ethel was grinning from ear to ear as the words came out of
her mouth. 'Only one,' she said. 'When can I start?'

Epilogue

Ethel could not have been happier to be invited back to Tate & Lyle, and she gave the rest of her working life to the company. Promotion followed promotion until before long she was doing Ivy Batchelor's old job, with over 200 girls working under her. By then, her house in Oriental Road had been demolished, and she, Archie and Colin were living in a brand-new flat directly opposite the factory – which she could watch over from her kitchen window.

For many years Archie continued to work at Hollis Bros timber yard, until suddenly he was made redundant. True to form, Ethel threw herself into the challenge of finding him employment. She marched from door to door, pencil in hand, drumming up window-cleaning work for him in the local area, and later managed to get him a job at Tate & Lyle, cleaning out the sugar hoppers.

'I ain't working with you, Et!' he said anxiously, when she told him about the position.

'Don't worry, Arch,' she laughed. 'You'll be right up the top with the other men. You won't barely see me.'

Since she had first moved out of the family home following her mother's death in 1947, Ethel had not had any contact with her father Jim. But one day, in the mid-1980s, she received a call from one of his stepchildren announcing that Peggy, his second wife, had died, and that he wanted to get back in touch with his daughter. After 40 years of separation, the two of them were finally reconciled, and from that day until his death at a ripe old age they saw each other every weekend.

Ethel retired from Tate & Lyle in 1986, and her sugar girls showered her with gifts, among them a figurine of her made out of a Lyle's Golden Syrup tin. Her friends feared that her life might feel empty without the factory in it, but they soon found that they were mistaken. After years of hard work and the strain and stress of management, she found a new lease of life in retirement, and thanks to a line-dancing class at the local activity centre she discovered a social network of former Tate & Lyle workers. These days, as the group of old sugar girls gather every Friday to play bowls and darts together, the temptation to take charge and boss them about sometimes creeps back in. 'Ethel, we're not at work any more,' they remind her gently.

One day, after Ethel had retired, she received a phone call from Miss Smith. The former manageress was approaching her 80th birthday and was planning a joint party with her old friend and colleague Betty Phillips, which she hoped that Ethel would come along to.

Ethel was honoured to be invited, but the highlight of the day was when Miss Smith said to her, 'Ethel, I've always admired you for how you worked your way to the top.' Coming from Miss Smith, who had held the highest female role in the factory for so many years, that meant a lot.

Archie died in 2009, but Ethel, now in her eighties, still lives in Silvertown, just around the corner from her old workplace. In the last few decades she has seen the neighbourhood change almost beyond recognition as the familiar factories have closed down one by one. Although a small team at Plaistow Wharf still produces Golden Syrup, there are no longer any Hesser floors there, and the beautiful frontage has been demolished to make way for the Docklands Light Railway.

Today, where the factory gates once stood there is nothing but a wire-mesh fence, and beyond it not a bustling yard full of workers but a derelict no-man's-land where weeds grow waist high. Set back some way, behind concrete walls covered in graffiti, a small nucleus of buildings is all that remains of the factory, taking up just a quarter of the old site. When Ethel started there in 1944 she was one of 1,500 workers – now there are fewer than 50.

But when she needs a reminder of how things used to be, Ethel turns to the book that she keeps permanently on her bedside table: *The Plaistow Story*, written by Oliver Lyle himself shortly before he died in 1961.

* * *

A couple of years after leaving the Blue Room, Gladys was astonished to receive her own invitation from Miss Smith, asking her if she would like to return to the factory. She couldn't quite believe it – after all the mischief she had got up to, almost landing her with the sack more times than she could remember, was it really possible that Miss Smith would consider re-employing her? Part of her would have loved to take the opportunity, but she and John had moved to Forest Gate by then, and commuting all the way to Silvertown wasn't practical. Besides, without Betty and Eva there with her it just wouldn't have been the same.

Gladys tried her best to keep in contact with the rest of the old gang, but with a pair of boys to raise and new jobs to hold down, somehow she lost touch with her old friends. In 1985, after working in a string of different occupations – baking asbestos rings for Thermos flasks and working in a matchbox car factory in Stratford, blagging her way into silver service in the city, even helping out at a family-planning clinic – she came to a decision: she would organise a Blue Room reunion and get as many of the old girls to attend as possible.

Betty and Eva were on board within seconds of receiving Gladys's call, although Eva, remembering the old rivalry in the Beauty Shop, asked anxiously whether Maisie had replied.

'Oh yeah, she's coming all right,' said Gladys. 'Here, do you think I should invite Flo? She was probably the person I saw most often at the factory.'

Betty thought the idea was hilarious. 'Miss Smith coming round your house, Gladys? There's fat chance of that!'

But Gladys decided it was worth a shot. After all, it wouldn't really be like old times without The Dragon present to put the wind up the lot of them.

To her astonishment, once Tate & Lyle had passed on the message, Miss Smith readily agreed to the invitation, only asking if she could bring her friend Betty Phillips along too.

Gladys threw herself into the preparations for the party, even ordering a special cake in the shape of a two-pound bag of Tate & Lyle sugar. She was looking forward to the event, but there was another feeling mixed in with her excitement, and it had started when Miss Smith had agreed to attend. As the prospect of The Dragon arriving at her door became ever more real, Gladys found to her surprise that she felt nervous. Was it possible that she, a grandmother in her fifties, could be intimidated by an old lady, just because four decades before they had been arch-enemies?

When she arrived, Miss Smith turned out to have lost both her bark and her bite. Now that she was no longer in charge, she was able to come down to the same level as everyone else. 'Please call me Flo,' she told the other women. 'After all, we're equal now.'

She was friendly and charming and remembered all the girls' names. 'How's your sister Mary?' she asked Betty kindly, before remarking to Eva, 'You always did have a mop of hair, and I can see that hasn't changed.'

Maisie turned to Eva too. 'I was so jealous of you,' she admitted. 'But we're grown-up now, aren't we?' The two old rivals squeezed each other's hands.

Finally, Miss Smith turned her attention to Gladys. 'You were such a cow, you know,' she told her, with an affectionate laugh.

The evening was a rollicking success and it was four a.m. before they all went home. As Miss Smith was on her way out, she caught Gladys's arm. 'I want to ask you something,' she whispered urgently. 'Back at the factory, did all the girls think that I was gay?'

Gladys was flabbergasted. It was the last thing she had expected to hear from Miss Smith's mouth, and she didn't know how to respond. She decided it was best to play dumb. 'No, Flo, not that I know of,' she lied, solemnly.

The reunion reminded Gladys what special friends she had made at Tate & Lyle, and from then on Betty and Eva became regular visitors to her house. They still hang out together to this day, meeting up to bicker and tease each other and to reminisce about their adventures at the factory. All three of their husbands have died now, but they still have each other – a gang of Blue Room girls to the last.

* * *

The curse of the Tull family continued throughout Lilian's life, and as the years rolled by she lost count of how many relatives had died as a result of the genetic heart condition. But she never let the losses drag her under, reminding herself every time of what she had to be thankful for: that she was one of the lucky survivors.

Lilian and Alec had decided not to risk having children, but they later gave a home to their teenaged niece Lesley, whose father Leslie had died on holiday in Dorset. For the childless couple, the pleasures of surrogate parenthood were all the more sweet. However devastating the curse was, perhaps it brought the odd blessing as well.

Although Alec was without doubt the most significant man in her life, Lilian never forgot entirely about Reggie, and throughout her marriage she held on to his picture, keeping it hidden where no one would find it. But when Alec died after half a century of married life together, Lilian realised that she had been wrong to cling on to Reggie's memory. 'Alec was my husband,' she told herself, 'not Reggie.' Ultimately, Alec was the man who meant more to her, who had given her all he had in the world, and who had loved her with all his heart. Once Alec was gone, there was no longer any room for Reggie's memory, and Lilian finally tore up the photograph.

Despite losing her husband, Lilian's recent years haven't been lonely ones. She has made new friends through the Ascension Centre lunch club in Custom House, and chief among them is her dear companion Flo Waller. Until they both began attending the Ascension Centre, the two women had never met before, but for almost eight decades their lives had seemed to shadow one other. Flo had worked at Tate & Lyle at the same time as Lilian, and outside of work their paths must have crossed a thousand times as well: every Saturday, Lilian would go to the market at Green Street, where Flo would be visiting her cousin, and she was often to be found in the cinema opposite the flat Flo grew up in. Their photographs even appear in the very same issue of *Tate & Lyle Times*, where Flo is snapped cutting her wedding cake and Lilian departing on the beano to Margate.

The two women have become the best of friends, and since Flo was diagnosed with Alzheimer's disease, Lilian, ever the carer, has devoted her life to looking after her.

* * *

Having given up one baby and lost another to a miscarriage, Joan had learned the hard way how to bounce back from misfortune, and the skill was to stand her in good stead. She and Lenny had been married for ten years and had two children together, when tragedy struck.

It was a hot summer's night and Lenny had spent all afternoon spray-painting his car in the garage. He came into the house with a pain in his chest, swallowed an alka-seltzer and refused to eat his dinner. By the time the couple went to bed, Joan was a bit frisky, but Lenny wasn't feeling up to it. 'Let's go to sleep,' he whispered.

Joan reached out and put her arm round him. 'I ain't sleeping while you feel bad,' she told him. 'If it was one of the kids I'd be up all night with them, and you don't mean any less to me than they do.'

Moments later Lenny let out a kind of strangled gasp, and when Joan shook him there was no response. She jumped out of bed and called an ambulance, but when the paramedics arrived there was nothing they could do to revive him. Lenny had suffered a massive heart attack.

The next morning, Joan explained as best she could to her children that their father had died. She was determined to keep them away from the funeral, since she didn't know how she herself would react, let alone what effect it would have on them. But if anything they took the loss better than she did. Her little boy drew a picture of his dad going off into the sky on a forklift truck, while her daughter proved to be remarkably mature for her years, helping her distracted mother keep track of her money.

For months after the funeral, Joan couldn't face laying just three plates at the kitchen table, and took the family out for almost every meal. She and her kids became regulars at the local Wimpy and the fish and chip shop, as well as her old favourite, Chan's Chinese restaurant.

One evening over dinner in Chan's, Joan ran into Alfie's half-brother, who she hadn't seen since she was a teenager. 'I don't want to disturb you, but is it true?' he asked her. 'We heard a rumour you and Alfie had a baby.'

Joan was stunned. So, even after all these years the little rat still hadn't told the truth to his family! And yet, just as her mother had always feared, the gossip had got out eventually.

She looked Alfie's brother squarely in the eye. 'Yeah, we did have a baby,' she replied proudly. 'And his name is Terry.'

Joan never spoke to Alfie himself again, but she did see him one more time, when she was out with her kids at the Romford dog track. She was pretty sure he noticed her too, but before they could make eye contact she turned her gaze back to the dogs. She had nothing more to say to Alfie, no desire to have anything to do with him. As far as she was concerned, he no longer existed.

A few years ago a friend asked Joan if she resented her parents for making her give up her baby. 'No,' Joan replied. 'My mother loved me and cared for me for 17 years. Who was I to degrade her like that?' She had come to feel that her parents and their generation deserved her understanding and respect.

But even now, more than half a century later, she still hopes her son Terry will come to find her.

Once she got used to life without Lenny, Joan found that being a single mum actually suited her rather well. She was fully independent once again, and now with her own house to rule as she saw fit. All the other kids at her children's school thought she was the coolest mum they knew, driving around in a bright-yellow Volkswagen Beetle. In the 1980s, Joan even went into business, taking over a corner-shop with her friend Dolly – they named it Jolly's – and running it very successfully.

Nor did she give up her writing habit. She still jots down little rhymes all the time, just as she did at Tate & Lyle, but nowadays she crafts them into stories for children, which she carefully illustrates herself. She has also become a silver surfer, spending her time online in nostalgia forums and reminiscing about the past over the internet.

* * *

For many years after Gladys's reunion, she and her friends would look out for news of Florence Smith. Eva sometimes saw her walking her dog in Barking, with exactly the same stern, upright demeanour with which she had once stalked the corridors of the factory.

After a while, though, Miss Smith disappeared altogether. The girls later learned that she had been moved into a nursing home in Redbridge. When some of her old employees tried to visit, they were told that she didn't want to see them. Treating them as equals was one thing, but perhaps showing that kind of vulnerability was more than her pride could bear.

She died in 2009, at the age of 92. A handful of old sugar girls attended her funeral.

Acknowledgements

Above all, our thanks are due to the women whose stories form the heart of this book: Ethel Colquhoun, Lilian Clark, Gladys Hudrell and Joan Cook. What we have written is based on interviews both with them and with over 50 other former workers at Tate & Lyle, and we owe a great debt to the following for their generosity, patience and understanding: Eliza Attenborough and her niece Pamela Rozee, Barbara Bailey, Flo Barley, Shirley Benson, Louisa Blaker, Janet and Stanley Copp, Jean Crump, Lily Dalsett, Jean Danrell, Maureen Deeble, Betty Dillon, Joan Dyson, Jim Fittock, Joan Flanders, Betty Foster, Eric Gregory, Pat Griffiths, Win Hardy, Doreen Harris, Jean Hatt, Edna Henry, Pat Johnston, Martin Jones, Esther Kennard, Joan Lee, Sylvie Lowe, Jean Mitchell, Lily Moore, Ted Phillips, Anne Purcell, Barbara and Dave Price, Bill Price, Maureen Richfield, Eva Rodwell, Elizabeth and Cyril Rozee, Betty Southgate, Carol Smith, Renie Smith, Clare Sullivan, Frances Swallow, Winnie Taylor, Edie and Peter Wallace, Florence Waller, Win Webster and her son Mike Hardy, and many others who did not give us their full names or who wished to remain anonymous.

Although we have tried to remain faithful to what our interviewees have told us, at a distance of over half a century many memories are understandably incomplete, and where necessary we have used our own research, and our imaginations, to fill in the gaps. We have also changed some names and details to protect anonymity. However, the essence of the stories related here is true, as they were told to us by those who experienced them at first hand.

For Tate & Lyle, Ken Wilson at the Thames Refinery and Ian Clark at Plaistow Wharf have very kindly shared their time and resources, and allowed us to look around the factories and their respective archives. The accounts written by Oliver Lyle and Anthony Hugill, *The Plaistow Story* and *Sugar and All That*, provide a wealth of detail on the history of the company.

A number of local experts have also been extremely helpful. Jenni Munro-Collins and the staff at Stratford Library have borne with our enquiries patiently, calling up dozens of editions of the *Tate & Lyle Times* and *Stratford Express* at a moment's notice. Kathy Taylor's Newham Story website has been an invaluable resource, and the posts from other members on the forums there have been very useful. Staff at the Museum of London, London Metropolitan Archives and Imperial War Museum have also given generous assistance.

Stan Dyson, whose book *Silvertown: A Boy's Story* is a fount of local memories and lore, has been generous in answering our questions. His contributions to the Docklands Memories website (www.docklandsmemories.org.uk) are an invaluable resource, as are the short stories of Keith Lloyd, also collected there.

Nadia Atia's help was much appreciated in the early stages of our own research, while Clare Barrett and Becky Barry made our lives much easier with their precise interview transcriptions. Jolien Harmsen kindly helped with the patois translations.

It was Louise Stanley at HarperCollins who first conceived of the idea for this book, and we are grateful to her and her colleague Iain MacGregor for entrusting it to us. Our agent Jon Elek has offered sterling support throughout the process, and Ruth Petrie has given advice and encouragement. Michèle Barrett, Alex Hayton, Anna Rice and Darren Rugg offered insightful comments on an early draft. Our copy-editor Steve Dobell has provided sage advice and good humour.

Tracking down former Tate & Lyle workers was not always easy, and the staff of many wonderful day centres and lunch clubs have assisted in the search, among them Gary Ewer at the Royal Docks Learning and Activity Centre in Silvertown, Beryl Callison and Sybil Nightingale at the Ascension Centre in Custom House, Anne Cross at the Kitchen Table Café in East Ham, and Jessica Wanamaker at The Hub, Ray Maybe at the Trinity Centre and Sam Clark at The Place, all in Canning Town. Thanks to their hard work and dedication, many of the women we have spoken to are still in touch with former colleagues, and enjoy the company of new and old friends alike.

Our thanks are also due to Terry Abbott at the Silvertown branch of the British Legion, Suki Kula who runs the Cromwell Stores corner-shop opposite the Thames Refinery, and Norma Reeve and Matt Nicholls at the *Newham Recorder*. Bill and Rose Perry's Garden Café on Cundy Road, Custom House, is an oasis for the local community, and we are grateful for their assistance and generosity.

To see photographs of the sugar girls,
and read more about them, visit:
www.thesugargirls.com

About the Authors

Duncan Barrett is a writer and editor, specialising in biography and memoir. He recently edited Ronald Skirth's First World War memoir *The Reluctant Tommy* and Vitali Vitaliev's travelogue *Passport to Enclavia*. He is co-author of *Star Trek: The Human Frontier* and, with Nuala Calvi, *Zippy and Me*, the biography of *Rainbow*'s Ronnie Le Drew.

Nuala Calvi trained as a journalist at London College of Printing and has written for *The Times*, the *Independent*, the BBC and CNN, as well as numerous *Time Out* books. She has a strong interest in community history and took part in the Streatham Stories project to document the lives of people in South London. She is co-author, with Duncan Barrett, of *Zippy and Me*.